Distant Viewing

Distant Viewing

Computational Exploration of Digital Images

Taylor Arnold and Lauren Tilton

The MIT Press
Cambridge, Massachusetts
London, England

The open access edition of this book was made possible by generous funding from the National Endowment for the Humanities and the University of Richmond.

The MIT Press would like to thank the anonymous peer reviewers who provided comments on drafts of this book. The generous work of academic experts is essential for establishing the authority and quality of our publications. We acknowledge with gratitude the contributions of these otherwise uncredited readers.

This book was set in Stone Serif and Stone Sans by Westchester Publishing Services. Printed and bound in the United States of America.

Library of Congress Cataloging-in-Publication Data

Names: Arnold, Taylor, author. | Tilton, Lauren, author.
Title: Distant viewing : computational exploration of digital images /
   Taylor Arnold and Lauren Tilton.
Description: Cambridge, Massachusetts : The MIT Press, [2023] |
   Includes bibliographical references and index.
Identifiers: LCCN 2022052202 (print) | LCCN 2022052203 (ebook) |
   ISBN 9780262546133 (paperback) | ISBN 9780262375177 (epub) |
   ISBN 9780262375160 (pdf)
Subjects: LCSH: Computer vision. | Image data mining. | Image processing—Digital
   techniques. | Visual sociology—Technique.
Classification: LCC TA1634 .A76 2023 (print) | LCC TA1634 (ebook) |
   DDC 006.4/2—dc23/eng/20230111
LC record available at https://lccn.loc.gov/2022052202
LC ebook record available at https://lccn.loc.gov/2022052203

10 9 8 7 6 5 4 3 2 1

Contents

Acknowledgments

Projects take time to percolate and refine. This one is no exception, and was easily over a decade in the making. For all our appreciation of the speed of algorithms, the time to think slowly and carefully were key. The final letters on the page are a fraction of the words typed, code processed, and ideas explored. And most importantly, this book was only possible because of the support, generosity, and patience of colleagues, friends, and family.

A significant amount of this book was written amid a global pandemic. Zoom calls, texts, and emails with Claudia Calhoun, Jordana Cox, Molly Fair, Joshua Glick, Eva Hageman, Devin McGeehen-Muchmore, Kristine Nolin, Jeri Wieringa, and Caroline Weist kept us grounded. Miriam Posner, Lauren Klein, and Jessica Marie Johnson have been constant guides, pioneering the intersection of digital humanities and data science.

Teaching and research are intimately connected. Working to understand and then explain to someone else one's theories and methods, and then the grappling with the questions that follow, is a humbling and rewarding process. Thank you, Jennifer Guiliano and David Wrisley, for the opportunities to teach the concepts that became foundational to this book as well as to learn from the HILT (Humanities Intensive Learning and Teaching) and the NYU Abu Dhabi Winter Institute in Digital Humanities communities. Thank you to the students at the University of Richmond who shared their excitement to try out new methods and conduct research. Salar Ather and Aalok Sathe's work on sitcom laugh tracks as independent studies still has us giggling at some of the results.

Workshopping and presenting this work at various stages offered influential opportunities to develop this project. Along with the great feedback at conferences, we are grateful to the colleagues who invited us to share our work, including Susan Aasman, Saskia Asser, Nicolas Ballier, Elisabeth Burr, James Connolly, Alexander Dunst, Jasmine van Gorp, Ann Hanlon, Tim van der Heijden, Vilja Hulden, Mike Kane, Ulf Otto, Nora Probst, Vincent Renner, Douglas Seefeldt, Thomas Smits, Stewart Varner, and Jun Yan. Thank you, and thanks to your colleagues, for thinking with us. A special thank you to our co-conspirator Mark Williams for his relentless efforts to amplify this project at every stage. Gratitude as well to the reviewers and editors of our first article on distant viewing in *Digital Scholarship in the Humanities* and our next article on sitcoms with co-author Annie Berke in the *Journal of Cultural Analytics*, which would become the basis for chapter 5. We appreciate Annie's support for our adapting this work for the book and her brilliant insights into post–World War II TV, which she expands on in her new book, *Their Own Best Creations: Women Writers in Postwar Television*. Finally, thank you to the peer reviewers including Lev Manovich for your insightful feedback that helped us clarify key ideas while helping us reach an interdisciplinary audience.

Research support made this project possible. The University of Richmond's institutional commitment to digital humanities and data science has been key. Deans Kathleen Skerrett and Patrice Rankine understood that hiring us together was critical to the success of our individual research, and that we would do even more together. Our departments helped us navigate being new professors, making sure we had time to pursue research and to integrate our scholarship into teaching. The Department of Rhetoric and Communication's embrace of digital humanities under the leadership of Chairs Nicole Maurantonio and Tim Barney, with the enthusiastic support of Mari Lee Mifsud and Paul Achter, has made for an environment that one could only dream of. With enthusiasm and patience, Brenda Thomas in the Foundation, Corporate, and Government Relations office navigated us through grant applications and management. Associate Provost Carol Parish's efforts to build an institution that supports interdisciplinary computational research steeped in the liberal arts has allowed us to scale up our research to the next level. Grant support from the Mellon Foundation funded the Collections as Data Initiative, which provided an invaluable opportunity to think and imagine with Carol Chiodo about how distant viewing could support museums and libraries. We are also appreciative of the visiting positions at the Université Paris-Diderot and the Collegium de Lyon made possible through Nicolas Ballier and Vincent Renner. We are grateful to Patricia Hswe and the Mellon Foundation for the opportunity to develop software to make distant viewing more accessible in the years to come. Finally, the National Endowment for the Humanities' Office of Digital Humanities has been with us at each step over the past decade. We are incredibly grateful to Brett Bobley, Sheila Brennan, Perry Collins, and Jennifer Serventi for their support of *Photogrammar* (HAA-284853-22 and HD-51421-11) and the Distant Viewing Toolkit (HAA-261239–18). Along with sharing your excitement about innovation and a culture of openness, you provided us with the time, space, and resources, and, perhaps most importantly, built the interdisciplinary digital humanities community that made this open-access book possible.

As with so many exciting opportunities in our careers, Laura Wexler has been central. In addition to sharing her passion for the power of visual culture to explain our world, she connected us with a remarkable network of intersectional feminist media scholars including Elizabeth Losh. Our deepest gratitude goes to Liz, who took significant time to provide formative feedback on the first few chapters of this book before anyone else had seen a page. The chance to work with colleagues who take the time to help you make a work the best version of itself is one more reason we are also indebted to both of these pioneers of the digital humanities for connecting us with the MIT Press and Noah Springer, who has been a tireless advocate of this project. Thank you as well to Kathleen A. Caruso and Paula Woolley for their careful reading of this book. We are lucky to work with such a supportive and ambitious team.

Looking nationally and internationally, we are indebted to the individuals and institutions across the world that have advocated for open access, open data, and open source. We are grateful for the United States Library of Congress, particularly the Prints and Photographs Division and LC Labs. Colleagues such as Beverly Brannan and Meghan Ferriter have worked in the background to make our kind of research possible. Our scholarship would not have been possible without the continued work and support of the open-source software communities within data science and computer vision. Further, a future of computer vision that is explainable and committed to intersectional feminism and anti-racism continues to require relentless advocacy. Thank you to groups such as Data & Society, the AI Now Institute, and the Algorithmic Justice League for your work to hold all of us accountable while building a more just and equitable future.

Finally, we want to acknowledge our families. Along with their unconditional support and love, they kindly listened to us tease out the core ideas of this book over lobster rolls in Maine or red beans and old-fashioneds in New Orleans, for years. While the actual book project started shortly after we became an official family, the process leading to the first typed pages taught us that forging a collaboration would take a loving amount of work, kindness, and vulnerability. Only our dear dog Sargent, who passed away as this book came to completion, knows all the coffee, walks, and dinner debates that this has taken; Roux has big shoes to fill.

Introduction

In the fall of 2010, we began working on our first collaboration. In what would eventually become the public digital project *Photogrammar*, we set out to build an interactive space that allowed visitors to visualize the more than 170,000 digitized Farm Security Administration / Office of War Information (FSA-OWI) photographs produced by the US government between 1935 and 1944. Our collaboration served as an ideal mixture of our interests. Taylor was a graduate student in a statistics department with a research focus on exploring and visualizing complex datasets. Lauren was a graduate student in American Studies with a concentration in public humanities with a focus on twentieth-century American film and photography. Combining the FSA-OWI collection's rich metadata and meticulously digitized public-domain images to create a publicly accessible interface overlaid perfectly with both of our areas of research. A proof of concept developed in Laura Wexler's public humanities graduate seminar turned into a full-fledged digital humanities public project thanks to the National Endowment for the Humanities Office of Digital Humanities.

Our work became a popular public project that would welcome millions of visitors and encourage numerous extensions and revisions. We created interactive visualizations that allowed exploration of almost all the collection's available metadata. Visitors could view one of several interactive maps, follow the journeys of individual photographers, search by themes, and explore the photographic captions. The critical context and the contribution of these elements to visitors' understanding of the FSA-OWI collection should not be understated. However, something seemed missing. We were working with an extensive collection of documentary photography, and it was ultimately the photographs that drew us and others to this collection.

Our work, however, facilitated an aggregative analysis of every element *but* the photographs. The images were only accessible by looking at them individually, with no way to search by visual themes or identify objects and people present within the frame. There was a disconnect between the main objects of interest and the affordances provided by our work.

The absence of image-based methods in our initial iterations of *Photogrammar* was driven by a scarcity of readily available tools, not a lack of interest. Digital images are challenging to work with computationally, for reasons that we interrogate in the following chapters. The best available methods we could find performed poorly on historic black-and-white photographs. Face detection methods missed more faces than they found, failing to find faces that were not at a particular angle and unable to detect anyone wearing a hat. Algorithms for detecting objects in images were more likely to produce comically bizarre predictions than usable information. Methods for aggregating based on dominant colors fared better but were not well suited to our collection of predominantly black-and-white photographs. Illustrations of these predictions were a consistent element of the earliest talks we gave on the work. Our favorite example came from the photograph featured in chapters 1 and 2 of a shepherd riding a horse in a field next to his sheepdog. Even though it was in vivid color and contained three distinct objects within the lexicon of popular computer vision algorithms, most failed to identify any element of the image correctly. The experience led us to ask more questions about exactly how these algorithms were built and for whom. We kept asking ourselves: what ways of seeing are these built to view and what if we thought differently about why we should use them.

By 2016 the landscape of available tools for working computationally with images had undergone a dramatic expansion. Software libraries such as darknet (2016), TensorFlow (2015), keras (2015), PyTorch (2016), and Detectron (2017) suddenly provided out-of-the-box access to increasingly accurate and powerful computer vision algorithms.[1] Scholars working with digital collections of images began to use this new set of approaches. Applications appeared in venues such as the Culture Analytics program at UCLA's Institute for Pure and Applied Mathematics, workshops held by the special interest group for audiovisual material within the Association of Digital Humanities Organizations (ADHO), and articles in the newly created *International Journal for Digital Art History*. Our work shifted as well.

Presentations that previously ended by critiquing algorithmic results were replaced with forward-looking examples of how computer vision was helping us reimagine the FSA-OWI collection by providing approaches for a visual search and discovery interface. Rather than relying solely on existing computer vision algorithms, we began to customize and build algorithms that viewed in the ways that furthered our areas of interest.

Our excitement about the improvements in computer vision algorithms was tempered by our prior experiences that had highlighted the comparative difficulty of training computers to understand digital images. The tools seemed to be producing helpful information, but what features of the images continued to be lost through their algorithmic transformation? Many of these new tools were created or sponsored by large corporations and government entities. What are the implications of aligning our analyses with the interests of these organizations? Software for data exploration and visualization was not built around the study of digital images. How can our exploratory methods catch up with the new methods in computer vision? Numerous scholars in media and visual culture studies—such as John Berger, David Bordwell, Lisa Cartwright, Stuart Hall, Lev Manovich, Lisa Nakamura, Leigh Raiford, Marita Sturken, and Laura Wexler[2]—have stressed the importance of thinking carefully about how images are created, circulated, and interpreted. When applying complex computational approaches to the study of digital images, it is as vital as ever to consider these questions. To enable the careful and critical computational exploration of digitized visual collections, we need a cohesive theory for how computer vision creates meaning and a methodological specificity that takes into account the intricacies of digital images as a form and format.

In this text, we present a theory and methodological description of what we refer to as *distant viewing*, the application of computer vision methods to the computational analysis of digital images. Our goal is to offer a constructive and generative critique of computer vision that focuses on enabling fruitful applications. To the best of our knowledge, this text is the first book-length treatment that approaches the application of computer vision to the study of visual messages as its own object of study. The distinction here is important because our approach allows for a critical understanding of the possibilities and limitations of existing computer vision techniques. It also provides a framework for a reflexive understanding of computer vision as a way of circulating and producing knowledge.

The focus of distant viewing on *digital* images is a pragmatic one, resulting from the fact that the application of computer vision requires machine-readable inputs. However, this does not limit our objects of study to born-digital materials. Distant viewing can be applied to digitized collections originally produced in almost any medium. For example, we can apply our approach to digitized collections of photographs, photographic negatives, newspapers, comics, and posters. We can also work with digital images of material culture, something we return to in chapter 6. Distant viewing is also not limited to still images; it can be used to study collections of objects from media such as television, film, and video games. An example of distant viewing applied to a pair of television series is illustrated, for example, in chapter 5. In most cases, when one is applying computer vision to a digital image, we argue that this is distant viewing.

Our terminology is motivated by the concept of *distant reading* from the field of computational literary studies. The specific meaning and importance of the term *distant reading* has been extensively discussed; it is not our goal to make specific connections or proclamation within these debates.[3] Rather, our terminology signals a general interest in adapting the computational literary studies approach of applying computational and statistical techniques to large corpora in the service of humanistic research questions.[4] While certainly not without their critics, these approaches have opened exciting new lines of scholarship.[5] Our terminology also signals a departure from the textual focus of literary studies. The process of interpreting a visual message is semiologically and phenomenologically different from the act of reading a text, which we theorize in chapter 1. As we will explore in the following chapters, these differences lead to important changes in the way that we can apply and interpret the results of computational analyses.

In the tradition of visual culture studies and computer vision as well as our history of collaboration, we take a transdisciplinary perspective to our work. Both of us were trained in interdisciplinary fields that taught us the power of thinking across boundaries of disciplines and fields. We primarily draw from and engage with scholarship from film and media studies, visual semiotics, digital humanities, information science, computer science, and data science. The text's structure and focus are designed to be legible and useful to audiences coming from any of these varied perspectives.

The first two chapters establish our main theoretical and methodological claims about distant viewing. Chapter 1 begins by investigating what it means to say that computer vision "understands" visual inputs. We draw from information science and semiotics to illustrate why the way that digital images convey information necessitates a different approach. Specifically, we see that this process involves creating annotations that capture some, though never all nor ever perfectly, of the information present in the images. We conclude the chapter by showing how the process of annotation can be seen as a machine-mediated way of viewing images; this leads us to understand how existing scholarship in media studies shapes the application of computer vision. In chapter 2, we engage with the methodological aspects of working with computer vision annotations. We investigate how standard approaches used in data science to explore data must be adjusted when working with computer vision, resulting in four phases of analysis. Namely, we must *annotate* our collection using computer vision algorithms, then *organize* the annotations and metadata, *explore* the data and our research questions, and finally *communicate* the results. The first two chapters engage in a close analysis of a single image, the FSA-OWI photograph of a shepherd mentioned above. We hope to model how computational analyses should also help highlight, rather than supplant, the close reading of individual images.

Chapters 3 through 6 present the use of distant viewing within four different application domains. As readers move from chapter to chapter, the complexity of the computer vision models build. Each chapter is structured around the first three phases of the distant viewing method described in chapter 2: annotate, organize, and explore; the fourth phase, communication, is this book. After establishing a research question, we start by understanding one or more annotations provided by computer vision algorithms, organize other metadata attached to the collection, and finish by conducting an exploration of the organized data. Along the way, we discuss the limitations of these algorithms as we think carefully about exactly what these computer vision algorithms view, and do not view. Chapter 3 investigates the use of color in movie posters and its relationship to genre. We see how distant viewing can address complex research questions even when using relatively low-level annotations. In chapter 4, we apply a region segmentation algorithm to the photographs from the FSA-OWI archive. This chapter shows how computer vision annotations can both support and supplant the organizational logic of the archive. We illustrate in chapter 5 how distant viewing can also be used with moving images. We see how formal film elements can be applied to study issues of gender and power within a pair of network-era sitcoms. Finally, in chapter 6, we apply distant viewing to a collection of images from a large encyclopedic museum to see how computer vision can open digital collections through public interfaces.

Our excitement about the possibilities for the computational analysis of collections of digital images has been shared by many other research groups. Some of the earliest examples come from the manual annotation of film and television metrics by Barry Salt, Gunars Civjans, Yuri Tsivian, and Jeremy Butler.[6] Recently, the journal *Digital Humanities Quarterly* (DHQ) sponsored a special issue focused on film and video analysis in 2020, with articles describing projects such as Barbara Flueckiger's FilmColors project and Masson et al.'s *Sensory Moving Image Archive project* (SEMIA).[7] Along with Stefania Scagliola and Jasmijn Van Gorp, we edited another DHQ special issue titled "AudioVisual Data in DH" with over twenty research articles from a wide variety of disciplines and nation contexts.[8] Interest has also expanded from the growing field of digital art history, which has had several special issues, conferences, and a new journal that have included a significant amount of computational work. Notably, in the first issue of the *International Journal for Digital Art History*, K. Bender made the first use of the term "distant viewing" within his study of the iconography of Aphrodite/Venus.[9] Numerous other exciting research papers have been published in other journals, such as Nanne Van Noord, Ella Hendriks, and Eric Postma's study of artistic style and Laure Thompson and David Mimno's analysis of the study of Dadaism.[10] We hope that our work in this book further enables and encourages more developments in these and other areas.

The book is designed to be read and used. Along with being open access, the text is organized such that the chapters should be readable in any order. One reader might be interested in the theory and then an application. Another reader might interested in a particular application and therefore wish to start with one of the applications before engaging with the more theoretical opening chapters. Many of the results in the following chapters are presented as tables. We chose to communicate results using numeric tables because of the limitations of other visualization types within the existing print form, such as the lack of interactivity and color. Other ways of visualizing these results are also given in the supplementary materials.

While making novel contributions to the fields of data science and digital humanities, we have avoided superfluous technical jargon.[11] There is significant translation work to do when talking across fields and forging transdisciplinary scholarship. We aimed for a writing style that is inclusive yet precise, while the footnotes provide more technical descriptions. A glossary of common terms, particularly for terms that may be used differently in different communities, is included at the end of the text to aid in this process. In addition, we have published datasets, code, and many additional visualizations under an open-source license that replicate and further explore the applications described in the text. All of these can be viewed and downloaded on the book's accompanying website, found here:

https://distantviewing.org/book

Finally, we have developed the Distant Viewing Toolkit, open-source software made possible through generous funding from the National Endowment for the Humanities and the Mellon Foundation, that puts theory and method into practice. Information on how to install a current version of the Distant Viewing Toolkit can also be found at the link above.

By theorizing and offering a method, our approach of distant viewing participates in the call for a more careful use of algorithms in our society. When we understand computer vision as a way of seeing, we are then accountable to the histories of vision and the ways we train algorithms to see, look, and view. We are also accountable for what they do not see, look, and view. We have had a plethora of conversations with colleagues who attest to the neutrality of algorithms and resist ideas of algorithms as a technology of vision and mode of communication inculcated in social and cultural pasts, presents, and futures. Distant viewing challenges such claims and calls on us to ask each time a computer vision algorithm looks at an image what is this algorithm viewing, mislabeling, and missing as well as why did we design this algorithm to view in this way. By doing so, we can more carefully engage with the computational analysis of digital images. Now, let's go distant viewing.

1 Distant Viewing: Theory

Whether gazing at a piece of art through the lens of an iPhone in the Louvre or tapping away at Instagram Stories among the flicker of the screens in Times Square, we are surrounded by images. Visual messages impact our daily lives and have done so for centuries. More recently, technologies that have enabled born-digital images are also facilitating mass digitization as institutions such as libraries, archives, and museums produce digital images stored on servers across the world. How does one go about analyzing the messages carried by these visual forms?

There is a plethora of different approaches for studying the messages conveyed by visual media. Often these consist of applying theories from fields such as art history, film studies, and media studies to a focused set of images. These approaches can inform insights such as the topics depicted at a certain moment in time or contribute to an analysis of how formal elements lend the medium its claims to truth.[1] Examples of powerful close analyses of visual messages include Elizabeth Abel's study of Jim Crow politics in the American South, John Berger's study of gender and western art, Herman Gray's study of race in 1980s and 1990 TV, and Laura Wexler's study of Alice Austen's photographs from Ellis Island.[2] Many questions require studying a small set of images in relation to a larger whole, which can be accomplished by meticulously combing through and viewing images stored in a physical or digital archive.[3] Combined with information from other archival sources, this approach captures a large portion of research methods in the study of visual messages and has frequently formed an important aspect of our own work.

Some questions regarding visual messages require identifying subtle patterns across a large collection of images. For example, we might want to understand how improving television quality during the twentieth century changed the way shot angles were used to tell a story. Or, how lighting deci-sions in Hollywood films from the 1970s were used to challenge or establish gendered or racial stereotypes. Similarly, we might be interested in under-standing the themes in a photographic archive with hundreds of thousands of images or visualizing different themes in paintings held by a large ency-clopedic art museum. Addressing these questions begins to exceed our abil-ity to remember and to view all of the relevant images. One approach to working with these collections is to use a quantitative social science meth-odology, such as content analysis, in which a random subset of images is manually labeled according to the information being studied.[4] However, this approach has the downside of viewing only part of a collection and, because of the labor involved in creating the labels, is only able to address a small set of predefined research questions. What we want, rather, is to view, explore, and interpret visual messages across a collection of digital images. This should be an iterative, exploratory process that mirrors the approaches that we turn to when working with a smaller collection of images. Such a process, it would seem, requires a different methodology.

Excitement has recently increased about the use of computer vision algorithms—computational methods that try to replicate elements of the human visual system—to assist in the study of visual collections. Algorithms applied to digital images through software can process large amounts of data in significantly less time than would be required to perform a simi-lar task manually. Computers can aggregate patterns and surface connec-tions that may be difficult to detect otherwise. These insights can lead to new ways of seeing and exploring visual data. Melvin Wevers and Thomas Smits, for example, have called for a "turn toward the visual" within the digital humanities through the application of computer vision techniques that "open up a new world of intuitive and serendipitous exploration of the visual side of digital archives."[5] Similarly, in his recent book *Cultural Analytics*, Lev Manovich argues for and demonstrates the use of computer vision and other computational approaches for the "exploration and analy-sis of contemporary culture at scale."[6] As highlighted in the introduction, we have also been excited by the possibilities of using computer vision algorithms in our work on twentieth-century US documentary photogra-phy. A cornerstone of visual culture studies is that images make meaning differently than other forms of expression do; we must account for this fact when applying computational techniques to large collections of visual materials. By combining the growing body of applications of computer vision to the study of digital images with the work of visual culture studies, we will offer a cohesive theory that explores the methodological and epistemological implications of using computer vision as a tool for the study of visual messages.

In this chapter we present the theory of distant viewing as a way of understanding how computer vision works and enables the exploration of collections of digital images. Specifically, we will develop a theoretical understanding of how *distant viewing*— the application of computer vision methods to the computational analysis of digital images—works, and why it is needed. This work emerges from the intersection of theories from several fields, including visual semiotics, media studies, communication studies, information science, and data science. By drawing on work across the humanities, social sciences, and sciences, we offer an interdisciplinary theory that interweaves the ways of knowing and understanding that animate a range of fields to understand the relationship between computer vision and digital images.

Attention to features of image analysis becomes critical when using computational methods. Visual culture studies and visual semiotics have established that visual materials make and transmit meaning differently than other forms of communication.[7] It is necessary, then, to consider how these differences affect the modes of research afforded by computational techniques and how the unique ways that images make meaning are accounted for within specific computational methods such as computer vision. At the same time, using algorithms to assist in the processing of visual materials mediates the task of understanding through a digital, computational process. The technologies of computer vision are being trusted to "view" collections of still and moving images. This raises several pressing questions about the ways of seeing that specific algorithms engage in and why. For example, applications to support the military and surveillance state have motived many of the most studied and accessible computer vision methods, such as face detection and object-tracking. Applying these methods is never culturally neutral. Distant viewing responds to the need for a theory of how computer vision algorithms serve as a means of analysis to study visual materials, and can account for the ways that these algorithms mediate the interpretation of digital images.

Our use of the terms *distant* and *viewing* each signals a component of generating annotations from images. The first is the distance from the eye, for computational methods "see" by calculating images as numbers. The second is distance as scale. Through computer vision, interpretation of images can exceed a person's physical ability to view and remember. At the same time, distance is not objective. Viewing makes explicit that the computational processing of images is shaped by ways of seeing and practices of looking and, therefore, by a set of social and cultural decisions. Using a term explicitly linked to visuality also signals how images convey messages differently than forms such as text. By theorizing computer vision as a computational mode of communication for decoding messages, claims to objectivity through computational interpretation no longer hold. Instead, the terms together, *distant* and *viewing*, make explicit that computer vision is a technology of communication shaped by people and imbued with cultural and social values. Chapter 2, where we turn to a methodological understanding of distant viewing, provides a detailed analysis of how the process of annotation integrates with existing data analysis pipelines. Before addressing the practices of distant viewing, we consider the epistemological and semiological implications that come from exploring digital images computationally using algorithmically generated information.

In the following sections, we start by drawing on concepts from visual semiotics and information science to establish that the use of computer vision to create structured annotations is necessary because of the way digital images are stored and the way images convey meaning. We then establish a framework for the specific ways that distant viewing uses computer vision. We show how images are converted into structured annotations that serve as mediators throughout the process of computation. Then, we illustrate how the application of computer vision can be understood as machine-based ways of seeing. The process of seeing through a computer is subject to culturally influenced factors, often mirroring human-based ways of seeing. Recognizing how these influences affect what information is privileged and hidden by modern computer vision algorithms allows us to understand the possibilities and limitations of distant viewing.

Meaning Making through Images

The process of interpreting meanings encoded in an image is a part of our daily lives, often implicit, and occurring incredibly quickly. For example, what do we interpret when we view a photograph in an online newspaper of a sandy beach with palm trees bent over precariously in the same direction, large waves crashing onto the shore, and dark clouds on the horizon? Many people, even before reading an accompanying caption or headline, will have a near-instantaneous realization that the news is covering the existence of a severe weather event. How is this kind of information transferred through an image, such as the watercolor or photograph in figure 1.1? Meaning is primarily interpreted based on elements that resemble a storm: the effects of dark skies and oncoming heavy winds. The same image could be meaningfully printed in newspapers around the world, regardless of the language of the newspaper. Attention to how images make meaning becomes a necessity to understand how to apply computer vision and interpret the results. Comparison with text demonstrates the challenges.

Textual data is described by characters, words, and syntax. Read within a particular cultural setting, these elements are interpreted as having meaning. Linguistic elements, such as words, serve as explicit signs that correspond to objects primarily by convention.[8] The word *pencil* in English is typically used to refer to a long cylindrical object that contains inner solid marking material (such as graphite or charcoal) surrounded by an outer material (such as wood) for writing or drawing. Millions of English speakers

Figure 1.1
On the left, a Winslow Homer watercolor depicting a scene from Nassau, Bahamas, in 1898 (Metropolitan Museum of Art, 06.1234; *Palm Tree, Nassau* (1898), https://www.metmuseum.org/art/collection/search/11131). On the right, a photograph by Brigitte Werner taken at Hayman Island, Australia, in 2019 (https://pixabay.com/photos/hayman-island-australia-travel-745789/).

induce the link between the six-letter word and the definition by their shared usage. That is, most words function as *symbols*, a socially agreed-upon connection between the word and the concept represented by the word.[9] Grammatical constructs such as verb conjugation, plurality, and object-verb relationships operate similarly within a particular language to produce higher-level meanings between individual words.

Visual forms such as film and photographs convey meaning in a different way than text.[10] They do not convey information primarily through agreed-upon relationships.[11] A photograph, for example, in its most basic form is a measurement of light through the use of either chemically sensitive materials or a digital sensor.[12] The objects represented within a photograph can typically be identified by people who speak different languages.[13] As Roland Barthes argues, there is a "special status of the photographic image: it is a message without a code."[14] In photography, it is not necessary to construct an explicit mapping between the visual representation and what is being represented. The relationship between the photograph and the object represented by the photograph is signified by shared features between the object and its photo.[15] In other words, meaning is conveyed through the photograph's mimetic qualities.

A similar relationship holds for other visual forms. Both paintings and photographs illustrate and circulate concepts through characteristics such as lines, color, shape, and size.[16] Images serve as a link to the object being represented by sharing similar qualities. It is possible to recognize a painting of a particular person by noticing that the painted object and person in question share properties such as hairstyle, eye color, nose shape, and clothing. The representational strategies of images, therefore, differ from those of language. While often rendered meaningful in different ways through language, visual material is pre-linguistic.[17] The French poet Paul Valéry eloquently described this phenomenon as "looking, in other words forgetting the name of the things that one sees."[18]

Interpreting images is further complicated by the amount of variation in images intended to convey the same or similar concepts. Photography offers an example again. The culturally coded elements of photographic images coexist with the raw measurements of light. The cultural elements are exposed through the productive act of photography—what Barthes refers to as the image's "connotation."[19] Consider the images in figure 1.1. They were created over a century apart on nearly opposite sides of the world.

On the left, the painting was created by pushing pigments suspended in water across a piece of paper. On the right, we have a digital image created by capturing the components of light observed over a small fraction of a second by an array of digital camera sensors. Yet, despite these differences, viewing each image conveys a similar scene of palm trees blowing in the wind in front of an ocean bay. Further connotations of the images can be built up from these elements. We may view either of these images as connoting scenes of idyllic luxury and relaxation, like the scenes one might post on social media from a vacation at a tropical beach. Or, possibly with some additional context, we might understand the movement of the palm trees as representing a destructive and dangerous oncoming storm. Interpreting the messages of a single image requires decoding its individual elements, an act that becomes even more important when working with a large collection.

Interpreting the connotation of visual messages is further shaped by people's beliefs and values.[20] As media theorist Stuart Hall argues, the messages encoded and decoded from images are not objective but shaped by the cultural, social, and political meanings that people want to convey and are positioned to interpret. For example, the photographer may have taken the photograph shown in figure 1.2 to convey loyalty. Whether the viewer decodes that message is not necessarily a given, depending on their background. A viewer from a different position may interpret the image as about the man's dominance of the landscape and, therefore, ideas about masculinity. How one interprets an image is shaped by the larger cultural and social ideologies that inform how one interprets the world.[21] The messages that are encoded may not be decoded, and messages that were not intentionally encoded may be decoded. How information is encoded and decoded is shaped by cultural ideologies, embodied ways of knowing, social scripts, and grammars of everyday life from which we learn and which we rely on to interpret the world.[22] How one views an image through computational processes is a part of the same process.

We can extend these considerations to the computational analysis of digital images. While a person looking at an image can decode the objects and meaning of the visual messages, the process of making these explicit decisions is what makes images so challenging to study computationally. We rely on learned semiotic and ideological systems to interpret the meaning of visual material. This interpretive process must be made explicit in computational

Figure 1.2
A color photograph digitized as part of the Farm Security Administration / Office of
War Information (FSA-OWI) archive, held by the US Library of Congress. The photograph is credited to staff photographer Russell Lee and cataloged as being taken in
August 1942. The item's caption reads: "Shepherd with his horse and dog on Grav-
elly Range, Madison County, Montana" (Library of Congress, https://www.loc.gov
/pictures/item/2017878800/).

processes. Therefore, the computational analysis of images requires an algorithmic interpretation of the meaning of digital images. Distant viewing asks
that we acknowledge and take into account the interpretative, ideological
work of algorithmically analyzing digital images. To further deduce how the
process of computationally decoding the messages in an image works, we
must understand how images are stored and analyzed by a computer.

Working with Digital Images

The unique features that humanistic inquiry have identified about working with visual materials apply to analyzing digital images. The way images

are stored as pixels mirrors the semiotic differences between forms such as text and image. In lieu of the human eye, computational interpretation through computer vision is used to decode the meaning of images. Seeing through computer vision converts the act of viewing into a computational process. The speed of computational processes thus enables analysis at scale and the decoding of millions of images in a short period of time. Whether applied to a single image or at scale, the information captured by computer vision becomes a mode of communication for interpreting messages in digital images.

Digital images are stored in formats that make it possible to see images on a digital screen. A computer displays images as pixels, the "minute individual elements in a digital image."[23] The word "pixel" itself reflects this relationship. It is a combination of *pix*, the plural form of *pic* (which is short for *picture*), and *el*, which is an abbreviation of *element*.[24] The term emerged alongside the terms *pix* and *pel* in the 1960s among researchers working on image processing who were trying to find ways to describe the basic elements of images. The digital image processing and artificial intelligence communities embraced the term *pixel* during the 1970s, followed by the television and image sensor communities in the 1980s.[25] Debates and norms across research disciplines and industries over the last several decades have resulted in slight variations in definitions and uses of the term. The most common definition today is that a pixel is the smallest element of a digital image.

Computers work with digital images as a set of numbers that comprise pixels. As shown in figure 1.3, a pixel is stored as three numbers, indicating the amount of red, green, and blue light needed to represent the color of one point in the image. It is possible to create almost any color with this method.[26] Adding the maximum amount of red and green and turning off the blue, for example, results in yellow. The complete digital image in figure 1.2 is represented by a computer by storing three rectangular grids corresponding to the red, green, and blue light intensities for every pixel in the image.

Returning to figure 1.2 helps illustrate a disconnect between the computer's storage and our understanding of the image. Figure 1.4 shows a grayscale version of the same image at four different zoom levels. Each zoom level is centered on the left eye of the horse. When we look at the largest image, it seems apparent that this is a photograph of a horse and that its left eye is at the center of our cropped image. When we look at the

Figure 1.3
The upper-left figure is a cropped and lower-resolution version of the shepherd seen in figure 1.2. The other panels show the red (upper right), green (lower left), and blue (lower right) pixel intensities. The numbers indicate how bright each color channel is as an integer from 0 to 255.

two highest zoom levels in isolation, it seems impossible to guess that these are images of a horse's eye. However, these same pixels were identified as an eye in the lower zoom levels. How is it possible that the same numbers can be interpreted so differently?

When we look at the display of a digital image, we understand the pixels in context with one another. We can only identify the eye after putting

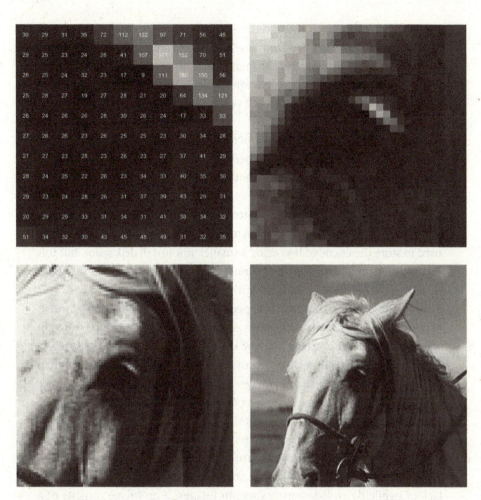

Figure 1.4
Four zoomed and grayscale versions of the image in figure 1.2. The highest level of zoom (upper left) also includes the grayscale pixel intensities, an integer from 0 (black) to 255 (white). All of the images are centered on the left eye of the horse in the image.

it into perspective with other pixels that resemble the horse's ears, nose, hair, and neck. These features are similarly understood only by putting them in perspective with all the other pixels. The implication for analyzing digital images, then, is that a substantial gap exists between the numeric representation of the image by the computer and the parts of the image that one sees when viewing the image. The pixels that represent figure 1.1's two images—from a digital scan of the watercolor image and the born-digital image on the right—provide another example. The specific pixels used and printed from the two images are completely different, yet we are able to understand the images as both representing scenes with elements of palm trees, an ocean, and the sky. With all of this variation, how do we tell the computer which pixels to look for and what those sets of pixels mean?

The challenge of interpreting pixels is further complicated by how images are stored compared to other data types. We return to the comparison between images and text, but this time focusing on how they are digitally stored. Text is written as a one-dimensional stream of characters. These characters are written in an encoding scheme that defines an agreed-upon mapping from 0s and 1s into symbols.[27] Compression software can be used to store the encoded text using a smaller amount of disk space, but this compression must be reversible. Going from the compressed format back into the raw text must be possible without losing any information.

Since images are composed of pixels, they are in a different format. While displayed as an array of pixels on the screen, images can be stored in several compressed formats. Many standard compression formats, such as JPEG, use a lossy compression algorithm. These algorithms only approximately reconstruct the original image. Similarly, it is possible in any storage format to rescale an image to a lower resolution. This process saves storage space but results in a grainier version of the original. Differences in storage methods between text and image data correspond to the semiological differences argued by scholars in media studies and visual culture studies. The fact that digital images can be scaled to a smaller size highlights the lack of explicitly coded elements within images. If an image consists of a code system, lossy compression will require losing some coded elements. However, images reproduced from compressed files have no detectable differences from the original file for a moderate amount of compression.[28] An illustration of how lossy compression affects an image is given in figure 1.5. The colors, shapes, and objects within the frame remain discernable even under extreme forms of information compression.

The format of digital images reinforces the semiological properties of visual materials. Pixels convey meaning only when put into context with one another by mimicking the act of viewing objects, people, and environments directly through the human visual system. The rectangular grid of pixels printed in different shades of gray in figure 1.4 convey the image of a

Figure 1.5
The image from figure 1.2 is shown (upper-left) along with five levels of increased compression. The compression algorithm uses a singular value decomposition on the individual color channels, reducing the dimensionality of the matrix of pixel intensities to 100, 50, 25, 15, and 5, respectively. We used this approach because it does a good job of showing what happens to the image under extreme forms of compression.

horse, for example, because looking at the resulting print shares similarities to the act of looking at a horse in real life. The complex ways that images make meaning are a large part of what make visual forms popular kinds of cultural expression and what makes visual materials particularly exciting objects of study. These complexities, however, must be accounted for when applying a computational analysis to the study of visual materials, a task that we now turn toward to fully theorize distant viewing.

Computational Exploration with Computer Vision

Returning to our primary task of working computationally with a collection of digital images, recall that standard methods for the visualization and exploration of data cannot be applied as-is to image data. Having seen the ways that visual materials convey meaning, we now have a more concrete way of understanding why applying computational methods to a collection of images presents certain difficulties. Fortunately, as is often the case, identifying the source of these obstacles will become the first step in producing a solution. An example will help further illuminate the challenges that we need to solve.

Consider the task of trying to automatically detect and characterize themes found within a large digital collection of newspaper articles. The explicit codes of written language provide a powerful tool for this task. Each of our texts can be split into individual words, the smallest linguistic unit meaningfully understood in isolation, and the number of times a word is used can serve to encode information about each document.[29] Then, we could use the word counts to automatically find sets of terms that tend to co-occur within the same documents with a high probability. In other words, if one word from a detected topic is used in each document, other words within the same topic are also more likely to be used. With no explicit tagging of the dataset, this kind of model could, for example, detect a set of co-occurring words such as *cloudy*, *cold*, *wind*, and *afternoon*. Manual intervention is only needed to interpret this topic to conclude that these words all focus on the concept of "weather." Both the interpretive acts of determining the keywords to associate with each article and assigning a meaning to the co-occurring words may be delayed until after a model has been applied. These are crucial features of many methods for textual analysis; the power of word counts to convey a reasonable approximation of document-level meaning has been one of the most important tools for the computational analysis of textual data.

Now, consider the parallel visual task of finding and identifying themes within a collection of digital newspaper photographs. As we have argued in the previous two sections, there is no equivalent way of grouping together and counting raw pixel values in the way that we were able to do by grouping letters into words. For this reason, before we do a computational analysis of a collection of images, one needs to interpret the messages encoded in the images. In other words, the images must first be *viewed*. There is no equivalent option, as there is with structured and textual data, to delay interpretation of the images' meaning(s) before applying computational methods. In other words, the first step of interpreting each image must be to create a structured, or indexical, system that we can then aggregate and analyze. Because these interpretations will not perfectly capture all the information present in the image, care must be given to the ways that the images are interpreted relative to the guiding areas of inquiry.

To be more concrete, the computational analysis of a collection of digital images requires as a first step that the messages encoded within the images are interpreted through the construction of structured labels.[30] We will refer to these labels as *annotations* and use *annotation* to describe the process by which these labels are created. Annotations can take a variety of different forms. They can be a single number, such as an indication of how many people are in an image. A single word can also be used as an annotation, such as an indication of the name of an object at the center of the image. Other annotations include automatically generated sentence-length captions or a large set of numbers representing the amounts of predefined colors present in the image's frame. Annotations can even take the form of images themselves, such as through the tagging of images with other images that contain the same people. Often, a collection of different kinds of annotations will need to be produced to address a specific question that one is exploring with a given collection of images. How, then, do we go about producing these annotations?

Manually creating structured annotations for a collection of digital images can be a laborious task. Even the production of a single, relatively clear label such as counting the number of people in the frame, can become prohibitively time-consuming when working with a large collection of images. More intricate annotations, such as outlining and describing every object in each image, are essentially impossible to construct manually for all but the smallest collections. Methods such as content analysis avoid these difficulties by only labeling a random sample of images and generally restricting the annotations to a small set of straightforward and relatively easy to produce categories.[31] These approaches make it impossible to iteratively explore a collection of images and limit our analysis to only a subset of possible research questions. Further, many more complex relationships between visual features and archival data can only be established by working with the entirety of a collection. Another approach is clearly needed.

The process of creating and interpreting digital images through annotations generated by computer vision is at the center of distant viewing.[32] Using algorithms to generate annotations allows us to work with the entirety of a collection. It also allows us to create intricate annotations that can be visualized, modeled, remixed, and aggregated through an iterative exploratory analysis. Our name for our approach to working with collections of digital images highlights the fact that the creation of annotations should be seen as a process of viewing, or interpreting, and that this viewing is done at a distance because it is mediated through the algorithmic process of computer vision. An understanding of the field of computer vision will further elucidate the possibilities and limitations of distant viewing.

The field of computer vision focuses on how computers automatically produce ways of understanding digital images. The field is interdisciplinary by design, drawing on research in areas as diverse as computer science, physics, engineering, statistics, physiology, and psychology. Most tasks in computer vision are oriented around algorithms that mimic the human visual system. Tasks include detecting and identifying objects, categorizing motion, and describing an image's context. While visual understanding is at the center of the field, computer vision algorithms may also take a multimodal approach. Algorithms may use, for example, image captions or film soundtracks to augment visual components in much the same way that humans integrate all of their sensory inputs to understand the world around them.

Our ability to construct high-quality computer vision annotations is driven by current research focuses within the field of computer vision. These directions, likewise, are influenced by the industry and government applications that fund the research. Some of the earliest computer vision algorithms were designed to identify images of numbers; this research was explicitly funded to sort mail envelopes based on detecting handwritten postal codes.[33] High-accuracy algorithms exist for the detection and identification of faces within an image. The research behind these tasks has been driven in no small part by applications in surveillance, which we should engage with cautiously. Several tools provide high-quality annotations for the detection of cars, people, crosswalks, and stoplights. These annotations are the direct consequence of computer vision applications within the technology of self-driving cars. When we use computer vision algorithms to produce automatically generated annotations, it is crucial to remember the role these funding streams play in the content and structure of available algorithms.

The availability of accurate annotations is also a function of the level to which an annotation is abstract or culturally mediated. Some tasks are well-positioned to be addressed with computer vision. For example, computer vision algorithms are better than human evaluators at detecting defects in agricultural products.[34] Similarly, a simple model can be used to identify the orientation of photographs with almost perfect accuracy.[35] Both of these tasks have concrete "answers" and can be identified by looking at only a small portion of the image, making them relatively easy tasks within computer vision. Other annotations present more difficulties and bring to the fore ethical and social questions. The goal of automatically identifying a person's emotion based on a still image is very difficult and shaped by cultural politics.[36] Computer vision algorithms struggle to attain human-like accuracy even when classifying strong emotions within a single cultural context.[37] When dealing with more subtle emotions across a range of cultures, the task becomes nearly impossible even for human annotators, much less a computational algorithm. The types of questions and analyses available through distant viewing are shaped by the relative difficulty and constructiveness of building the algorithms that are annotating. The challenge of determining if a task is amenable to exploration through computer vision is further complicated by determining exactly what we are decoding.

Decoding through Viewing

The process of distant viewing applies computer vision algorithms to automatically interpret a layer of meaning within images through the creation of structured annotations. As signaled in our terminology, computer vision algorithms engage in the process of viewing an image. This characterization allows for a reflexive formulation of distant viewing. Whereas we have so far used visual semiotics to argue for the necessity of computer vision, we can similarly take computer vision as an object study itself which can be analyzed through the application of media theories. Theories of communication around decoding become key.

The process of annotating images with computer vision can be understood as a mode of communication that transmits a message between the materials of interest—the digitized images—and human audiences. To computationally decode the messages, people must decide which annotations to look for in an image using computer vision. The human eye is replaced by computational processes that identify the features in images through numbers. As a result, computer vision decodes to interpret and convey encoded messages in digital images. At the same time, computational methods are created by people and are therefore not outside of cultural, social, and historical ways of seeing and practices of looking.[38] By theorizing computer vision as a computational process of decoding messages ("viewing"), the method of distant viewing makes explicit that computer vision is a technology of communication produced by people and therefore imbued with cultural, political, and social values.

How to interpret visual media in a digital form is a question about conveying and interpreting meaning. In his model of communication, Stuart Hall argued that messages are encoded and decoded.[39] The sender produces a message in a form such as television. The message is circulated, and audiences then interpret the message. The message encoded may not be the message decoded. The values and beliefs of the creator and receiver shape the messages that are conveyed and interpreted. The form of the medium also impact which messages are communicated. For example, digital images make and convey meaning differently than audio. The same image, such as a meme, will often be interpreted differently by an audience in the United States than an audience in France. Computer vision has become another powerful actor in the process of encoding and decoding digital images. Nevertheless, exactly how is it possible to understand this newer technology of interpreting meaning in images?

Images encode messages. Exactly how they send those messages and which parts of the message are decoded are shaped by what is recognized and how the signs and symbols that comprise an image are interpreted. Visual culture studies, informed by semiotics and rhetorical studies, explores how images signify and communicate, which differs from how other forms of knowledge, such as text, do so.[40] We return again to the relationship with text. Even at the level of an individual object, meaning is encoded in images differently than in text, as theorized by semioticians across fields such as linguistics, media studies, and visual culture studies.

Computer vision has become a way for people to create annotations to decode visual messages. As a set of computational processes designed to interpret images, computer vision emerged to address the issue of how to understand images. In other words, computer vision is a computational model of communication designed to interpret information from digital images. To do so requires building annotations that replicates the features necessary to interpret the meaning of an image. Therefore, computer vision algorithms look for specific features by following processes to recognize patterns that we determine based on a task.

The process of computational viewing through computer vision algorithms produces new structures that attempt to capture layers of meaning within images. Creating structured data is often described as information "extraction" and aligns with the popular channel encoding model of communication proposed by Claude Shannon. The model provides a communication framework describing how a fixed message is passed between two parties. It focuses on the amount of intrinsic information contained in a message and the amount of redundancy needed to ensure a high probability that the resulting message will be transmitted between the two parties without any errors.[41]

Due to the nature of visual messages, however, Shannon's communication model does not accurately capture the process of producing structured data through computer vision.[42] The decoded messages do not symmetrically represent an image's intended meaning. Instead, in the language of Stuart Hall, computer vision algorithms are active participants in the process of knowledge production through the act of decoding. During this process of decoding, computer vision algorithms produce structured data from visual inputs. The knowledge produced by the algorithms—such as label names for detected objects or a probability that the image was taken outdoors—are not objective or intrinsic to the images themselves. Instead, the kinds of data labels that are privileged, and the internal mechanisms used to produce them, are significantly influenced by the social contexts that motivated, produced, and circulated the algorithms themselves. In other words, the algorithms produce knowledge by interpreting visual materials within the frame of their own artificially produced social context. Framing the use of computer vision as an imperfect decoding process highlights the need to consider the underlying decisions privileged by existing algorithms.

Computer vision expands the rate and scale of interpretation by becoming an intermediary between the eye and an image. Algorithms can iterate over millions of images looking for features. The rate is increasing as hardware such as high-performance computing and GPUs reduce the time for analysis. The ability to zoom out and view at a large scale is a powerful affordance of these recent advances. Messages that may have been difficult to interpret by looking at just a few images can be decoded through large-scale analysis. This changes not only the kinds of messages that we can decode but also what we can encode, since we now have a new mode of communication with which to interpret and convey messages.

Distance from the human eye combined with large-scale computation could lead to claims about objectivity. After all, powerful discourses have lent fields built on numeracy and quantitative evidence claims to neutrality and objectivity.[43] However, theorizing computer vision as a mode of communication inculcated in the process of sending and receiving messages challenges such claims. Instead, computer vision becomes a cultural and social process. The annotations that we adopt, create, and resist through computer vision are in conversation with existing cultural, social, and technical values shaped by visual cultures. The concept of "viewing" becomes particularly important.

Decoding images requires decisions about which annotations to view with. How and what we choose to see and look for—where we direct our gaze, how we see, and how we perceive and discern visually—are culturally and socially shaped.[44] Decoding, therefore, is not independent of visual cultures. Instead, viewing is not simply a biological process but relies on ways of seeing and practices of looking that people learn from each other to interpret the world through.[45] Viewing, therefore, conveys that decoding through computer vision is a set of decisions about how to interpret visual messages that is shaped by cultural and social values, in addition to producing them.

The distinction, as theorized in visual culture studies, between seeing and looking becomes necessary for further expanding on the stakes of using the term *viewing*.[46] *Seeing* occurs through the physical process of receiving light when one's eyes are open. This does not mean that one is *looking*, which can be defined as actively seeking to see through visual perception. For example, one might be in a room and see a photograph but choose not to look at the image. One can also try to look and not see. For example, one may return to the room to look at that photograph but not be able to locate it because the lights are turned off. Seeing occurs when the eyes are open and whether we want to see or not. The act of looking is an intentional process where we decide what we want to see. Types of looking not only include what to look for but ways of looking, such as watching. Viewing, therefore, indicates the entanglement of seeing and looking in analyzing digital images. Scholars such as John Berger, Lisa Cartwright, Lisa Nakamura, and Marita Sturken have further theorized these distinctions as producing visual cultures that we learn, circulate, and rely on to decode the meaning of images.

Ways of seeing and practices of looking shape the encoded meaning in images. As John Berger argued in the popular 1972 BBC television series and subsequent book *Ways of Seeing*, "an image became a record of how X had seen Y."[47] He analyzed how X, a community such as White male European oil painters, had seen Y, women as forms to depict in the nude, and argued that they produced this way of seeing for the male gaze and thereby revealed as well as produced problematic gendered power relations. Lisa Cartwright and Marita Sturken expanded on this concept, calling for visual culture studies to address "practices of looking" to emphasize the intentionality of looking in place of the passiveness of the biological process of seeing. One can see and not look. One can look and not see. Scholars such as Stuart Hall and Lisa Nakamura have further argued that these ways of seeing and practices of looking are shaped by and produce ideologies such as gendered and racialized visual cultures.[48] Therefore, the ways of looking replicated through media shape which messages are encoded and decoded as well as being imbued with beliefs, ideologies, and values.

How we view is also a culturally, socially, and historically informed decision.[49] Until the 1950s, most technologies of looking still involved the eye, such as a magnifying glass, telescope, and camera. The advent of computing and computer vision has enabled a way of looking that no longer relies on the physical process of the human eye.[50] Yet, the term *computer vision* and scholarship in machine learning naturalize a computational process through the language of biological seeing and the eye.[51] This research is not a biological process but rather is focused on *emulating* humans' ways of seeing and practices of looking through the fundamental way that computers "see," which is through computations based on the pixel intensities. Ways of seeing, such as color perception, and practices of looking, such as identifying people, are computationally decoded to interpret images. The result is an epistemological and ontological shift in what and how we view that does not easily fit into current theories.[52]

Therefore, we see that annotation through computer vision can be characterized as decoding messages in digital images, as a form of communication that changes how we "see," and as a new scale with which we can view images. When annotations are built through computer vision, ways of seeing and practices of looking are encoded into the computational processes to decode information about the images. This allows us to shift how we understand computer vision. Rather than focusing on whether a computer vision algorithm can be objective, we focus on defining which ways of viewing are encoded and decoded, and assessing the possibilities, limitations, and effects of these decisions.

Conclusions

In this chapter, we have focused on the epistemological and semiological implications of applying computer vision algorithms to the study of digital images, which we have theorized as distant viewing. The theory is based on the ways that visual objects make meaning, which is further supported by the way that digital images are stored and displayed. These features necessitate the creation of annotations that capture a way of viewing images, which requires the use of computer vision in order to apply distant viewing to larger corpora.

As a method, distant viewing also provides ways of reflexively and critically engaging in the computational analysis of images. While the next chapter will go into further detail, a discussion of a few possible avenues of inquiry using distant viewing is warranted. Ways of seeing and practices of looking shape our daily lives and are entangled in questions about power. Who gets to look, who is the subject of looking, and which practices of looking circulate are not neutral processes. Whether efforts by US communities of color to assert full citizenship through twentieth-century African American portrait photography, the use of the close shot in film on female bodies for the male gaze and thereby producing misogynist ways of seeing, or the use of the skin brightening and warming Instagram filters to assert ageist and racialized standards of beauty, visual cultures are being encoded and decoded through images constantly.[53] Images, therefore, are shaped by and circulate practices of looking. However, these decisions are often implicit and therefore difficult to recognize and make explicit. Distant viewing allows for decoding digital images and their visual cultures, which we demonstrate in chapters 3 through 6 by viewing a range of still and moving images.

As we go about distant viewing, there are significant reasons to be cautious about using the method to identify and challenge ways of viewing. The annotations for computer vision are largely driven by industry and government applications. Whether they are trying to identify trucks and light posts for self-driving cars or people for surveillance technology, computer vision methods are often driven by entanglements with capitalism, state power, and militarism.[54] However, computational image analysis should not just be the domain of multinational corporations and government. We can use distant viewing to ask different questions and to critique and question our visual cultures of computer vision. Furthermore, perhaps the most exciting part is that we can recreate and reimagine the role and possibilities of computer vision. Reconfiguring how to use and remake ways of viewing through computer vision algorithms can be a timely and laborious project. Distant viewing offers one way that we can question existing annotations *and* remake computer vision.

Designed with the intention to mimic the human eye and neural processes, computer vision algorithms look for certain features by following processes for calculating pixels to recognize patterns. Computer vision "sees" through numeracy and "looks" based on the assigned numerical patterns. Therefore, computer vision enables identification of practices of looking in visual materials and algorithmically creates practices of looking. Computer vision encodes social, cultural, historical, and political values algorithmically. Distant viewing, therefore, enables a reflexive view of computer vision. We can use distant viewing of digital visual materials to interrogate the ways of viewing embedded in computer vision.

Distant viewing provides a call to action. We are slowly cracking away at the facade that algorithms are unbiased and recognizing that algorithms can do incredible harm as well as good. Yes, there are algorithms of oppression.[55] Yes, there are weapons of math destruction.[56] However, we have fewer capacious theories for understanding the computational processes that produce ways of viewing at a large scale. So, we heed media scholar Steve Anderson's call to interrogate and theorize vision technologies through the lens provided by media and visual culture studies, and zoom out and in through data science and digital humanities.[57] As long as we are involved in the process of building annotations for seeing, and therefore viewing, then having a method and theory for analyzing, interpreting, and critiquing these computational processes matters. So, we need distant viewing.

2 Distant Viewing: Method

Images. Images everywhere. We see, look, analyze, and interpret images, often in seconds. A newspaper cover photo of a palm tree bent over in the wind and waves crashing ashore can quickly convey a storm. A historical photograph from the 1930s of a man, horse, and dog standing upright together in a rural plain sends messages of dominance, fortitude, and loyalty. To add a different kind of example, think of the feed on Instagram and how quickly one swipes up while still interpreting the images posted by the accounts that one follows. Messages are quickly decoded based on ways of seeing and practices of looking that we have learned, constructed, and resisted.

What happens when we slow down and ask: What is this an image of, what are the messages being conveyed, and how do we know this? In other words, what if we want to analyze how the messages interpreted were visually constructed? What if we want to explore whether there are messages that were missed on the first view? And, what if we want to view these images through certain ways of seeing and practices of looking? A person can sit down and closely analyze an image, but this takes time and becomes a challenge when the number of images increases.

Consider the challenge of analyzing images from another angle. Libraries, archives, and museums have made significant commitments to digitizing visual media. Priorities for digitization include collections with a large audience, those that the institution wants to bring attention to, or collections in a quickly degrading format. What if we want to describe each of these images? The decisions that one might make for an exhibition may not be the same as decisions designed for facilitating access, discovery, and analysis. What, then, do we do if we decide to change how to describe the images? How does one do this at large scale?

The approach we offer to this challenge, distant viewing, uses computer vision to computationally explore digital images. The previous chapter presented a theoretical treatment of the possibilities, limitations, and implications of the distant viewing approach. Here, we focus on the practical aspects of applying computer vision to a set of digital images. Building upon the stakes outlined in the previous chapter, we situate distant viewing within the field of data science. Our analysis focuses on how the method of distant viewing engages with existing data science methodologies while accounting for the unique ways that images make meaning and explicates the modeling assumptions that underlie the computational analysis of visual data.

As a starting point, consider a typical workflow for computational analysis from data science, an interdisciplinary field that applies and develops methods to understand collections of data.[1] The first diagram in figure 2.1 illustrates a series of high-level steps involved in the processing of data. The steps and names are adapted from Hadley Wickham and Garrett Grolemund's well-known text on the subject.[2] The pipeline shown here is focused on the algorithmic aspects of working with the data and therefore does not include steps such as designing a research question and collecting data. The starting point, instead, involves loading and organizing information. This structured data is often stored in the form of a relational database or files in a well-known format. The pipeline's first step, organization, includes standardizing names and units, identifying data errors, and combining or separating data according to the format needed for subsequent analyses. After the data are organized, the pipeline moves to the process of exploration. Here, an iterative mix of visualizations, transformations, and modeling is used to understand the data and address various research questions. Finally, the third step involves communicating the results of the exploration. The communication step can take various forms depending on the desired audience, such as short presentations, peer-reviewed papers, and digital projects. The arrows in the figure show the conceptual flow of information. However, data analyses almost always require a more flexible iteration back and forth between each part.

The ways that visual materials make meaning combined with the mechanics of digital images and computer vision require a modification of the standard data science pipeline. Implicit in the organization step of the pipeline is the notion that producing structured data from the available inputs requires only a reorganization of the original dataset.[3] However, as shown in

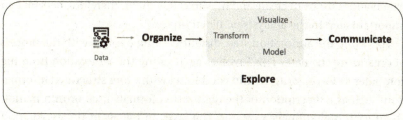

Data Science Pipeline (Structured Data)

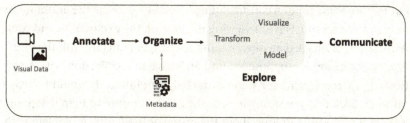

Pipeline for Distant Viewing

Figure 2.1

Two pipelines for working with data. The top represents a typical workflow when working with structured data, adapted from work by Hadley Wickham and Garrett Grolemund. The pipeline on the bottom illustrates a modification built using distant viewing, which first annotates the visual materials. (Steps such as developing a research question or hypothesis and collecting the data are integral parts of data science but omitted here for clarity.) The arrows show the conceptual flow of information; analyses of data almost always require an iterative approach moving back and forth between each part.

chapter 1, knowledge produced from computer vision algorithms works differently. Creating a structured representation of messages encoded in digital images involves a process in which information is lost as well as created.

Informed by the theory of distant viewing, our method adds a new step into the standard data science pipeline, which is incorporated into the second row of figure 2.1. This new first step encapsulates the process in which digital images are annotated with computer vision techniques. The construction of these annotations is inserted prior to the step of data organization.[4] Rather than assuming the data exists or is given, we make explicit through this addition the creation of annotations from the visual data.[5] Unlike the process of organizing structured data, annotations are not just a reorganization of the original inputs. Rather, annotations capture elements of the images using algorithms that only view in a certain way. Determining which annotations to create and how to create them, therefore, becomes an important step in the analysis of digital images.

Following the annotation step, distant viewing engages with the process of organizing the data. This involves aggregating the annotation from the computer vision algorithms and combining with other structured information, such as a description of the digitization formats used or information about each digital image's creator. The tasks and goals of the exploration and communication tasks mirror those of a standard data science pipeline but require some unique considerations. Notably, because the annotations only capture specific ways of viewing the images, the exploration and communication of image data often require re-engaging directly with the visual inputs. For example, suppose we find an image in a collection with a particularly extreme value for some extracted annotation. It would be helpful to go back and physically look at the original image to help determine if there is something unique about the image or to identify a problem with the computer vision algorithm. As a result, distant viewing is an iterative process rather than a linear pipeline.

The following sections begin by situating the method of distant viewing as a data science approach to analyzing collections of digital images. While the method of distant viewing, as with any data analysis technique, cannot be reduced to a checklist of tasks, there are benefits in dividing this method into discrete tasks. By identifying and naming different parts of distant viewing, we clarify the humanistic and computational assumptions that underlie the study of digital images, open each task in the process to inquiry and critique, and reveal how theory and method are intertwined and mutually reinforcing. We then describe the individual parts of the distant viewing method and how they are motivated by the distant viewing theory developed in chapter 1. Along the way, we will discuss strategies for approaching each part and draw on the specific examples that are further explored in the following chapters.

Annotate: Create Data with Computer Vision

The first part of the distant viewing method consists of annotating a collection of digital images using computer vision algorithms. As discussed in chapter 1, the explicit construction of a set of annotations is a necessary part of the computational analysis of a sizeable corpus of digital images because of the unique way that images make meaning and how digital images are stored. The annotations chosen for an analysis must be guided by the elements we are interested in studying because no general set of annotations captures all the information present in the original images. Decisions, therefore, must be made about which annotations to encode through computer vision.

Annotations can take many forms. There may be just a numeric value, for example, capturing the number of people in the image or the percentage of the image dominated by the background. Alternatively, there could be a single label indicating a particular category, such as "portrait" or "landscape." Slightly more complex systems return a sequence of numbers or categories. These may indicate the most dominant colors, the names of all the objects found by an algorithm, or the locations of people within the image. We demonstrate the application of these annotations in chapters 3, 4, and 5, respectively. More flexible annotations can be built from linguistic systems, such as an annotation that describes each image with a detailed caption of its content and style.[6] It is even possible to use images themselves as the elements of annotations by describing one image in terms of other images that are the most similar, an approach we will turn to in chapter 6.

As an example, let us return to the image in figure 1.2. Many ways of viewing the photograph are possible. One possible type of annotation might describe the number of people (one) and the number of animals (two) shown in the image. Another may indicate the height of the man's face relative to the height of the image (64 pixels / 1024 pixels = 6.6%). An annotation may supply the coordinates—perhaps in pixels, from the frame's top-left corner—of the man's face (200, 250, 500, 550). It may list all the objects found in the frame (dog, horse, man) or the dominant color of the foreground (#503C28; dark, muted orange) and background (#374A66; dark blue). It could give the average brightness (0.4022) and the image's average saturation (0.4168).[7] Categorical tags could be assigned to capture elements depicted in the image, ranging from the relatively explicit (grass; field; blue sky; clouds) to the increasingly subjective and abstract (work; shepherd; cold; loyalty). A linguistic system could be used to describe the contents of the image ("an older man sits on a horse overlooking a field with a dog") or its composition ("subject framed in the upper-right quadrant with a double background of a field followed by a blue sky"). To construct an annotation that features different types of information stored within the image, one can put many of these individual elements together. For example, we could use the size and location of faces to identify portraits or elements in the background to identify location. However, we will never be able to perfectly represent all the information in the image through structured annotations.

The annotating of images is both destructive and interpretive. Regardless of our attempts to produce a rich set of annotations, there will always be a difference between the original image's information and the extracted annotations' information. On the one hand, many image elements are lost, and no amount of information could ever fully capture the entirety of the original image.[8] The example annotations constructed from the image of the man on the horse, for instance, did not capture details about the size of the dog, the type of clothing the man was wearing, or the color of the horse. On the other hand, some annotations make interpretive choices about what is being represented that are often shaped by specific cultural contexts and their visual cultures. An encoding of the image as representing the concepts of "work," "loyalty," and "cold" are all interpretations based on a particular reading of the image that may not match that of the photographer or the intended audience. The people involved and the areas of inquiry that animate distant viewing shape the annotations that should be created.

To accomplish the task of automated annotation, we turn to methods from computer vision. By building annotations that can be automatically applied, we open the possibility of working with data sources that are beyond our ability to tag manually. There are several strategies for determining which computer vision algorithms to use for automatic annotation. Because computer vision research has been driven primarily by industry, government, and medical applications, prominent areas of computer vision include automation tasks such as in manufacturing applications, medical imaging, militarism in the form of drone warfare, and surveillance capitalism.[9] As a result, a large proportion of research and software within computer vision has been focused on a relatively narrow set of tasks. One way to address this challenge is to develop new models, which we demonstrate in chapter 5, but this is a time-consuming and often resource-intensive task. As an alternative, existing models can be adapted for our exploratory analyses.

Many existing models are generalizable enough as to be amended to map onto areas of inquiry from different domains. Working with algorithms out of the box can lead to generative annotations, though they often require additional post-processing or modifications of the tuning parameters that change the way model outputs are formed. For example, if studying the framing of actors in classic Hollywood films, we could start by creating an initial set of annotations using an existing pose-detection algorithm. Next, we could transform these poses into an ontology based on film-theoretic concepts such as shot blocking and shot length. Another common annotation task that can be used in a variety of applications is object recognition. While we will return to further challenges and drawbacks of object recognition in chapter 4, here we briefly describe an example of how an existing set of algorithms for object recognition offers a set of annotations that are amenable to distant viewing.

The algorithmic task of *object recognition* consists of three phases. The first is *object detection*, identifying which objects are present in an image. Algorithms for image detection are built by showing a computer example images from a set of predefined categories. For example, researchers working on self-driving cars are interested in training algorithms to see different parts of the environment, such as pedestrians, sidewalks, traffic lights, and other cars.[10] To accomplish this, they train computer algorithms to detect patterns within the images and then apply the algorithms to find similar objects in new images. In addition to knowing what objects are present, researchers also want to identify where an object is in the image. This second phase, *object localization*, is often done simultaneously with object detection and requires a dataset of thousands of pre-located objects.[11] After an object is detected and localized, computer algorithms can be further taught to conduct *object qualification*. Algorithms that detect pedestrians, for example, may include identifying their age, detecting where they are moving, and the direction in which they appear to be looking.[12] As object detection algorithms demonstrate, computer vision models come with a set of annotations that we may want to use, adjust, or reject.

Let us return to our example image from figure 1.2 to discuss the decision-making process involved in using automated annotations. We have already seen several annotations that could be used to describe the image in question, such as identifying the number of people and the number of animals in the photograph. We now investigate the coded elements returned out of the box by several popular image-processing algorithms. While the outputs of these models are shown as images, the detected regions, labels, and poses can be described by giving the coordinates of the respective bounding regions. The output of the YOLO model, trained to locate eighty-two object types, is shown in the top-left corner of figure 2.2. Objects detected

Figure 2.2
The output of several computer vision algorithms. The top row consists of object bounding boxes (YOLO9000) and detected object regions (Mask R-CNN). In the bottom row, the detected regions of the COCO Panoptic task are shown, followed by the detected COCO Keypoints.

with a high degree of confidence are illustrated by showing a rectangle, known as a bounding box, on the original image. The algorithm correctly identifies a person, a horse, and a dog. In the top-right corner of figure 2.2 is the output of the Mask R-CNN model. This model is trained on the same dataset as YOLO, but its goal is to find the exact region where an object exists rather than only using rectangular boxes. Mask R-CNN also identifies all objects with confidence scores given as percentages; for this image, it correctly detects and locates a person, the horse, and the dog. However, it also incorrectly believes that there could be a cat in the same position as the dog; interestingly, the model is more confident in the label saying the image is a cat (81%) than in the correct label of a dog (59%).

Figure 2.2 also shows the output of data trained on a slightly larger set of 133 categories, known as COCO Panoptic, which includes high-level scene regions such as "wall," "sky," and "pavement."[13] The algorithm again detects the person and the horse. It incorrectly labels the dog as a cat, failing altogether to identify the correct category. Additionally, the Panoptic model detects the sky, the grass, and a mountain region. These categories reasonably match the image, but it is unclear whether there is a meaningful distinction between the grass and the mountain category. We will explore this type of annotation and what kinds of exploratory analysis are possible in chapter 4. The final part of figure 2.2 shows the output of a model trained on the DeepPose dataset for estimating the location of body parts within the image. The algorithm detects the single person in the image and reasonably marks the man's left leg, hip, torso, neck, arms, and eyes. It also does an excellent job of detecting that the right leg is not visible within the shot. These features can be mapped and aggregated to study questions such as themes within a collection or the way a set of photographs are composed.

At a high level, what conclusions can be made from the detected features in the four images shown in figure 2.2? For one thing, the algorithms produce accurate predictions. This is striking, given that the models were all trained only on modern images, and our photograph is from 1941. The results show the remarkable predictive power that these algorithms have achieved in the past few years. Contrasting with state-of-the-art methods from a decade ago demonstrates the rate at which image segmentation has advanced within the field of computer vision. Of course, the algorithms are not foolproof—even our one example has an error, with a dog incorrectly labeled as a cat—and fall far short of mimicking general human-level intelligence. However, they have reached a point where off-the-shelf algorithms can be applied to new domains to produce meaningful results.

The creation of annotations through computer vision algorithms is a necessary step in the exploratory analysis of digital images and offers a crucial departure from the steps outlined in the standard data science pipeline. Choosing which annotations to produce and which computer vision algorithms to use has profound effects on the types of exploration we will be able to perform with our data. Selecting annotations requires understanding the history of the underlying computer vision tasks, evaluating the accuracy of the algorithms within an application domain, and determining how the output of the algorithms can be interpreted. Careful consideration of the assumptions and implications of decisions made in the annotation step is required when applying distant viewing. In the following chapters, we will carefully demonstrate how each annotation was selected and then organized to explore our research questions.

Organize: Aggregate Annotations and Combine with Metadata

As with the standard data science pipeline, we need to organize our data before undertaking the process of exploration. We commonly have two distinct types of data to organize: annotations from the application of computer vision, and structured data that has been independently collected. We first need to aggregate the annotations; often this is a straightforward process, in which we create a table from the structured data produced from each image. In some cases, however, organizing the annotations requires a careful consideration of how to produce higher-level features out of lower-level annotations. We will use the term *metadata* to refer to structured data produced independently from the annotations created with computer vision algorithms. More generally, metadata is a term used to describe "data whose purpose is to describe and give information about other data."[14] In our case, this consists of information that provides additional context to a collection of digital images. The second step in the organization our data is to combine the aggregated annotations with this independently produced metadata.

While many features can be automatically extracted directly from a single image, others require access to all images in the corpus. This mirrors a common way of seeing that we engage in daily. A single photo of a birthday party takes on new meanings and offers new information when viewed in a family photo album, for instance.[15] While the annotation process applies computer vision algorithms to each image or a small set of adjacent frames in a moving image input, there is often a need to aggregate these annotations to identify features based on information from other images in the corpora. For example, identifying that a person in one image is the same person in another image or finding objects that are near-duplicates require examining the entire collection.

Consider the two photographs shown in figure 2.3, from the FSA-OWI collection, which features over 170,000 photographs taken in the United States during the Great Depression and World War II. While the image on the right is probably unfamiliar, the image on the left is one of the most iconic photographs of the Great Depression in the United States. However, when looking at the two images together, we can identify that these photographs depict the same woman in different poses and from different angles. This realization allows us to form a connection across the corpus. While it is difficult to understand the environment in which the first image was taken based on the image itself, the image on the right shows that the background

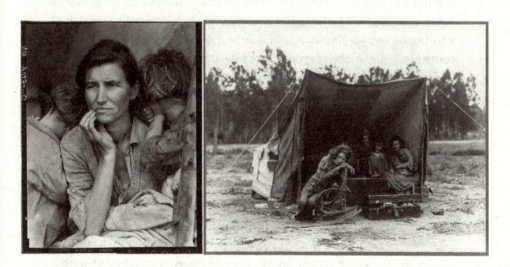

Figure 2.3
Two photographs taken by Dorothea Lange in Nipomo, California, during 1936 while she was employed as a staff photographer with the Farm Security Administration. On the left is the iconic *Migrant Mother* photograph of Florence Owens Thompson; on the right is another view of the same scene showing more context of the family and their living conditions.

in the first is a canvas and wood-beamed tent. The generalizability of the image on the left—produced in part due to the lack of spatial and temporal information and visual allegories to the bible, namely situating the woman as a Madonna figure—is changed by the information provided by the image on the right, which begins to situate the image in particular material and temporal conditions. Putting these images in conversation draws out connections across the corpus and new understandings of the individual images.

Another example is image similarity, featured in chapter 6, in which each image in a collection is assigned several other images that it most closely resembles. Image similarity is a particular type of annotation that also requires considering the entire corpus as a whole. First, it demonstrates the possibility of building annotations based on visual forms instead of purely numeric values or linguistic descriptions. This is possible by turning the images within the corpus into an indexical system; each image is tagged with the other images that it most closely resembles. Second, image similarity illustrates the possibility of producing flexible annotations. In producing similar images, we can avoid making a set of tags that explicitly describe the elements of interest within an image. Instead, image similarity serves as an implicit system of annotations. There is no need to enumerate why two images are similar, which may be a result of composition, color, or containing similar object types. Therefore, distant viewing can be applied in situations where the specific features of interest may not be available in an existing algorithm or may not be clear to look for. Finally, image similarity requires viewing the entire collection as a whole. By its very nature, image similarity cannot be fully accomplished through the annotation of individual images; it requires a discrete step in which annotations are aggregated across all the available visual inputs.

Figure 1.2 once again provides a clear example of how one can learn about a photo by viewing it in relation to other images. In figure 2.4, we apply a neural network-based image similarity algorithm to several color photographs from the FSA-OWI collection. Five images were selected. We display the four most similar images from an image embedding algorithm using the intermediate representations from a well-known neural network, ResNet-50. In inspecting the results, we see that the technique has picked up on both the content and composition of the photographs. The first row starts with our image from figure 1.2. Most of the recommendations

Figure 2.4
Visualization of image similarity using 1,612 digitized color photographs from the FSA-OWI collection. The left-most column consists of images selected from the corpus. To the right of these are four other photographs that are the most similar according to an image embedding algorithm based on the penultimate layer of the neural network ResNet-50.

associated with the image of a shepherd and his horse are based on connections with texture and color. One image was found with two similarly clothed ranchers inspecting a cow. The other recommendations—a mechanic on a boat, farmers hoeing a field, and soldiers with a tank—seem to be similar only in sharing a color palette similar to the yellow-beige field mixed with a bluish-gray sky. The relations revealed through image similarity can then provide more information about the images in aggregate.

We can apply the same method to other images in our corpus. The algorithm is also able to detect images that were taken at the same place. The second row recommends shots that seem to be the same red brick building from different sides. The window shown in the third row is associated with two photographs taken from slightly different angles and with a broader frame. All of the images selected in the third row are of windows with signs hanging from them. In the fourth row, close shots of people are given; three of the recommendations are men wearing hats, and the fourth is a woman with braids in her hair. The fifth set of recommendations are all images of well-lit people intensely focused on their work. Each of these examples demonstrates that detecting similar photographs through neural networks helps us draw connections across a corpus by automatically annotating explicit and implicit annotations.

Determining the set of most similar images has several critical applications. For example, a public search interface can recommend to users other records in the collection that might be of interest.[16] We will return to this approach in more depth in chapter 6 when discussing the possibilities of unsupervised models. One can find clusters and trends across the collection by modeling the network structure of the image similarities.[17] This helps identify recurring themes, motifs, and styles that are present in the collection. They can then be used to compare corpora as well. The key is that the annotations need to be combined to be understood.

Aggregating annotations can support combining with metadata. When an extensive collection contains slightly different versions of the same event or scene, the similarity scores may unearth connections across the collection that can help fill in missing metadata that may only exist for some of the records.[18] For example, we were able to add additional metadata columns that augment information about the materiality of objects held by the New York Metropolitan Museum of Art in chapter 6. Aggregating annotations can augment the metadata as well as make meaning when annotations are put into relation with one another. This can then open up new questions and areas of inquiry to explore.

We now turn to working with another kind of data, metadata that comes with the digital images. When we view, we bring additional context to the analysis, such as information about when, where, and by whom an image was made. Think of the label next to a piece of art in a museum, the description next to a film on the Internet Movie Database (IMDb), and details attached to each social media post. Many digital technologies can even embed this information in the digital file itself, along with additional details such as format, shot type, and the technology that created the image. This information provides essential social, cultural, historical, and technological context for our visual annotations. While there have been significant advances in machine learning, automatic annotation is still constrained by the limitations of computer vision. The annotations we want to analyze often need additional information to address the questions we are interested in exploring. Then, the organization of the data also requires being combined with contextual metadata information into the annotations produced by the computer vision algorithms.

Returning to the image in figure 1.2, we have constructed annotations that identify the person and animals in the image. However, the conclusions drawn about the image are limited without information such as date and location. Even after looking closely at the image, one would be hard-pressed to identify when and where the image was taken. The landscape suggests some limits to the geographical possibilities. Since the image appears to be a photograph, one can begin to narrow down the possible date. The clarity of the animals and grains of grass suggests a camera with quick shutter speed and, therefore, at least from the twentieth century. However, the image could be a colorized image from the 1910s, a Kodachrome from the 1960s, or processed through an Instagram filter in 2020. The border suggests the format is a color film, which places the photo at least in the 1930s. The clothing might help to determine a date but has come in and out of style over the last century. The style suggests a documentary photograph, but it could be a still frame from a Hollywood western. Our understanding of the image and its meaning changes when we learn the photo is a color transparency from 1941 and taken by acclaimed documentary photographer Russell Lee in Montana. Metadata, therefore, becomes a powerful strategy for adding context to draw insights from the automatically constructed annotations in the first part of distant viewing.

The types of metadata to combine with annotations depend on the areas of inquiry and will often require creating, collecting, and merging metadata. Attention to the relationship with the annotations, as well as existing metadata, is critical. Since it is often a laborious task, we suggest exploring what kinds of information already exist and then creating metadata. To provide a way to think through the possible sources of metadata to collect and merge, we divide our discussion into whether metadata needs to be collected from an external source or is internally connected with the visual data, such as through an archival tag.

Metadata may be gathered from external sources. Governments, corporations, nonprofit institutions, and individuals are creating, storing, and sharing data. A common reason for the existence of metadata, for example, is to enable digital search and discovery, whether for cultural heritage institutions such as national archives or multinational corporations such as Google. For example, the metadata used in chapter 3 to analyze movie posters is created, collected, and merged from multiple sources, including structured metadata from the crowdsourced DBpedia project, curated data collections released by companies such as IMDb for academic research, unstructured textual descriptions from Wikipedia, and information about DVD releases from the open-access Amazon Review Dataset.[19] Modifications of the information collected will often be necessary for use as metadata in distant viewing.

One space engaged in creating data is the Linked Open Data community, which determines and models best practices for publishing structured open-access data on the web.[20] In the last decade, nonprofit institutions such as the British Library, the Netherlands' Rijksmuseum, and the United States Library of Congress have been at the forefront of the Linked Open Data movement.[21] Libraries, archives, and museums create standardized metadata about collections using schemata amenable to an organization as tidy data.[22] The metadata is often descriptive and provenance information that is not easily created using computer vision.[23] External information can also be included by using available metadata fields to enrich a dataset with additional information.[24] If a collection of films includes a record of the director attributed to each work, additional information about each director, such as their nationality and year of birth, can be gathered from sources such as the Library of Congress's Name Authority File.[25] By leveraging the power of Linked Open Data, we can add rich contextual metadata to collections of visual materials, even when there appears to be only a limited amount of information attached to each record.

Metadata about visual materials can also come directly from digital image files. We return to the particularities of digital images. Because of the way a computer reads images, the pixels are stored in compression formats such as JPEG and TIFF. As a part of the file, information about the image can be embedded, such as details about hardware and software used to create the file, the file's resolution, and when and where the file was created. Born-digital materials may have information such as a precise latitude, longitude, and timestamp. The file might also include important production information such as shutter speed and lens type. Also, recent movements for added accessibility have prompted more images on the web to include an *alt text* field that provides a textual description. Moving image files can include additional information such as the frame rate, timestamps corresponding to "chapters" in a movie or television show, and closed captions. Attention to the internal metadata can open interpretative possibilities for distant viewing.

Merging external and internal data can be challenging, particularly if bringing together different kinds of metadata for the same corpora or aggregating metadata to study multiple corpora. The principles of data normalization offer a roadmap for how to create, collect, and merge metadata for distant viewing.[26] Fortunately, it is increasingly common for existing data to be organized in a structured format. Creating, collecting, and merging data according to these principles will result in metadata that is particularly amenable to exploratory analysis, the next step of the distant viewing method. A general recommendation is to keep any metadata that has been previously recorded in a machine-readable format when creating, collecting, and merging metadata. It may be tempting to delete some of the information from an existing source because it does not seem immediately relevant. However, metadata is significantly smaller in file size than images or videos. Given how little storage the data usually requires, it is often best to keep all the available information. The benefit may become apparent later.

Our study of the FSA-OWI photographic collection offers an example of the power of keeping all the available metadata together, even when a field initially seems to be of little use. The United States Library of Congress has meticulously digitized and provided metadata for the 170,000 photographs and placed them on their public website. When we began exploring the collection, the metadata records included a field called "other number" that was, at the time, entirely undocumented in the Library of Congress's digital archive. Despite having no initial thoughts about how this field could be used, we retained it in our local database. Nearly two years after our work on the collection began, we realized that this field corresponded to a category in the original classification system set up by Paul Vanderbilt in the late 1940s. By digitizing an out-of-print manual written in the 1970s, we reconstructed the original classification system and reconnected those categories with the digital images. This opened an entirely new research direction for the project that would never have occurred if we had only kept those fields that were initially useful to our mode of analysis.[27] Keeping metadata that at first did not appear necessary turned out to be an asset, as we further demonstrate in the analysis in chapter 4.

Which metadata to create, collect, and merge is dependent on the visual annotations produced in the annotation step, and vice versa. Creating metadata to describe a feature in the image is unnecessary if a computer vision algorithm can accomplish the same goal. Developing a deep learning model to predict a feature is not beneficial when the data already exists from another source and can be added as metadata. Combining the automated annotations with metadata adds layers of context to our analysis, providing vital social, cultural, historical, and technological information. Together, all of these decisions will shape what one can and cannot learn from distant viewing. Exploring the annotations and metadata together is the subject of the third part of our iterative pipeline.

Explore: Understand Data and Address Areas of Inquiry

Once we have created annotations and organized them with internal and external metadata, the next challenge becomes interpreting and exploring the data in the context of our areas of inquiry. One cannot easily view thousands of images, much less the pixel counts, bounding boxes, and metadata for each image. Part of the pipeline for the distant viewing method draws on the concept of *exploratory data analysis* (EDA), which undergirds data science.[28] Through EDA, summary statistics and visualizations reveal patterns, trends, and outliers, which are often not apparent when manually analyzing the collection image by image. The third part of our pipeline is called "explore" to make an explicit connection to EDA.

Popularized by John Tukey, EDA is an approach from statistics for analyzing, interpreting, and summarizing information from data. Tukey's field-forming 1977 book demonstrated how statistical analysis through data visualization, such as box plots, histograms, and scatter plots, is a method for exploring data.[29] Rather than already assuming which data would be of interest through a hypothesis or modeling assumptions, Tukey argued that EDA is a way to explore characteristics of the data and then develop hypotheses. At stake was changing how statistics produced knowledge and what kinds of knowledge. Paired with foundational works in statistics graphics such as Jacques Bertin's *Sémiologie Graphique* (1968), William Cleveland's *Visualizing Data* (1993), and Leland Wilkinson's *The Grammar of Graphics* (1999), visualizations of statistics serve as a form of evidence and argument.[30] The summary statistics and statistical graphics can support and challenge prior interpretations, highlight interesting outliers, and indicate new avenues of research. EDA, therefore, is a strategy for analyzing the annotations and metadata produced and organized in the first two parts of our method.

Attention to the assumptions in the annotation and organization parts of distant viewing becomes essential when exploring the data. Tukey's original formulation of EDA sharply contrasted data exploration with the kinds of rigid confirmatory analysis required in applications such as clinical drug trials. Rather than using statistics to test existing findings and arguments, as is the case with confirmatory data analysis, EDA is designed to minimize preconceived assumptions about the exact relationships and patterns of interest before engaging in statistical analysis. Assumptions always exist, though, so attention to the characteristics of the data being analyzed becomes very important when interpreting EDA results.

The annotations that are used to represent the visual material shape the interpretative possibilities of EDA. We often want annotations that are general enough to identify and annotate relevant features within and across corpora. For example, we may want a tag that identifies animals rather than specific kinds of animals. If we annotated the FSA-OWI collection with just horses and dogs, we would have missed other animals, such as cows. As a result, we would miss patterns about agriculture and the environment during the Great Depression and World War II in the corpus when doing EDA. The specificity of the categories can become either an asset or a possible hindrance for EDA and, therefore, which insights can be gleaned from the corpus.

EDA facilitates the interpretation of the annotations and metadata, resulting in questions about and offering insights into the meaning of images. A goal of EDA is to reveal avenues of inquiry according to the patterns and anomalies in the data. As a result, new annotations and metadata will often be necessary. While manually tagging a new type of annotation is possible, the analysis is often limited to a small set of features because the process is incredibly laborious and often cost-prohibitive. The construction of annotations through computer vision becomes a way to identify another set of features at a large scale. The use of computer vision to produce annotations and other algorithmic techniques for aggregation allows for the iterative exploration of corpora because it is relatively easily to rerun an analysis with new algorithms or updated tuning parameters. As a result, we often return to the annotation and organization parts of our data analysis pipeline. Our own work on the FSA-OWI collection has consisted of iterating between these steps for over ten years.[31] The following chapters demonstrate how exploration at a distance offers new insights into visual cultures and serves as an active example of the final part of the method: communication.

Communicate: Present Results and Share Data

The final part of the distant viewing method focuses on communicating the findings of a computational analysis of digital images using computer vision. Deciding how and to whom the results are communicated is shaped by the areas of inquiry and goals of distant viewing. A nonprofit using the method to identify stereotypes in media will communicate the results differently than a researcher writing a paper on the same topic for an academic journal. An artist remixing images for a collage will communicate the results differently than a museum focusing on search and discovery in a collection. Moreover, scientists studying bird colonies will communicate the results differently than activists working on a climate change campaign. Attention to which communication practices reach which audiences becomes essential.

Communication is an explicit part of the typical data science pipeline shown in figure 2.1. The inclusion of this aspect in the pipeline signals that the field understands the importance of building methods and tools to convey knowledge through forms such as visualization and open-source code.

Communication is a necessary part of producing, conveying, and transmitting knowledge from data. Distant viewing has the same goals and is dependent on specific communication strategies to convey insights about the analysis of images.

While different distant viewing projects will necessitate different kinds of communication, we offer two interconnected ways to communicate based on the data science framework. The first is communication for a particular audience beyond the individual or group conducting distant viewing. Defining the audience is essential for selecting which forms of communication to pursue. While writing an article for a popular magazine or a book for an academic press may be appropriate for some audiences, visualizations circulated through a social media campaign or an interactive digital website may be better for others.

Fortunately, we do not need to guess which communication strategies convey which kinds of knowledge or effectively reach specific audiences. The scholarship on communication is extensive, with fields such as communication studies and public humanities offering essential insights into giving, receiving, and exchanging information.[32] A significant amount of work in communication studies, for example, focuses on identifying effective strategies for conveying information and arguments, such as through writing, speaking, and media.[33] Attention to these fields is a benefit when thinking through how to convey the insights from distant viewing and to whom.

For example, we show how distant viewing can increase access to and discovery of the New York Metropolitan Museum of Art's Open Collection in chapter 6. Since the collection belongs to a large, nonprofit museum, the intended audience is the general public and people interested in the study of art. After identifying sets of similar images, we move to the identification of discrete clusters of images. These two ways of annotating and organizing the collection could be integrated into a digital interface and serve as a communication strategy that enables search and discovery while conveying the scope and scale of the collection.[34] Creating an interactive digital platform to visualize the results as the primary mode of communication allows users to interactively explore the collection. Consideration about which communication formats enable the actual viewing of the images and reach which audiences is essential.

Another form of communication is through technical documentation. As a part of the theory of distant viewing, we argue that understanding images is shaped by cultural, social, historical, and technological ways of seeing and practices of looking. Therefore, the goal of the theory is to make explicit the modeling assumptions that underlie the computational analysis of digital images. To put this theory into practice requires an explicit description of the decisions made during distant viewing, such as annotating through object detection, and how the decision was implemented, such as the specific algorithm. Technical communication is an established set of communication practices designed to clarify which technical choices were made and why, often with the goal that the audience can replicate the process outlined.[35]

Forms of technical communication vary. Strategies include descriptions in audio and video such as an instructional video, a textual form such as a report or white paper, and visualizations such as diagrams and charts. Given the importance of algorithms to distant viewing, attention to strategies that communicate code is significant, which is a general concern within the field of data science. Data scientists have actively developed methods and tools for describing code and algorithms. R Markdown documents, for example, include executable code, narrative text, and metadata to build the file, which can then be exported as a report in formats such as HTML, PDF, or plain text.[36] Including the programming code and describing the decisions are key to making the decisions visible, such as how the choice of annotations shapes a distant viewing analysis.

While communication appears at the end of the pipeline, it will often not be the last step. Thinking through communicating to specific audiences and documenting technical decisions will reshape the other parts of distant viewing. For example, one may decide to build another set of annotations to analyze upon realizing one wants to reach a specific audience, necessitating a return to the annotation process. Attention to the audience throughout the analysis is thus necessary, and shapes how one can convey claims and arguments through the method of distant viewing.

Conclusions

The theory of distant viewing motivates the four parts of the method, with each part's name emphasizing these connections. We start by *annotating* a collection of digitized images, proceed to *organizing* the metadata and annotations, then move to *exploring* the extracted annotations, and finally engage in *communicating* the findings. Such an approach allows for auditing, questioning, identifying, and changing the ways of seeing and practices of looking throughout the process of encoding and decoding through computational viewing. In other words, each step in the method opens the computational analysis of digital images to questions about exactly what we want to annotate and why. It asks us to pause and think through exactly what we, as humans, are doing with computer vision, and to ask critical questions about what kind of work computer vision is doing.

Another aspect of distant viewing that the method reveals is that this theory can be used to analyze computer vision algorithms. Deciding if the creation of annotations is possible or which annotations to build with which computer vision algorithms is complicated if one cannot determine the ways of seeing and practices of looking encoded into the algorithm. Building automatically produced annotations make visible the ways of viewing embedded in computer vision. Being clear about the assumptions encoded into computer vision algorithms is not always easy. However, whether we use them to decode an image collection or analyze the algorithms themselves, it is essential. Distant viewing offers a method to open computer vision algorithms to critical inquiry.

While the scale is an essential factor, distant viewing aims to not fetishize size. The dominant discourse about technology makes it tempting to think that bigger data is better data, but this is not a given.[37] Just because the data exists does not mean that it always should be used.[38] The same caution extends to annotations: just because we can produce a specific set of annotations does not necessarily mean we should. Paying attention to social and ethical issues may mean deleting and not using specific annotations as well as not combining certain internal and external metadata. Laws such as copyright and institutional policies, such as those determined by an ethics committee, are another set of considerations. Attention to the inequalities and violence that annotations and data can enact should always be considered.[39] Collaboration offers one way to address these issues as well as following the call for approaches such as data feminism.[40] Keeping these considerations at the fore is essential at all stages of distant viewing.

In many cases, the scale of the collection is a challenge. Mass digitization and born-digital images abound. Viewing at scale opens new areas of inquiry, so new theories and methods are needed to understand how to approach and interpret the sheer number of digital images. The number of images far exceeds the ability of an individual or even a team to view them all, which can be challenging without access to significant resources.[41] The method modeled by distant viewing is one answer.

3 Advertising in Color: Movie Posters and Genre

"The posters should be out doing missionary work," wrote Epes Winthrop Sargent in his 1915 book *Picture Theatre Advertising*.[1] While early film was in black and white, movie exhibitors in the United States in the early twentieth century were well aware of the power of advertising in color to build an audience.[2] Effective advertising meant producing visual messages to lure audiences to the movies by drawing on existing visual cultures and fine-tuning how they would convey their messages. Color was an important attribute that drew attention and connected to culturally established relationships between colors and emotions.[3] The choice of palette served as a way to appeal through a visual message. Deciding which colors to use in movie posters has also been shaped by relationships to communities such as elite art circles and commercial advertising. Further, these relationships have continuously changed over the twentieth and twenty-first centuries, with movie poster creation increasingly becoming its own unique artistic and commercial form.

A variety of theories from both popular and academic sources propose specific relationships between the colors used in movie posters and their genres. Take the color red, for example. In the United States, it is often associated with the concepts of love and romance through imagery such as cartoon hearts and Valentine's Day decorations. By relating these connections and several hand-selected examples, some commentators suggest that red is used as a signifier for light-hearted romantic comedies.[4] The color red has many other cultural connections, however, such as its association with blood, leading some commentators to suggest that red is used on movie posters to attract the attention of people looking for horror movies.[5] Finally, red is often considered a lucky color in East Asian cultures. Combining several examples with this observation has led others to suggest that red may highlight films produced in Asia that are distributed in the United States and Europe.[6] Similarly broad relationships between most primary colors and genres have been argued for by selecting a few example movie posters and connecting them to existing cultural associations. Zooming out and viewing thousands of posters offers a way to see if these broad claims hold.

This chapter takes a distant viewing approach to study the relationships between film genres and the colors used in movie posters. Initial questions that guide our exploration include how the overall use of color changed over time, to what degree certain colors dominate, and whether specific genres are associated with individual colors. We analyze the color composition of the top 100–grossing films in the United States from each year between 1970 and 2020. Examples of several movie posters from our corpus are shown in figure 3.1. Using this set of five thousand feature-film movie posters allows us to explore how color has been used over time and across different film genres within the US market. We will show how computational techniques identify and illustrate overarching patterns while highlighting specific outliers. The exploration builds on debates over the role of color, emotion, and genre that animate fields such as communications, film studies, and popular culture studies.

Previous computational analyses of visual culture have also used color information. An analysis based on color can be performed using relatively simple computations applied to pixel intensities; therefore, color has been an accessible choice of annotation. Most studies have focused on using color as a way of organizing and visualizing a collection of images. For example, take Barbara Flueckiger's analysis of color film technology from a collection of four hundred feature-length films.[7] Or, Adelheid Heftberger's study of the Russian director Dziga Vertov.[8] In 2019, Cooper Hewitt Labs released a digital prototype for exploring the entire Cooper Hewitt collection based on color.[9] Their digital interface, Dive into Color, was integrated into the interactive exhibit "Saturated: The Allure and Science of Color." Projects such as Dive into Color and Flueckiger's Film Colors illustrate the power of organizing images based on color features. We are not aware of any previous academic studies that computationally analyzed movie posters. Here, we show how aggregating the features of movie posters can help us explore larger patterns that are difficult to detect when only manually viewing a collection.

As shown in the previous two chapters, an essential step in applying distant viewing is the creation of structured information from a corpus

Figure 3.1
Example movie posters from twelve top-grossing films. The films are arranged in temporal order, ranging from 1970 through 2018.

of digital images. For the study in this chapter, our annotations need to capture information about color. We will need to determine the computational features that capture the color composition of digitized scans of movie posters. We approach this task in two steps, first by describing the color of an individual pixel and then specifying how to aggregate the colors across all the pixels of a particular image. Determining how to describe the color of an individual pixel is surprisingly tricky. While the actual computations are relatively simple, determining the appropriate way to calculate and describe color through annotations requires engaging with scholarship in fields including physiology, psychology, philosophy, and engineering. We explore these connections in further detail in the following section.

After establishing our annotations and approaches to quantifying color, we will look at several increasingly complex ways to summarize the colors found within the pixels of movie posters. These different methods for aggregating the individual colors across pixels and the entire corpus combined with metadata lead us to different analyses that collectively help address the relationship between movie poster colors and genre. We start by looking at the overall brightness of the entire image and the relative proportions of black, white, and other colors. We will see that these patterns reveal strong relationships with time and among clusters of closely related genre categories. As a second approach, we look at the proportion of specific color hues—such as red, blue, or purple—within and across genres. The analysis of dominant colors shows some genre-related patterns, but they are not as strong or specific as some literature suggests. Finally, we look at the relationship between two or more colors within a poster. Here, again, we see several reliable patterns but only limited relationships to specific genre categories. By iteratively annotating, organizing, and exploring, we demonstrate that the balance of black versus white and warm versus cool colors in this corpus is a far more potent signifier of a genre than individual color choices. By viewing at scale, the findings challenge common claims that a single color defines the genre that a movie poster is communicating and shift our understanding of how color works when marketing a film made by the US movie industry. The specific application also demonstrates how determining the annotations, organizing and combining with metadata, and exploring the results for a seemingly straightforward feature such as color is suffused with human decision-making, which is intimately guided by our objects of study.

Annotating Color

In chapter 1, we explained how the smallest components of digital images, pixels, are described by specifying the level of red, green, and blue (RGB) light needed to display the color. This format is ideal for displaying an image but not well suited to analyzing an image, even for features such as color. In order to quantify the color of a pixel, a different representation is typically used. Formulas for these components based on red, green, and blue intensities can be easily written down, but understanding the meaning and motivation behind them requires a more careful study of color theory and the history of color photography. Theories of color abound across various disciplines, including the visual arts, cultural studies, engineering, physics, and medicine. It is not feasible to give an exhaustive history of these approaches here; instead, we will focus on those aspects directly related to constructing representative features from a digitized corpus of images. We start with a brief description of the physiological process of color perception before exploring how this process impacts how color is represented and used in the storage and display of digital images.

The human visual system collects and interprets data by sensing light waves that enter the human eye.[10] The light-sensitive cells in the eye can detect several different aspects of light. For example, by understanding which cells detect light relative to the eye's current focus, the visual system can determine the direction from which a particular sensation of light is coming.[11] Combining this information across the entire visual field allows for the detection of textures, objects, and a higher-level understanding of one's environment.[12] By understanding the rate at which the cells are activated, the visual system can also estimate the intensity of the light waves coming from a particular direction. Light sources with high intensity are perceived as bright, and sources with low intensity are perceived as dark. Finally, the system is also able to distinguish between different wavelengths of light. These distinctions are what contribute to the human perception of different colors, such as red, yellow, green, blue, and purple.[13]

Physiologically, the eye interprets color information using cone cells. Different types of cone cells are sensitive to a narrow range of wavelengths. Most humans are trichromats, with three different types of cone cells. One type of cone is most sensitive to blue light (S cones), another to green light (M cones), and the third is most sensitive to yellow-green light (L cones).[14]

Different colors are perceived by contrasting the relative differences between the activation of the cone cells.[15] For example, an object will appear red if the L cones are activated more than the M cones. The exact range and relative sensitivity of the three types of cone cells will differ slightly between different people. If two of the cone types have light sensitivities that significantly overlap, or if someone has a reduced number of cone types, this can result in a reduced ability to distinguish hues.[16]

A conceptual understanding of the physiology of color is essential for our study because it has implications for how color information about digital images is recorded, stored, and displayed. Naturally occurring light typically involves a mixture of many different wavelengths. However, there is no one-to-one correspondence between the perception of color and mixtures of light wavelengths.[17] Many different combinations will appear completely indistinguishable.[18] Consider a light source that emits a uniform stream of light with wavelengths of 600 nanometers (a nanometer is one-billionth of a meter) and contrast this with another source that emits a mixture of light with two different wavelengths, some near 550 nanometers and some near 650 nanometers. Both sources will activate a combination of the M and S cones in a typical human eye; it will be perceived as a shade of orange. If the second light source is blended at a specific proportion, dependent on the observer, the perception of the two colors will be indistinguishable. Similar mixtures can be devised to explain limitless combinations of wavelengths that will be perceived to be the same color by the human eye for every hue in the spectrum of visible colors.

How computers store and display images is shaped by the history of photography and therefore by human-created technologies of vision.[19] Attempts at producing color photography started in the 1840s.[20] The success of the daguerreotype, which projected a black-and-white image onto the photosensitive surface of silver-plated copper, was followed by a similar process to capture the exact color of the light that had been exposed to the surface.[21] Early attempts by experimenters such as Edmond Becquerel and Levi Hill produced scientifically exciting results. However, these methods required long exposure times, produced only dim images, and were never found to be sufficiently stable to produce color-accurate reproductions of their subjects.

In 1855, James Clerk Maxwell proposed a different approach to the production of color photography.[22] His method was based on the popular and essentially correct theory that the human eye is covered by different types of receptors sensitive to a different spectrum of light.[23] Maxwell proposed taking three photographs of the same scene using different colored filters. These filters, one each for red, green, and blue, allowed only certain light hues to pass through the camera. Colored light corresponding to these hues could then be passed through the resulting negatives and combined to produce a positive slide projected in a dark room. Likewise, each negative could be sequentially exposed on photosensitive paper with different colored dyes to produce a permanent color print that will appear, to the human eye, the same color as the original objects.

Maxwell's three-color process proved to be a great solution for the production of color photography. Following several decades of research, researchers perfected the chemical processes of capturing, storing, and printing each spectrum of light.[24] Mechanical and engineering methods were also devised to produce three negatives simultaneously to reduce the already long exposure times. By the start of the twentieth century, surprisingly vivid color images were being produced by photographers such as Sanger Shepherd, Sergey Prokudin-Gorsky, and Louis Arthur Ducos du Hauron. Commercially available equipment became widely available soon after, with products such as the autochrome being produced, marketed, and improved through the 1940s.[25]

The creation and display of digital images follow the same approach as Maxwell's three-color process. Digital images, whether created from scans of printed materials or born-digital, are stored as an array with three digital signals. Each type of sensor responds to a specific range of light wavelengths corresponding to red, green, and blue. The intensities of these sensors are stored as three rectangular arrays showing the observed amount of three different wavelengths detected in the image. We saw an example of this representation in figure 1.3. Finally, to display the image on a digital screen, an array packed with a larger number of small red, green, and blue lights is illuminated to replicate the observed intensities of the image observed by a digital camera. From a distance, the displayed light intensities blend together and are perceived by the human brain as (approximately) replicating the original.

Taking, storing, and printing both analog and digital images are processes grounded in replicating the physiological processes for the perception of light performed by the human eye.[26] While it is tempting to use RGB as a basis for annotations, we must pay attention to the relationship between seeing and interpreting color. The human visual system does not end with the eye.[27] There is a significant conceptual distance between the perception of color intensities in the eye and our mental model that identifies properties of color. We do not continuously observe the intensities of three wavelengths; instead, we perceive a rainbow of hues in a continuous gamut of brightness and richness. In order to perform a meaningful computational analysis of color information, we must approximate how the human brain perceives color rather than working directly with raw color intensities, which can otherwise be deceptive. For example, if a digital image has a high amount of red intensity, it would be a mistake to assume that it will appear red. If the blue and green are present in equal proportion, the light will instead appear as the color white.

A method is needed for representing the red, green, and blue intensities in an alternative format that better matches the way color is mentally perceived and culturally understood.[28] In this chapter, we will use the HCI— hue, chroma, and intensity—color model to apply distant viewing to the posters.[29] This model applies mathematical equations to a set of three intensities of color associated with an individual pixel to produce a new set of three numbers representing different aspects of the perceived color. We will summarize the numbers in various ways across an image and across a corpus of images to identify and understand general patterns of color usage within a collection.

Hue is a single number that attempts to capture where a color occurs along the visible spectrum.[30] The exact formula is slightly more complex than intensity and chroma, but the concept is easy to describe. By convention, we define hue as zero for a pixel with only red light, one-third for a pixel that has only green light, and two-thirds for a pixel that has only blue light. We fill in other hues according to the relative contributions of the red, green, and blue intensities. For example, yellow has a hue of one-sixth, halfway between red and green, and cyan has a hue of one-half, halfway between green and blue. Hue is undefined for shades of gray. An essential feature of hue is that it circles back on itself, often visualized in the form of a color wheel, so a hue of 0.99 will be very similar to a hue of 0.01. Both will appear as slightly different forms of red.

Chroma is a measurement of the richness or colorfulness of a color.[31] Bright colors that appear in places such as cartoons and neon signs have a very high chroma. Pastel colors appear pale relative to these colors and have a comparably low chroma. White, black, and shades of gray have no color element and have a chroma of zero. To define a formula for chroma, we compute the smallest and largest numbers from a pixel's red, green, and blue values. Chroma is defined as the difference between the largest and smallest value. Taking the difference between the smallest and large values gives a measurement of the degree to which the eye will distinguish one color from another. Chroma is closely related to the slightly more common term *saturation*, with saturation being a scaled version of the chroma.[32]

Intensity is a measurement that attempts to compute how bright the color will appear, calculated by taking the average of the red, green, and blue pixel values.[33] This measurement can be justified by considering how pixels are displayed on a digital screen. Small lights are turned on with a brightness proportional to the red, green, and blue values. When more lights are turned on at higher levels, we expect the image to appear brighter. Likewise, when many of the lights are not turned on, the image will appear dark. The exact perception of an image's brightness will depend on the specific device used to display an image and the lighting conditions under which the image is viewed. However, intensity will serve as a helpful proxy that can be easily aggregated across our corpus for our purposes.

In summary, converting the RGB values into HCI values allows for the computational approximation of the human visual system. As a basis for annotations, HCI helps the computer see as we do by accounting for the signals detected by cells in the eye and the mental model of visual inputs consciously processed by the brain. HCI provides a literal version of the concept of distant viewing to the study of color. Aggregating these coordinates in different ways across a corpus will provide our main features for analysis in this chapter. Before delving into determining how to summarize the three components across each poster and across the collection, we turn to the history of movie posters to better guide the research questions about the ways that movie posters use color. This history will inform how to aggregate annotations, how to organize the metadata, and how to explore the corpus—all parts of the distant viewing method.

Organizing the Movie Poster Corpus

Movie posters are a popular form of advertising dating back to the turn of the twentieth century. By the 1910s, nickelodeon operators and film companies agreed that posters could powerfully guide audiences to the movies. Debates ensued over their content and scale, informed by advertising practices from other forms of entertainment such as the circus.[34] As with the films, their advertising came under scrutiny from advocates of Progressive Era social mores who sought to censor the advertisements on the cinema exterior as well as the images that flickered on the screen.[35] Depictions of sexuality and violence were seen as not only crude and lurid but a threat to public morality, a view that movie producers sought to counteract.[36] The advent of "feature-length" films, combined with the formation of a film industry, resulted in savvy studios ready to control circulation, promotion, and branding. Locally crafted posters by nickelodeon owners were replaced with posters sent directly from the studios across the United States.[37] The establishment of the Associated Motion Pictures Advertisers in 1916 in New York City indicated an industry practice that had no intention of going away.[38]

What once was a local practice featuring hand-drawn posters became big business by the early twentieth century as studios began to standardize their advertisements in an effort to reach targeted audiences while controlling their image.[39] National advertising for films became standard practice by the 1930s. The Motion Pictures Producers and Distributors Association (MPPDA), today known as the Motion Picture Association of America (MPAA), agreed to oversee advertising to monitor compliance with an ad code that the major studios had adopted. The code was designed to demonstrate that the industry could self-regulate to ward off content censorship through federal laws. Control over their advertising also meant control over how and to whom films were marketed while diminishing the risk that the local theater owner might misrepresent or too graphically market their product.[40]

The idea of a standardized movie poster in color featuring an image with text also took shape over the twentieth century. From the early day of the nickelodeons, local theater owners used the combination to catch people's attention, drawing on practices from entertainment industries and commercial culture.[41] They also adopted printing practices from the circus by using the same dimension standards, such as a "half sheet" of 21×28 inches and a "one-sheet," a single-sheet of 27×41 inches.[42] Writing on movie picture theater management took off, offering advice about best practices for display, including printing sizes, color, font, and the relations between images and words.[43] For example, Harold Franklin, while president of Fox West Coast Theater chain, called for the use of the "show window" to more elegantly display posters, suggesting visual connections between plays, which enjoyed societal acceptance, and the movies.[44] As middle-class audiences began to embrace the movies, theater owners followed Franklin's call and sought to differentiate themselves and adjusted their advertising practices to suggest their target audience. In the 1910s, owners seeking to convey that their theater was more "refined" began placing their posters in frames, which was suggestive of a fine painting and conveyed notions of order, containment, and reverence.[45] Attuned to social and cultural as well as biological understandings of visual recognition, marketers have long paid attention to the latest research in visual perception.[46] Thanks to advances in printing technologies, they added forms such as photographic images to the repertoire alongside an expanding font and color palette.

Industrial shifts also shaped the mass production and display of movie posters over the course of the twentieth century. Lithography provided a cost-effective and timely method for nickelodeons, storefront cinemas, and traveling roadshows to create posters.[47] Often in charge of their own advertising, they purchased posters from lithography companies until the mid-1910s.[48] Seeking control over how to market their films, studios sought to standardize advertising by working with established companies and bringing marketing in-house.[49] Along with the rise of the studio system, advertising consolidation occurred in the 1940s with the development of a national poster exchange service. According to the vice president of Advertising Accessories, Inc., a subsidiary of the National Screen Service, "the deal climaxed 25 years of effort to centralize all distribution of advertising screen accessories and paper."[50] The National Screen Service had a monopoly over film posters until 1984. Ultimately it was the film studios that broke the advertising monopoly rather than the decades-long legal challenges.[51] In the 1980s, the studios rebuilt their in-house advertising and marketing units as the young and defiant directors of New Hollywood gave way to studio-controlled and funded blockbuster films.[52]

The postwar era would also be lucrative for the studios as audiences drove to the movies. Parking lots expanded as multiplexes became megaplexes serving a primarily white middle-class audience in sprawling suburbs. The rise of companies such as AMC Theatres, the financial bread-and-butter of the film industry, left less real estate on theater facades for each film. Rather than using multiple pieces of paper to create an advertisement, the "one-sheet," became the primary form of advertisement. A mini sheet, which has a dimension of 16.5×25.5 inches, was introduced for theater lobbies.[53] The development of the VHS market, with stores across the country such as Blockbuster in the 1980s, 1990s, and 2000s, would become another prominent site for movie posters. Posters would remain relatively standardized until the early twenty-first century with the rise of screens, including the expanded visual possibilities of the internet as well as digital displays, and social media alongside industry "disruption" from streaming services such as Netflix. As the paper movie poster gave way to pixels, film advertising took new forms, eager to convey messages that capture the attention of potential viewers and pique their interest in the latest releases.

Along with serving as advertisements, posters also have enjoyed a long conversation with the arts. Movie posters' claims to being art are indebted to the legacy of painters such as Jules Chéret and Henri de Toulouse-Lautrec. Their successful elevation of the status of the poster at the turn of the twentieth century in France shaped US publishers' embrace of the commercial value of art posters.[54] Movie posters may have been advertising cheap amusements, but they were still shaped by ongoing art movements. In the wake of World War I, German expressionism's aesthetics of distortion and asymmetry alongside a rejection of a naturalist color palette in favor of highly saturated reds and cavernous blacks would have a lasting effect on the film noir and horror genres. While the consumer culture spurred by Madison Avenue in the 1950s and 1960s treated movie posters as a commercial product, the work of post–World War II poster artists such as Saul Bass demonstrates the entanglement between advertising and the graphic arts. As art historian Karal Ann Marlin argues, poster illustrators worked under "art directors," where practices often mirrored those of art gallery directors.[55] Both types of artists created an image to hang on a wall. While not all movie posters would enjoy the status of "art" according to the critics, a small set of posters—such as those created by Bass, Ronald Brown, and Bill Gold—continue to be appreciated for their aesthetic value.[56] A Bass poster today costs thousands of dollars. This history shapes the questions and data that we analyze in this chapter.

The debates over whether movie posters are crass marketing schemes, corporate advertising, or art reflect their complicated conversation with visual cultures. They are also interesting for the way they reflect and produce messages through visual cues. To analyze the messages encoded in movie posters, we selected the top 100–grossing films in the United States from 1970 to 2020. We begin our analysis when the auteur-driven genre-bending films of New Hollywood and the subversive and liberatory possibilities of blaxploitation films gave way to the age of studio-driven genre-conforming blockbuster films such as *Jaws* (1975), *Saturday Night Fever* (1977), and *Star Wars* (1977).[57] We end in 2019 in part because it is close to the time this book was written. It is also convenient to end the analysis in 2020 since ways of creating, circulating, and advertising feature films were being revolutionized by technology companies such as Amazon, Apple, and Netflix. While movie posters still exist, the emergence of social media and platform-specific recommender systems is changing how companies reach audiences. The prominence of the movie poster as a specific form and genre of advertising appears to be waning.

We limit our analysis to the top-grossing films because this financial metric is an excellent gauge of audience reach and financial investment.[58] High-grossing films not only reach a large audience but often enjoy significant resources at every stage, from production to circulation. As for-profit multinational corporations, the studios spend tens of millions of dollars each year in advertising to reach and build audiences. These investments are guided by detailed research on everything from the content of the actual film along with its advertising campaigns to scientific research on visual reception.[59] These practices have been in place since at least the early 1930s.[60] We constructed our dataset of movie posters from the Internet Movie Database (IMDb). IMDb began as a user-run website spun off from a Usenet group in the 1990s. While now a commercial entity run by Amazon, the site makes much of its data freely available to download for research applications. Using the data available from the site, we selected the one hundred films from each year between 1970 and 2019 with the largest US box office numbers.[61] In general, these are films produced by the major US studios and work within Hollywood's forms of storytelling, and, therefore, its genres, tropes, and narrative arcs. Next, we downloaded and curated a collection of digital images of each movie's poster. A small number of movie posters were not available, mainly for films from the 1970s. These records were removed from our analysis.

With our annotations defined, we then annotated and calculated the HCI components for each poster. The digital movie poster images were scaled to have the same dimensions, and each RGB pixel was converted into an HCI representation of the pixel's hue, chroma, and intensity. In addition to looking at summary statistics of chroma and intensity, we will look at the distribution of discrete types of colors used in the poster. This required determining cutoff values to split the HCI space into discrete categories. We choose to group pixels into one of five buckets to analyze color types possible. If the chroma was sufficiently low, a pixel was grouped into the bucket labeled "white," "gray," or "black," depending on its intensity. Pixels with high intensity and high chroma (both greater than 30 on a scale from 0 to 100) were grouped into the "color" bucket. The cutoff values were determined by manually looking at the colors in a small set of posters to ensure that the categories matched our perception of the images. All other pixels, including very dark or pale colors, were placed in the "other" category. Finally, the annotations were combined with metadata.

There are many metadata fields available from IMDb for each film in our corpus. Of specific interest to our research questions are the title of the movie, the year of release, and the associated genres. A full dataset of the computed annotations and all the available metadata fields can be downloaded from our website, https://distantviewing.org/book, which allows for the replication and extension of the results presented here. To begin, in the next section, we use the combined dataset to identify patterns and outliers across the fifty years of movie posters in our collection.

Exploring Trends over Time

Having established the underlying color theory and historical context of movie posters, we now use computational techniques to explore our corpus of movie posters. For the first exploration, we will investigate patterns of movie posters over time. Specifically, we look at changes in the color and intensity of movie posters for the top-grossing films released from 1970 through 2019. Focusing on these changes allows us to see how the history of movie posters has affected their visual style and provides context for subsequent analyses of movie genres. Given the importance of color to communicating and marketing, our analysis is guided by questions such as which colors are in posters, the relationship between color and genre, and whether the colors in posters have changed over time.

To investigate change over time, we draw on the approaches of exploratory data analysis by summarizing the color composition of the movie posters over each half-decade.[62] We computed the average value of the corresponding chroma and intensity for each poster and the pixels within the image. Then, we computed the median value of the average chroma and intensity for overall posters within a particular period. For the color buckets, all of the pixels from every poster within a half-decade were combined, and the overall percentage in each bucket was computed. The posters are relatively standardized in size and aspect ratio, which allowed us to directly compare these measurements over time. We split the buckets into half-decades rather than full decades because we wanted a more precise unit of analysis to see gradual changes in time. Also, while it was tempting to look at decades such as the 1970s as 1970–1979, cultural change does not easily align to such a numerically driven characterization of cultural and social change.[63] The results of this analysis are given in table 3.1.

The trend of using white in movie posters has undergone a dramatic shift over the last fifty years. In the first half of the 1970s, the median poster had over 30 percent of its area covered by white. This proportion dropped steadily and consistently through the year 2000. Posters from the second half of the 1990s had only 5.2 percent of their area filled with white, a six-fold drop over thirty years. From its low point in the 1990s, white in movie posters increased slightly in the 2000s. The proportion between 2005 and

Table 3.1
Summary of movie posters from the Top 100–grossing films of each year, grouped by half-decades. Statistics compute the average percentage of the posters that are taken up by "color," "black," and "white"; the median intensity; and the median chroma. All posters were scaled to be the same size.

Years	Color %	White %	Black %	Median intensity	Median chroma	Count
1970–1974	13.2	31.9	11.3	60.9	13.6	315
1975–1979	12.9	23.7	13.9	52.5	13.1	368
1980–1984	11.9	15.1	19.2	44.5	12.4	486
1985–1989	13.8	12.7	24.9	42.0	13.9	500
1990–1994	14.7	7.9	30.9	38.5	14.0	500
1995–1999	18.0	5.2	36.8	34.0	15.2	500
2000–2004	21.2	7.7	28.5	39.0	16.3	500
2005–2009	14.2	11.0	25.4	42.5	14.0	500
2010–2014	11.0	7.2	30.2	37.5	13.2	500
2015–2019	15.4	7.3	23.4	39.7	15.2	500

2009 was twice the proportion of the period ten years prior. In the final decade of our data, the amount of white in movie posters seems to have stabilized to a value around 7 percent of the total area.

The use of black in movie posters over time has primarily been the inverse of the use of white. In the early 1970s, the amount of black used in movie posters was only 11.3 percent. By the second half of the 1990s, this had tripled to a level of 36.8 percent. As with white in the early part of our data, black comprises more than one-third of the average movie poster between 1995 and 1999. In the 2000s, the level of black used in movie posters has slightly decreased, but not as consistently and drastically as in the first half of our time period.

The amount of color used in movie posters over the past fifty years follows a similar trend as that for black and white, but with a more gradual change between each half-decade. Throughout the 1970s, only 13 percent of each poster was composed with a sufficiently bright and saturated color to be categorized as a color by our algorithm. This slowly increased to 21 percent in the half-decade between 2000 and 2004. The half-decade with the smallest percentage of white and the largest percentage of black (1995–1999) is followed by the half-decade with the most color (2000–2004). To understand how this is possible, keep in mind that the three percentages in table 3.1 for each time period do not need to add up to 100 percent because some parts of posters will be classified as "gray" or "other." As with white and black, the amount of color slowly oscillated through the later years of the dataset.

Finally, the trends of intensity and chroma of movie posters follow patterns that mirror the distribution of white, black, and color over the poster area. As the amount of white in posters decreased and the amount of black increased from 1970 to 1999, the median intensity of the posters similarly decreased. Also, as the amount of black and white stabilized in the first two decades of the 2000s, the median intensity held relatively steady around a median value of 38. We would expect the trend of the median chroma to follow the amount of color in the poster images; this largely holds, with the direction the median chroma changes in each half-decade matching the direction of the color percentage in each time period of the data.

The trends of the intensity and chroma add important information to the pattern of the color types. Our cutoff values for the chroma that "count" as black, white, and color may not perfectly match our perceptions of color in the context of a specific poster. The values were selected based on trial and error, but could easily be tweaked, producing slightly different results in our analysis. Hence our emphasis on the distant viewing approach to the role of people in determining the scope of the annotations. However, the median intensity and chroma have no such arbitrary cutoffs but reveal the same general patterns of a gradual change from 1970 to 1999, followed by smaller and less consistent changes between 2000 and 2019. This indicates that, while the specific percentages may change slightly, our overall conclusions are not sensitive to the specific values that were used as cutoff values.[64]

Movie posters are, at their core, created as a form of advertisement. Their form has been dominated throughout their history by an economic evaluation of the cost and benefit of producing them. The relatively significant change in the color composition of movie posters throughout the 1970s, 1980s, and, to a lesser extent, the 1990s, can be understood by considering the changing practices of how posters were printed and displayed over this period.

Since the early days of cinema at the turn of the twentieth century, movie posters have been a staple form of advertisement used both inside and outside theaters.[65] Posters served the dual purpose of advertising the theater itself and drawing audiences in for the viewing of specific films. Before the proliferation of the internet, these printed signs needed to display extensive information about the film content. High contrast was required to read the text. Posters often contained small headshots of the actors and longer descriptions of the film in a smaller type. These same posters, serving similar purposes, were posted in a variety of public spaces to attract customers into movie theaters from malls, subway stations, and public streets. Today, movie posters are still a staple decoration outside many movie theaters, but they increasingly play a different role. Now, these printed posters are also featured digitally on sites including IMDb and Rotten Tomatoes, review and ranking sites that shape viewers' watching habits. Other details, such as studio producers and related metadata, can be easily looked up on a smartphone. We can see this change in the increased use of color through the 1990s and 2000s and the decreased use of white, which was no longer needed as the default background for intricate text and headshots.

The decrease in the white background can also be explained by the change in printing practices over the past fifty years. In the 1970s and 1980s, most movie posters consisted of color printed on top of a white background. The more color and text printed on this background, the more expensive the poster was to produce. In addition to the need to include significant text, the added cost of non-white colors made it advantageous to have posters with a white background and economical use of color. By the 1990s, the popularization of laser printing significantly reduced the economic benefits of using white backgrounds. Now, posters are typically printed on glossy paper with ink covering the entire image from edge to edge. To make posters attract maximum attention, designers have shifted to creating posters with bright colors and dark backgrounds. These material changes, along with new printing technologies and the shifting use of movie posters over the past half-century, help explain the temporal patterns seen in table 3.1.

The dramatic shifts in the color composition of movie posters from 1970 to 1989 need to be accounted for in any analysis of our movie poster dataset. Given the importance of genre to how moviegoers select which film to watch, in the following sections we will investigate differences of color across movie genres. To allow us to isolate the effect of genre, we will reduce the corpus to include only those posters from the past thirty years.[66] Restricting our analysis to the past thirty years also removes the problem of the several hundred missing posters from the earlier part of the corpus.

Exploring Movie Poster Genres

Having investigated how black, white, and color are used in movie posters over the past fifty years, we now turn to our initial motivating goal of understanding the use of color across different movie genres. Common arguments about the movie poster in books, blogs, and creator videos associate a specific color with a specific genre. For example, creative director James Verdesoto states that blue is associated with action thrillers and yellow is associated with lower-budget films.[67] Determining whether these generalizations hold over time or at scale is perfect for a distant viewing approach. To start, we will look at the same metrics and summarizations from the previous section applied to a specific genre. These will reveal whether there are patterns in how color is used in a poster to signify a movie's genre. We will see specific genres that use color in similar ways. Some genres more closely adhere to a specific use of typical colors, but not always as expected.

There are several different approaches to associating movies with a specific genre. Even defining the collection of movie genres is an open question. We will look to our dataset to determine how best to handle picking a set of genre categories and associating movies with each genre. Our dataset from IMDb assigned up to three different genre tags to each movie. These tags are not given in any particular order of importance; they are listed in alphabetical order. Taking the films from the top 100–grossing films of each year released between 1990 and 2019 yields a total set of twenty unique genres.[68] Some genre categories appear relatively infrequently, such as the Western and Musical genres, which appear twenty-three and thirty-three times, respectively.[69] Others are tagged in over half of the dataset; Comedy and Drama appear for more than 1,700 of the 3,000 total films. The IMDb categories provide a good starting point, but the question remains of how to work with this information, because most posters are associated with multiple genre tags.

To determine how to work with the repeated genre tags, we will start by looking at how common it is for any pair of genres to co-occur. This will show how each of the genre tags relates to the other and the degree to which some are proper subsets of others. Table 3.2 shows the pairs of genre tags ordered by the percentage of times the tags occur together relative to the total number of films in which either genre appears. The highest overlap is only 28 percent, which belongs to the Action and Adventure categories, indicating that none of the tags appear to be duplicating similar information.[70] Pairs that do tend to co-occur most frequently correspond to popular subgenres such as Romance Comedies and Animation Adventure films. Other common pairs primarily consist of a more general tag paired up with a more specific tag. These include Action films paired with Sci-Fi, Crime, or Thriller, and then Drama paired with Romance or Crime. Finally, there is one case in which one small genre is primarily contained within another. Of the 276 Animation films, 217 are also classified as Adventure films. However, there are 730 Adventure films that are not classified as Animation, so while one tag may be a subtype of the other, the tags continue to convey different classifications of films.

Our approach to working with genre tags will be to associate each poster with each of the individual genres its associated movie is tagged with. If a movie is an "Action, Adventure, Sci-Fi" film, we will include the poster's

Table 3.2

Movies in our dataset are associated with one to three genres. This table shows those pairs of genres that co-occur most frequently; "Genre 1" is always the rarer of the two genre tags. The table is sorted by the overlap percentage, given as the percentage of films from either genre that are in both genres.

Genre 1	Genre 2	Genre 1 count	Genre 2 count	Overlap count	Overlap %
Adventure	Action	1006	1240	498	28
Romance	Comedy	756	2037	473	20
Animation	Adventure	276	1006	217	20
Crime	Action	848	1240	344	20
Mystery	Horror	382	478	138	19
Romance	Drama	756	2177	457	18
Drama	Crime	2177	848	454	18
Thriller	Horror	702	478	170	17
Drama	Comedy	2177	2037	593	16
Thriller	Mystery	702	382	148	16
Sci-Fi	Action	385	1240	218	15
Thriller	Action	702	1240	255	15
Comedy	Adventure	2037	1006	389	15
Thriller	Crime	702	848	187	14
Fantasy	Family	408	408	91	13
Family	Adventure	408	1006	156	12
History	Biography	100	211	32	11
Drama	Action	2177	1240	349	11
Crime	Comedy	848	2037	275	11
Sci-Fi	Adventure	385	1006	130	10
Family	Comedy	408	2037	224	10

color information three times in our summary statistics, once for each genre category. The metadata gives no clear way to associate the film with a single genre. Creating a unique category for every specific combination of three tags would result in too many combinations to be easily analyzed.[71] Likewise, the results in table 3.2 show that each genre has a unique meaning associated with it—no two genre tags occur particularly frequently together—indicating that there is no simple way to collapse or remove tags based on their distribution. We will not be applying the machinery of statistical inference, which requires assumptions about the independence of different summary statistics, so there is no inherent problem with counting the same poster multiple times in the summaries.

We applied the same summary statistics used in the analysis of half-decades to each of the movie genres. These summaries consist of the average white, black, color, median intensity, and median chroma in movie posters. The results are given in table 3.3, where genres are sorted from having the most colorful poster to the least colorful. Only the fourteen most common genres (of the total twenty) are included in the table to focus on those genres with sufficient data to establish a consistent pattern. The results show several genres with similar patterns in their posters' use of color and brightness. Looking at each of these clusters will help us explore how color conveys information about a movie's genre.

Movie posters for Animation films stand out from other genres in their heavy use of color. Nearly 35 percent of the Animation posters are taken up by pixels that our method has classified as belonging to a color. By comparison, Family films include only 22.2 percent of their posters with color. Animation film posters also have the highest median chroma of any genre, an unsurprising fact given their extensive use of color. They have a moderately

Table 3.3
For each movie genre, this table provides the average amount of the posters that are "color," "white," or "black"; the median intensity; and the median chroma, using the Top 100–grossing films for every year from 1990 through 2019. These are the same summaries as in table 3.1 but grouped by genre instead of half-decade.

Genre	Color %	White %	Black %	Median intensity	Median chroma	Count
Animation	34.8	7.9	11.1	46.4	25.7	268
Family	22.2	12.9	14.6	46.8	17.8	394
Adventure	20.9	7.3	23.5	38.7	17.7	992
Comedy	18.8	18.2	13.7	52.1	16.3	1974
Romance	15.8	20.1	15.6	51.9	14.1	739
Fantasy	15.8	7.4	28.9	36.8	15.0	402
Action	13.7	7.0	36.4	34.3	13.9	1226
Sci-Fi	12.8	5.6	39.1	31.5	13.4	379
Crime	12.6	10.3	34.5	38.0	12.6	837
Drama	12.3	11.8	27.0	42.0	13.0	2094
Biography	9.9	11.9	29.1	42.3	12.4	208
Thriller	9.2	5.9	46.2	29.1	11.0	699
Horror	7.6	3.8	53.4	24.7	10.5	474
Mystery	7.0	4.6	49.6	26.8	10.1	381

high intensity, but unlike the other metrics, this is not a particular outlier, with several genres having a slightly higher median intensity value. The heavy use of color in Animation films is not constrained to real-world colors; animators such as Pixar can create whatever color palette they want to represent their characters and imagined worlds. Typically, animation films play with brighter, more saturated, and more extreme colors to explore the affordances of the medium. Animation films are also commonly marketed to younger audiences, which respond positively to bright and saturated colors.[72] The corresponding posters feature the same characters and scenes from the film and transfer these color palettes directly from the film onto the poster.

Comedy, Romance, and Family films all tend to use a lot of color and white in their movie posters. Their median percentage of color used ranges from 18.8 to 22.2 percent, and their median percentage of white used ranges from 12.9 to 20.1 percent. These three genres have the three highest scores for the use of white in their posters. Also, due to a large amount of color and white, they are the three genres with the highest median intensity. Family films tend to use more color and less white on posters within the cluster of genres, Romance films use the most amount of white and least amount of color, and Comedy films fall in between these two in both metrics. These three genres of film also share a close connection in their typical themes. All three extend across the audience spectrum, from those aimed at general audiences to films targeting mature viewers. They also tend to focus on providing light-hearted themes and have cheerful endings.[73] The use of bright, white, and color posters can be seen as a way of conveying positive feelings to respective audiences.

Another cluster of genres has movie posters that contain substantial amounts of both color and black. This cluster consists of five genres— Adventure, Action, Crime, Fantasy, and Sci-Fi—that tend to focus on themes of escapism and action and are primarily plot-driven.[74] These posters all, on average, consist of between 12.6 and 20.9 percent of their area taken up by color and between 23 and 39 percent of their area taken up by black. All five genres have less than 11 percent of their average area taken up by white. As a result of the predominant mixture of black and color, these posters have a median intensity and median chroma close to the median over the entire collection. Adventure posters and Fantasy posters use slightly more color and less black within the cluster, whereas Action, Crime, and Sci-Fi use a larger amount of black and less color. The Adventure category contains several hundred Animation films, likely contributing to the relatively more significant presence of color used in the Adventure category than in the other four.

Looking at example posters from these genres reveals a typical pattern in how black and color are used together. Often, black is used as a background, and colors are used for the foreground. The color foreground may include bright colors from an explosion or a heavily tinted overlay of the main characters. This combination helps to build the idea of a stylized world, drawing viewers through the promise of mystery and excitement surrounding the ensuing plot. As a part of our exploration, we will look more closely at the specific colors typically used within these genres in the following two sections.

Posters for the Biography and Drama genres are similar to those in the Adventure, Action, Crime, Fantasy, and Sci-Fi cluster. They use slightly less color, slightly more white, and slightly less black. Drama is the largest category in our corpus and appears to be a catch-all category for several heterogeneous subgenres. Drama films especially tend to have posters that, for various reasons, incorporate a variety of colors in each poster. We will explore the usage of specific colors in the following section to further untangle the different analytical possibilities.

Our final distinct cluster of genres consists of Mystery, Thriller, and Horror. Their posters contain significantly more black pixels than any other set of genres, ranging from 46.2 to 53.4 percent on average. The following closest percentage of black is Sci-Fi, with 39.1 percent. This cluster also has the lowest median intensity scores, all under 29.1, and the lowest use of the white, with all under 5.9 percent. These three genres are often grouped when discussing movies, so it is not surprising that their posters exhibit similar properties. The use of very dark posters with limited colors and vague images draws on cultural assumptions that associate darkness with suspense, fear, and uncertainty—themes that all of these genres explore. Also, audiences tend to be polarized in their preferences for these films. Using a strong visual style that most movie posters align with is a sensible approach to marketing to a group already inclined toward a specific genre.

What do we learn about the use of color in movie posters by the clustering together of different genres based on the summary statistics in table 3.3? In aggregate, it appears that film posters use color to signal and evoke genres' themes and their associated affective responses. This is not particularly surprising, but our computational analysis has given a clear picture of precisely what general types of color are used to elicit a particular reaction and how the poster colors group together according to their tagged genres. For example, posters for light-hearted films (Comedy, Romance, and Family) combine white and color. Action and plot-oriented genres use a similar combination of black and color to draw viewers into their world. Genres focused on suspense and mystery convey this mood through dark posters dominated by shades of black. Of course, we also see that the specific elements from within the movie impact the content of the movie poster. This is seen most clearly in the Animation film posters, which display animated figures with a very high amount of bright, saturated color relative to all the other genres.

While we have learned a lot about the correspondence between movie genres and the color choices in their movie posters from our first set of summary statistics, there is more depth to explore. For example, we have focused on the interplay between black, white, and color. Of course, not all colors are the same, and we should try to look at the dominant hues of the colors used in each movie genre and how they contribute to the creation of genre stereotypes and the advertisement themes surrounding each movie. These are the questions that will motivate our exploration in the following section.

Exploring Dominant Colors

We now shift to an analysis of the dominant color hues used in movie posters. The exploration of dominant colors will focus on identifying which, if any, hues are associated with individual genres. As mentioned in the opening of the chapter, there are many popular theories about the meaning and messages associated with individual colors, such as yellow being associated with low-budget and independent films. Exploring dominant colors computationally allows us to see which associations between color and genre hold when we view at scale.

The shift to studying hue requires an additional approach to summarizing our annotations. First, we will focus on those parts of the posters that we grouped as "color." Secondly, we will move away from summary statistics that count averages and medians of values of groups of the corpus. Instead, we will assign each poster to the hue most dominantly represented in the poster. This winner-takes-all approach more accurately captures how color is used in movie posters. A poster with a small, single red object on an otherwise white background is more dominated by red than a poster that uses many different objects of different colors, one of which happens to be red. As in the previous discussion, we will continue to focus on movie posters by genre over the past thirty years to see trends, patterns, and outliers.

Working with the hue components of a digital image requires more care than the intensity and chroma. Recall that we have defined hue as a number between zero and one, mapping out a color wheel with red at zero, green at one-third, and blue at two-thirds. Unlike intensity and chroma, we cannot meaningfully take medians or averages of hue values. One reason for this is that the hue values circle back to red for values near one. Pixels with hues 0.01 or 0.99 both will appear to be shades of red, but the average of their hues will be the color cyan.[75] Even for hues that do not wrap around the circle, averages do not capture the way we understand color. If a genre has half of its posters in shades of orange and half in blue, it would not be correct to describe the posters from this genre as being, on average, green. In place of average hue, we need to think of how colors are typically described. Usually, we group hues into discrete buckets with names such as "orange," "violet," "blue." This is the approach we will take here.

Grouping similar hues into discrete colors is not a neutral process. We are back to the challenges and decisions that shape our annotations. Creating large groups that capture many different variations together risks losing essential differences within a group. Likewise, creating very narrow buckets makes it hard to determine the dominant color of a poster. Consider a poster mostly covered with red, with a small amount of blue in one corner. If the reds are placed into ten different buckets with slightly different names while the blue is all the same hue, it may be that the most common color bucket is blue rather than any specific shade of red. There is no easy answer from a linguistic, psychological, or computational perspective.[76] Different human languages differ on what the "basic" color types should be and which hues correspond to them.[77] For example, the Russian language has a distinct difference between light blue (голубой) and dark blue (синий).[78] There is no collective term for the hues that an English speaker would call blue. Nevertheless, our analysis requires deciding what hue categories to create and what values to use to divide them. As with the choice of the chroma values that distinguish colors from shades of gray, there will be no perfect choice, but we can try to use the data to make informed choices and check that our conclusions are not too sensitive to the selected values.

For our collection of hue cutoff values, we will look at the distribution of hues for several different poster genres. We started by selecting a granular set of hue buckets, splitting up the range of hues into thirty-two equally sized groups. Figure 3.2 shows the percentage of colorful pixels in each genre that falls into each bucket. Looking at the distributions, we see two clusters: one around shades of red and orange, and another around shades of blue. The colors around blue are more concentrated around a particular shade of blue, whereas there is more of a smooth spectrum around the reds and oranges. One reason for this is that human color perception is not uniform across the scale of hues. Our eyes are more sensitive to differences of hue near red than they are near green. Another explanation is that movie posters use colors that attract attention, something that we will return to shortly. Animation films use more green in general and more hues than other genres. This finding follows from the differences between drawings of animated characters and photographs of real people and scenes.

Using the distribution of the granular hues, we will define seven color categories. These include the most common colors mentioned in English (red, orange, yellow, blue, green) and categories for violet and cyan. Violet and cyan are included because we found them too visually different to group with red or blue, respectively. The hue cutoff values are shown as dashed lines in figure 3.2. These values were chosen based on visual inspection of the values and the extended color keywords defined by the World Wide Web Consortium (W3C).[79] We will use this consistent set of hue names in our analysis of dominant poster colors.

By taking our seven buckets of hue, we can now look at dominant colors in the movie posters in our corpus. We start by associating every pixel with a sufficiently large chroma value to a color category based on its hue. Next, we determine the color category for each poster that contains the most significant number of pixels. This largest bucket gives a poster's dominant color. So, if a poster has more pixels labeled "green" than any other color, we will describe "green" as the dominant color for the poster. Some posters contain little to no color; we removed from our analysis posters in which the largest color category covers less than 3 percent of the image. With the remaining posters, we look at the distribution of color categories within each genre. The results of this analysis are given in table 3.4. Note that,

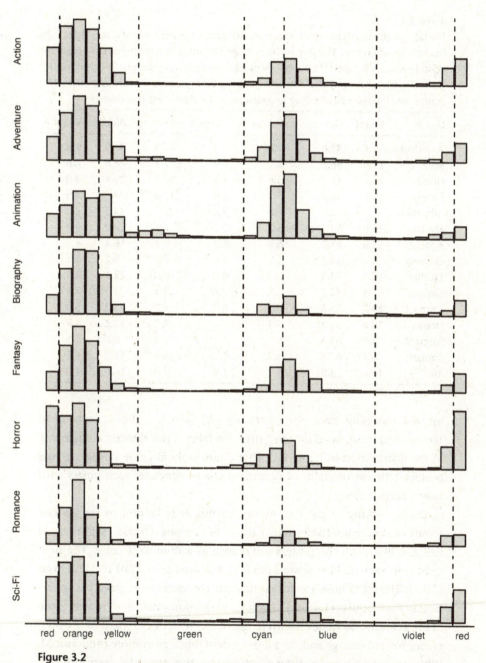

Figure 3.2
Histogram of hues detected in the Top 100–grossing movie posters from 1990 through 2019, grouped by genre, for six selected genre types. Reference colors are given on the x-axis. See supplemental materials for a full-color version of the figure.

Table 3.4
We take all the pixels in a poster that are categorized as a color and group them into buckets based on hue. The hue with the largest count is indentified as the dominant color hue of each poster. This table gives the distribution of dominant color hues by genre for the posters of the Top 100–grossing films from 1990 through 2019. The genres are ordered in ascending proportion of the dominant hue orange.

Genre	Red %	Orange %	Yellow %	Green %	Cyan %	Blue %	Violet %
Animation	4.1	33.8	7.8	3.2	17.4	32.0	1.8
Sci-Fi	11.9	38.7	2.1	1.5	17.5	25.8	2.6
Horror	22.2	41.9	3.6	1.8	7.2	20.4	3.0
Family	10.1	43.5	5.1	1.8	11.2	24.6	3.6
Adventure	6.2	46.5	6.6	2.2	12.7	23.3	2.6
Mystery	16.0	50.3	5.5	0.6	7.4	16.0	4.3
Action	12.0	51.2	5.6	1.0	9.8	16.4	4.1
Comedy	8.5	53.1	6.7	1.5	6.9	18.2	5.1
Thriller	18.0	53.3	3.7	0.6	8.0	12.1	4.3
Fantasy	7.8	53.5	3.2	2.8	7.4	23.5	1.8
Crime	14.7	55.5	5.7	0.2	4.7	12.3	6.9
Drama	10.0	61.4	5.1	1.0	5.5	12.2	4.8
Biography	5.4	63.4	9.7	1.1	4.3	8.6	7.5
Romance	5.4	67.7	5.2	1.2	3.5	11.0	6.1
All	10.1	54.3	5.7	1.4	7.6	16.6	4.3

up to a rounding error, the percentages in each row should sum up to 100 percent. Also, keep in mind that this table is not directly comparable to the distribution in figure 3.2. That figure looks at color averages across posters, whereas the table of dominant colors associates each poster with only a single color.

Before looking at patterns among genres, it is helpful to see general trends of dominant colors across the entire corpus. Overall, slightly over half (54.3%) of all the posters use orange as a dominant color. The next most common are blue posters (16.6%), followed by red (10.1%) and cyan (7.6%). The other hues are not particularly common, with green being particularly unpopular (1.4%). The results of the dominant hues match those of the average hue values shown in figure 3.2, with the strength of the preference toward orange and, to a lesser extent, blue, even more pronounced. While the specific ratios differ across genres, this general pattern can also be seen within each genre. Orange is the most prominent dominant color of every genre, and blue is the second-largest category for all but three categories, and a close third in those.

We will now look at each of the color distributions and see how these differ across genres. Orange, the most common color across all genres, is particularly dominant in movie posters for the Drama, Biography, and Romance categories. Orange is the most dominant color in over 60 percent of all movie posters from these three categories. These three genres all focus heavily on character development, which could explain the dominance of orange.[80] Our movie posters come from top-grossing films in the United States and feature predominantly white leading actors and actresses. When characters' faces and bodies are shown in a movie poster, the color is often adjusted to make them slightly warmer, showing up as a shade of orange. Manual inspection of several posters featuring Black actors also shows that our algorithm typically categorizes their skin as a dark-orange hue. Movie posters that primarily focus on showing the characters, in the absence of other intense colors, will therefore often be categorized as having a dominant color of orange. This may also help explain the overall high amount of orange across all genres due to posters that highlight one or more individuals. The genres with the lowest proportion of posters associated with orange are Animation, Sci-Fi, Horror, Family, and Adventure films. These genres tend to focus on the setting and plot of their films rather than individual people, for it is often the unknown that is the source of fear and excitement.[81] Horror films often seek to obscure their main characters to build suspense. This falls in line with the theory that one driving factor for the orange colors is the detection of people in the image.[82]

The proportion of blue as a dominant color in each genre largely follows the opposite pattern of the use of orange. The three genres that use the most orange—Drama, Biography, and Romance—also use the least blue. Of the six genres with a substantial proportion of posters dominated by blue, five have the lowest amount of orange. Looking at individual examples from these genres, the tone of blue often seems to be used to highlight the plots and locations of these categories. The outlier genre in this set is Fantasy, which has an unusual distribution compared to the other categories; it has the fourth-largest amount of blue and the fifth-largest amount of orange. The reason for this unexpected distribution leads to more questions and explorations, which will be explained in the following section once we have looked at color pairs.

The distribution of red as a dominant color varies substantially by genre. The three genres with the highest amount of red are Horror (22.2%), Thriller (18.0%), and Mystery (16.0%). These genres also had the largest median amount of black in their posters and the lowest median intensity. All three are built around the idea of suspense and fear. Red can be used to evoke these feelings, with its close associations in Western culture to blood, danger, and death.[83] Interestingly, despite several sources claiming that red is common in posters for Romance films due to its other association to themes of hearts and love, this does not reveal itself in the data.[84] Romance films are, instead, associated with one of the lowest amounts of the color red.

The colors cyan and violet do not appear frequently as a dominant color. Looking across genres, we see that they appear most frequently in genres that include a high amount of blue or orange, respectively. The Animation, Sci-Fi, Family, and Adventure categories contain the highest levels of cyan and are four of the five genres with the largest proportion of posters dominated by blue. Violet is most common in Crime, Romance, and Biography, which are also three of the four genres with the largest proportion of orange. These signals are probably a result of the cutoff values that we chose for each bucket. The relatively large amount of violet in Romance films may also partially explain the absence of red in these posters. Romance films may use a softer violet form of red that our cutoff values push into the violet category.

Posters dominated by yellow and green do not cluster as clearly as by genre. Yellow is the most dominant hue in Biography, Animation, and Comedies. Green is the most dominant hue in the posters for Animation, Fantasy, and Adventure films. To further understand these results, we will explore color combinations to see if we can better tease out the effects of color in these genres. It is likely that green and yellow pop in these categories because they are rarely particularly dominant and float to the top only when a poster uses a variety of different colors all at once. In the next section, we will explore further by looking at color combinations to see if our hypothesis holds.

The use of computational analysis is often associated with computing summary statistics and identifying general patterns across data collection. So far, we have followed this approach closely with our analysis of movie posters. However, computational techniques can also be used to identify exceptional individual data points that can be useful to investigate on their own. The patterns we have found in the dominant colors results have shown some interesting patterns. However, it is hard to precisely determine the cause behind some of these without drawing on existing scholarship, including film history and theory, and looking at some examples. Distant viewing is intricately linked to the use of theory and close analysis.

Let us look at several specific posters to further demonstrate the weak relationship between a single color and a genre except for Horror. We can use our measurement of dominant color to identify the individual posters most strongly associated with each of our color buckets. Those posters that have the largest proportion of each color are shown in figure 3.3. The results reveal several exciting observations that help to put the summary statistics in context. Those posters that primarily contain the largest amount of red and orange support our conclusions about the patterns in the use of these colors across the whole corpus. The poster that uses the most orange is for the drama *American Beauty* (1999), with the entire frame of the poster taken up by a woman's bare stomach. This shows that White skin tones will often be identified as orange in our method of assigning a hue to each pixel. A similar example from the fourth most orange poster, *Election* (1999), which is categorized as a Comedy and Romance, illustrates the same phenomenon with an extreme close shot of a White woman's face. Orange is associated less with a single genre than with a particular feature of posters—the inclusion of people—that spans genres. Of the six posters with the most significant amount of red, four are for Horror films. The only Romance film in the reddest posters is the crossover Romance/Horror film *Warm Bodies* (2013).

Many of the other patterns in the posters with the most dominant colors show that color, at least in extreme cases, is often driven by specific elements of a film. Categorized as an Action, Crime, and Thriller, *Kill Bill: Volume 1* (2003) is dominated by its yellow background, which is playing off the jumpsuit of Uma Thurman's character shown in the foreground; this film is not a low-budget, independent film as one might argue for based on its use of yellow. *Finding Neverland* (2004), categorized as a Biography, Drama, and Family, is dominated by the green color associated with Peter Pan. Animated films often have a character drawn in a single hue, making for particularly colorful posters, such as the yellow in *The SpongeBob SquarePants Movie* (2004), orange in *The Lorax* (2012), and violet in *Piglet's Big Movie* (2003); combining this close analysis with distant viewing suggests looking at a range of colors in posters to see if a spectrum of colors align with genres is a more promising line of inquiry. Dominant colors can even play with the name of the film, such as the red in the *Red Sparrow* (2018) poster

Figure 3.3

Each row shows the six movie posters with the greatest amount of each color: red, orange, yellow, green, blue, and violet. See supplemental materials for a full-color version of this figure.

and the yellow of *Little Miss Sunshine* (2006). The poster for the movie *Green Book* (2018), interestingly, contains the largest amount of the color cyan. It is playing with the film's name but perhaps avoiding something too close to green, given its general unpopularity as a movie poster color. Looking at specific posters as well as at scale through distant viewing reveals the tenuous relationship between a specific color and a genre.

The summary statistics across genres and looking at examples with particularly dominant colors reveal an intense concentration of dominant colors, with orange by far the most popular choice, followed by blue. The general balance between a warm orange and a cool blue within a genre can be roughly described by the balance between character-driven genres and plot-driven stories, with the first having relatively more orange and the second containing relatively more blue. Along with catching the eye, a large amount of orange, in general, and especially in character-driven genres, is often caused by skin tones being detected as a shade of orange. The use of red as a dominant color has a strong association with the suspense cluster of the genres Horror, Thriller, and Mystery. Otherwise, there are no robust relations between dominant hues and genre. A dominant color does not mean that a single color dominates a genre, as is often stated in popular forums such as creator videos and the popular press. Associating red with romance is an oversimplification of a set of decisions that includes communicating the themes and scope of a film and catching the attention of people through marketing. We turn to color pairs to further explore the relationship between colors and genre.

Exploring Color Combinations

As a final exploration, we will investigate how different color hues are paired together within a particular movie poster. In the previous section, we looked at the distribution of only the most dominant hues. This analysis showed that a large proportion of our posters use only a limited range of colors as their most dominant hue. Are the other hues used heavily as secondary colors, or are they just generally rare on average? Are some hues paired together in common combinations? Are some movie genres more likely to make use of a wide range of colors compared to others? Looking at combinations of hues will allow us to take a deeper look at how color combinations are used across the corpus to address these questions.

We will use the same grouping of hues into seven categories for color hue combinations as defined in the previous section. Assigning each pixel in a poster with a sufficiently high chroma value to one of the color categories, we can identify the dominant hue as the one that takes up the most significant proportion of the poster, and the secondary hue as the one that has the second-largest proportion. Measuring hue proportions is only interesting in posters that use more than a negligible amount of color; therefore, we removed any posters from this analysis that have less than 3 percent of the total poster area assigned to a color category. With the selection of dominant and secondary hues for each poster, we can look at the average proportion covered by these hues in each genre.[85] In other words, we will measure the average proportion that movie posters are covered by their dominant hue and the average proportion that is covered by its secondary hue. The results of this summary are given in table 3.5. The genres are ordered by the ratio between the dominant hue percentage and the secondary hue percentage. Note that all of the percentages in the table are given relative to the entire poster, not just the percentage of colorful pixels. For example, the percentage of Animation films filled with the dominant hue (24.1%) indicates that about a quarter of the entire poster is, on average, covered by the dominant hue. We see that 39.7 percent of the poster is covered by color, indicating that about 60 percent (24.1 divided by 39.7) of the color pixels are from the dominant hue.

One of the first striking elements of the results is the large degree to which the dominant hues dominate each genre. In every film genre, the most dominant hue, on average, takes up more than half of the color in the posters. These patterns may not be surprising for those categories, such as Horror, that generally do not use many colors. The pattern is more surprising in the case of Animation and Family films, which contain a significant amount of color overall. Also, remember that our boundaries between different color hues are not sharp. The cutoffs are judgment calls between a continuum of different hues, which we determined when we decided on our annotations. A poster that contains many different shades of blue—for example, the ice and snow scene on the *Frozen* (2013) poster—could easily have a relatively even split between pixels from the cyan and blue buckets. Seeing the large proportions of the dominant hue compared to the overall amount of color shown without correcting for these crossover effects at the boundary of different color shades shows how strongly a single color tends to dominate most posters.

Table 3.5

For color pixels in each image, this table gives the average proportion of the dominant color hue that constitutes posters in each genre. It also gives the overall average proportion that is taken up by all colors, and the average proportion of the second-most common hue, or secondary hue. The ratio between the dominant hue and secondary hue is used to sort the table; this gives a sense of how likely a poster is to make significant use of multiple hues.

Genre	Color %	Dominant hue %	Secondary hue %	Ratio	Count
Animation	39.7	24.1	8.9	2.7	223
Family	29.4	18.6	6.5	2.8	282
Adventure	31.3	20.2	6.9	2.9	671
Sci-Fi	23.7	16.0	5.3	3.0	211
Comedy	29.3	19.4	6.1	3.2	1241
Action	25.6	17.4	5.4	3.2	727
Crime	23.2	16.1	4.8	3.4	452
Fantasy	26.9	18.7	5.2	3.6	227
Thriller	21.7	16.1	4.1	3.9	351
Romance	25.6	18.4	4.7	3.9	444
Drama	24.5	18.1	4.5	4.0	1040
Biography	24.7	18.4	4.6	4.0	101
Mystery	19.3	14.6	3.5	4.2	178
Horror	19.6	15.2	3.2	4.8	182

Looking at the ratio between the dominant hue proportion and secondary hue proportion reveals three clusters of genres. Six genres have an exceptionally high ratio, indicating that their posters are generally designed to primarily consist of (at most) a single hue of color. These genres all correspond to "serious" themes: Thriller, Romance, Drama, Biography, Mystery, and Horror. Even within this group, Mystery and Horror films tend to have exceptionally high ratios (4.2 and 4.8, respectively). The use of a single color could be used to signal the serious nature of their corresponding genres. The appearance of Romance in this list may seem unexpected. However, if we look back at table 3.2, we will see that Romance has significant overlap with Drama. These categories also tend to be on the lower end of overall color use. However, there is no one-to-one correspondence between the overall amount of color and the ratio between the dominant and secondary color proportions. Sci-Fi, for example, uses less color than Romance, Drama, and Biography films but has the fourth-lowest ratio between the color categories.

The three genres with the smallest ratio between the dominant and secondary hue proportions are Animation, Family, and Adventure. In contrast to the genres with the smallest ratio between the two hues, these categories tend to be primarily lighthearted and aimed at younger audiences. They also use the most significant amounts of color overall, have the most intense median posters, and are the most saturated. The other genres that fall between these two extremes—Fantasy, Action, Crime, and Sci-Fi—tend to focus on escapism aimed at adult audiences. This group's position between the other two groups falls in line with the observation that secondary colors convey the seriousness of a movie.

To understand the relationship between the primary and secondary hues, we may also look at the specific pairs of hues that tend to appear together. This can be accomplished by counting the number of times each dominant hue is paired with a specific secondary hue. Counts of these pairs across all the posters in our dataset (1990–2019) are given in table 3.6, with the primary hue given in the columns and the secondary hue given in the rows. Most pairs appear to come from a range of hues that blend continuously into another hue. For example, red is most frequently paired with orange, and next most frequently to be paired with violet. Cyan is most often paired with blue. Other than these, the next most significant overlaps occur between orange and blue. In other words, most pairs between dominant and secondary hues appear to be a continuum of hues across our

Table 3.6
Using the same data as table 3.5, this table shows how frequently two hues are paired up as the primary and secondary hues of a poster. The data only include posters where the secondary hue constitutes at least 5 percent of the poster. Columns give the primary color and rows give the secondary color.

	Red	Orange	Yellow	Green	Cyan	Blue	Violet
Red		498	10	2	13	35	30
Orange	151		101	9	62	173	52
Yellow	6	424		13	9	31	3
Green	1	17	4		16	9	0
Cyan	2	72	4	3		100	4
Blue	20	169	11	4	70		13
Violet	59	106	5	1	10	43	

hue boundaries rather than more exciting color combinations. This may be partially due to these being the most common hues overall but is also likely to be driven by their common use as complementary colors.

Looking at pairs suggests another area of inquiry. To what degree are color pairs shaped using warm and cool colors in the posters? If we look more closely at interesting pairs, it would be helpful to compute warm and cool explicitly. One way to do this is to group our color buckets into two meta-categories: warm colors (red, orange, yellow, and violet) and cool colors (green, blue, and cyan). As we saw in the histograms in figure 3.2, there is minimal use of colors in our dataset in the vicinity of green-cyan and blue-violet. Therefore, the divide of warm and cool colors should cleanly split the hues into easy-to-distinguish categories. Suppose a poster uses a mixture of warm and cool colors. In that case, this will usually correspond to the use of two distinct colors rather than a spectrum of colors that happens to cross one of our color boundaries.

Table 3.7 replicates the analysis of table 3.5 using two color groups (warm and cool) in place of the original seven. Arranging the genres by the ratio between the dominant and secondary temperatures shows a similar pattern to the analysis with more granular hues. A few orderings shift around, which should not be analyzed too closely given the small ratios and sample sizes. As before, in general, light-hearted, family-oriented films are the most likely to use a mixture of warm and cool colors, whereas the serious genres tend to stick with a single-color temperature, most commonly a warm tone.

The most compelling feature in table 3.7 is the enormous magnitude of the ratios between the dominant and secondary color temperature within each poster. The smallest value for Animation film posters is 4.6, and over half of the genres have a ratio greater than 9. Horror posters, which have the most significant ratio, have a value of almost 20. These values show that movie posters limit their mixture of warm and cool colors, with a strong tendency to focus on only one or the other. When posters do mix warm and cool colors, the second temperature is typically used only as an accent color, taking up around ten times less space than the primary temperature. Given the strength of the relationship between these ratios and genre, it was interesting to us that this pattern was not one we had seen discussed in the popular media sources describing the colors of movie posters. This finding is an example of how distant viewing can help identify more complex

Table 3.7
Using the same data as table 3.5, this table groups pixel colors into warm and cool colors and shows the amount of warm color in each genre, as well as the average degree of uniformity of the use of the warmth and coolness.

Genre	Color %	Warmth %	Dominant temp. %	Secondary temp. %	Ratio	Count
Animation	39.7	21.3	32.5	7.1	4.6	223
Family	29.4	18.1	24.5	4.9	5.0	282
Comedy	29.3	20.7	25.1	4.3	5.9	1241
Adventure	31.3	20.3	26.8	4.4	6.0	671
Fantasy	26.7	18.0	23.4	3.3	7.1	229
Sci-Fi	23.7	15.5	21.2	2.4	8.7	211
Romance	25.5	20.9	23.0	2.5	9.0	445
Action	25.5	19.8	23.2	2.4	9.8	729
Mystery	19.3	13.5	17.5	1.7	10.1	179
Drama	24.4	19.6	22.4	2.0	11.1	1044
Crime	23.2	19.3	21.3	1.9	11.5	452
Thriller	21.7	17.7	20.5	1.2	16.9	352
Biography	24.7	20.9	23.5	1.2	19.4	101
Horror	19.6	15.0	18.7	1.0	19.6	182

types of relationships between annotations and metadata fields that may not be immediately evident.

Summary statistics show there is a solid relationship between the perceived seriousness of a genre and the degree to which that genre's movie posters balance the use of warm and cool colors. Those genres that correspond to serious tones, such as Biography and Horror, are unlikely to use both warm and cool tones. In contrast, Animation, Family, and Comedy films are more likely to use warm and cool colors within a single poster. The order of magnitude of this pattern is strong relative to the relationships discussed in the previous sections; Horror film posters are four times less likely to use warm and cool colors together than posters for Family films. Looking at specific examples of these posters shows that the decision to use a narrow or wide range of colors is linked closely to the poster's scale, objects, and composition. A thorough study of these elements moves us beyond the realm of color, our primary object of study here, and requires an entirely new set of annotations. Distant viewing offers a way of looking at scale that allows us to explore current claims, find new patterns, and open new avenues of inquiry.

Conclusions

Movie posters serve as a robust visual signifier for their corresponding films and therefore hold an essential place in visual culture. Using a distant viewing approach to analyzing a collection of movie posters, we have investigated patterns in the poster color palettes over the last fifty years and across different genres. First, we explored color intensity by looking at the relationship between the use of black, white, and color over time. Then, we looked more closely at possible relationships between genre and color by focusing on dominant colors, and finally by turning to color combinations. As we explored, we posed new questions and avenues of inquiry to better understand movie posters' cultural and economic work.

Exploring the color palette of movie posters allowed us to see patterns, trends, and outliers. Some of these patterns, such as the relative darkness of Horror film posters and the chroma of Animation film posters, follow the conventional wisdom of how movie posters are constructed. The bright, vibrant, and otherworldly reds of Animation film posters align with the popular understanding of these films as creative worlds often designed for younger audiences by companies such as Pixar. Other results—such as the correspondence between warm or cool colors with the seriousness of a genre—may not be particularly surprising but, to the best of our knowledge, has not been established in previous quantitative studies.

The most surprising result in our analysis was finding that, in general, the spectrum of movie poster colors is relatively narrow. The dominant color of every single genre is the same (orange), and most posters contain pixels with similar hues. With the exception of the use of red in Horror and Thriller posters, theories about a specific color being clearly linked to a specific genre are complicated by the data. The overall dominance of orange is so prevalent that the many sweeping claims that individual colors are associated with specific genres should be met with caution.

Putting together the results from the previous section with the analysis of color combinations, we see a relatively consistent story: movie posters tend to be cautious and narrow with their use of color. The choice of dominant colors in posters follows the common trends of using attention-getting hues, which are typically shades of warm orange or, slightly less commonly, shades of blue. Other hues are relatively rare, except for the significant use of red in Horror, Thriller, and Mystery film posters. When secondary-color hues are used, these most frequently consist of a range of nearby hues rather than complementary colors. Mixing opposing warm and cool colors is done in relatively small proportions, even in the posters of Animation films. Exceptions to these general trends are seen most in the light-hearted, family-oriented genres or when the specific content of a film calls for bold uses of color. Even the few outliers support the general trend that the dominant colors are limited primarily to red, blue, and orange. Given the purpose of movie posters, it is perhaps no surprise that they use well-established colors for grabbing attention in marketing and visual perception scholarship. Movie posters, in other words, play it safe. Their formulaic style duly maps onto the formulas that define Hollywood genres, which are surer roads to box office success. The movie posters reflect the homogenized product and industry that they are designed to sell.

The exploration of movie poster color is just one way we could analyze the posters using distant viewing. Color is a relatively simple feature to analyze compared to algorithms for features such as people and objects, which we turn to in the next chapter. Nevertheless, as we could see with this seemingly straightforward annotation, even deciding which types of annotation to use and how to determine the cutoffs that defined each color involved a series of decisions. Unlike other forms of data, we had to decide which pixels to count and how to count them because we did not have a built-in set of annotations. Determining which annotation to use and how to define it is a critical component of distant viewing and demonstrates why it is crucial to identify, pause, and think critically about this step. The decision making is also deeply informed by the histories of the data along with theories and questions that animate fields such as communications and film studies. Looking at additional annotations would expand our analysis by investigating relationships between poster genre and other formal elements, such as the location of text or the number of people featured on the poster. We could further extend our analysis by enlarging the dataset itself. For example, we could include posters from different regions and include independent films. Our analysis is just the start and demonstrates how distant viewing offers a method for exploring current arguments and then provides new directions for future research. As we turn to more complex features in order to study early twentieth-century photography in chapter 4, we must keep in mind how distant viewing is shaped by our choice of both datasets and computer vision techniques as well as the histories and theories that help us interpret the results.

4 Seeing Is Believing: Themes in Great Depression and World War II Photography

During the height of the Great Depression, the United States federal government sought strategies to demonstrate why a set of programs and financial policies known as the New Deal were necessary and successful. Among these efforts was the Farm Security Administration's Historical Section, which funded a group of photographers initially charged with taking images of the administration's activities. Photographers were sent across the country to galvanize support for relief services and the expansion of federal resources by depicting impoverished people deserving of government relief and the subsequent recovery made possible by the New Deal. Tens of thousands of negatives were processed in Washington, DC. Staff selected, printed, and cataloged images in filing cabinets for access and circulation. The collection became known colloquially as the "The File," but was officially called the Farm Security Administration / Office of War Information (FSA-OWI) Collection, named after the two government agencies that housed the unit from 1935 to 1944. Along with amplifying the careers of now-acclaimed photographers of the twentieth century, the project was innovative in its elevation of photography as a powerful form of persuasion.

While supporting New Deal policies was an explicit goal, the purposes of the project exceeded bureaucratic expediency.[1] Spurred by contemporary social science's interest in understanding people's daily lives, the Historical Section's leader Roy Stryker and staff photographers shared a belief in the expository power of photography and sought to expand the scope of the project. Rather than just serving as a tool to justify the expansion of the New Deal state and depict a nation ready for world war, the goal of the collection became capturing a pictorial record of everyday life in America. While Stryker, shaped by his upbringing in Kansas, would be most interested in daily life in small towns, he sought to provide photographers with institutional flexibility to pursue their interests. At scale, with tens of thousands of photographs coming to DC, the Historical Section could become an archive of daily life during a period of great turmoil, participants in the unit argued. Yet, with over 170,000 negatives, of which nearly eighty thousand were also printed, the scale exceeds our ability to look easily at the entire set.

In this chapter, we use distant viewing to study the content and style of the printed photographs contained in The File. We look beyond the most iconic photographs, such as Dorothea Lange's *Migrant Mother* and Arthur Rothstein's *Fleeing a Dust Storm*, to understand the larger collection. Figure 4.1 shows twelve example photographs from the collection. Initial questions that guide our exploration include: To what degree did photographers follow the government's needs and pursue the expanded aims of the project? Are there particular features or themes on which the photographs and archive are focused? And can we see a specific visual style by a photographer or across the collection? These questions build on scholarship from art history, cultural history, and visual culture studies.[2]

To begin to address these questions, we turn to the first step of distant viewing: creating annotations. In the previous chapter, we focused on the relatively low-level approach of color analysis. As we move from chapter to chapter, the annotation steps increase in complexity to demonstrate the range of methods that may be utilized. We now turn to techniques facilitated by machine learning to build our annotations. This chapter focuses on *object detection*, the identification of objects found within an image. The identification of objects provides annotations that are more specific than dominant colors, but this specificity comes at the cost of needing to be careful about the categories of objects we are detecting and how accurate our algorithms are at identifying them. Algorithms for object detection are being actively developed within the computer vision community and are used in several application domains.

Several previous computational studies of visual culture have used object detection techniques. As part of putting together the MINERVA dataset, a group of scholars created a custom object-detection algorithm to find musical instruments within digital scans of paintings.[3] Similarly, Smits and Wevers applied object detection to digital scans of historic newspapers.[4] They surfaced hundreds of advertisements for objects such as cars and maps. In another study, a group produced a custom computer vision algorithm to

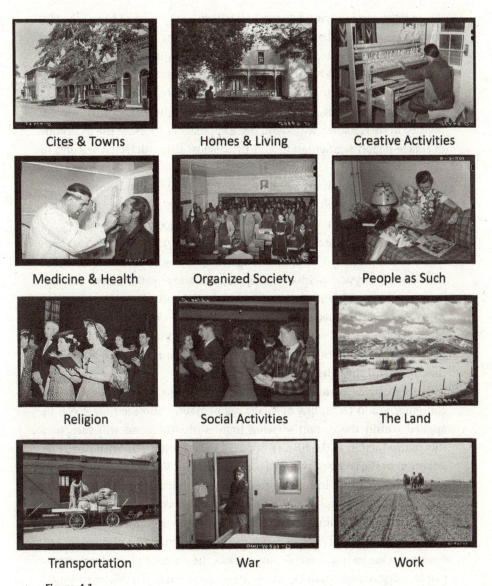

Figure 4.1
Twelve example photographs from the FSA-OWI collection. One photograph has been selected from each of the high-level thematic categories that organize the collection.

detect right-wing propaganda symbols within a corpus of 274 YouTube videos.[5] Their analysis detected hundreds of instances of these symbols and served to illustrate the changing symbolism of right-wing parties in Eastern Europe between 2007 and 2018. These applications illustrate the power of object detection for the analysis of visual culture, with a primary focus on serving as a visual search algorithm to highlight images with specific objects. In this chapter, we extend these approaches by using the technique of image region segmentation and by looking at the detected features in aggregate.

To pursue this analysis, we apply a computer vision algorithm that organizes each photograph into regions corresponding to the people, objects, and materials present within the image frame. Aggregating these regions across the rich metadata of the archive reveals patterns over time, across photographers, and within a historical organizational system initially designed to search the physical archive. Aggregating the data at various levels of specificity uncovers different ways to understand the content of the collection. As we increase the specificity of the labels for the detected regions of the photographs, we will see how distant viewing facilitates viewing in comparison to the traditional archival information from the 1930s and 1940s that undergird the collection.

We start by determining our type of annotations. We then explore the computer vision technique of image segmentation and see how it can be applied within the distant viewing framework. Then, we will turn to a short introduction to the history of the FSA-OWI collection, with particular attention to the archival system developed by Paul Vanderbilt in the 1940s. Finally, we will move into three areas of exploration. Our first analysis tags each photograph based on whether it appears to have been taken outdoors and whether it contains any people. This set of annotations offers a way to explore the relationship between the government's and photographers' priorities. Our second analysis investigates the content of outdoor photographs using a more granular set of categories to study the degree to which individual photographers forged their photographic style. In our third analysis, we use the most specific region tags provided by our algorithm. We remix the collection with these categories to explore themes and topics that help us see with, across, and against the archival organization of The File. Finally, we turn to a caution about object detection, including questions about algorithmic decision-making and how we might be able to create innovative interfaces for exploring the digital collection using the distant viewing approach, a topic we return to in chapter 6.

Annotating Image Segmentation

Significant work in computer vision research has been focused on automatically identifying objects such as people and cars in images. These are features that one often can count, and corresponding approaches are often collectively known as object detection algorithms. Yet, images include many features that are not countable, including the sky and the ground. Arthur Rothstein's famous photo *Fleeing a Dust Storm* is a prime example.[6] Identifying the three people in the photograph is just the beginning of understanding the image's messages. The dark haziness of the sky blends into the ground to convey that they are surrounded by billions of particles of dirt and dust. The relationship between foreground and background communicates the gravity of the situation, a struggle between people and the environment they have physically altered.

In response to the goal of identifying and accounting for the innumerable features that are so critical to interpreting images, new algorithms are now looking for what is referred to as *stuff* alongside the search for concrete objects. For our annotations, we will be using the image segmentation algorithms provided by a computer vision library called Detectron-2. While we could customize the model, which we will address in further detail at the end of the chapter, we decided to work within the model's default ways of viewing. This decision creates space to discuss the opportunities and challenges of mapping our annotations to the concepts and questions that guide our analysis of The File. Even when we retrain a model, understanding the assumptions that we are retraining is key to determining what we can and can't know from the algorithm's results. The history of the algorithms informs our analysis.

As discussed in chapter 2, computer vision research is often guided by a focus on "shared tasks." These tasks involve different research groups competing to develop the best algorithms to match manually labeled data tags on common dataset. Shared tasks are typically focused on application domains such as facial recognition and motion detection that have concrete industrial applications. Organizing the field around these challenges is partially a result of the funding streams for computer vision research.

The focus on shared tasks also reflects the emphasis on numeracy and (perceived) objectivity within the broader field of computer science. Evaluating new ideas and approaches based on concrete benchmarks is viewed as better than a holistic consideration of a method's merits.[7] Together, these factors have focused a significant amount of work toward solving a specific set of computer vision tasks.

Many of the shared tasks in computer vision research are framed as trying to answer the question, What is this an image of? One of the first such tasks in computer vision consists of the Modified National Institute of Standards and Technology database, commonly known as MNIST.[8] Released in 1998, the dataset contains seventy thousand images of handwritten digits, with each image containing only a single digit. The grayscale images are provided at a small resolution, only 28 pixels high and 28 pixels wide. Because the MNIST digits are a visual representation of an explicit written system of numerals, it is relatively straightforward to agree on what tags (the digits) to assign to each image manually. Research on this and other related datasets contributed to modern optical character-recognition systems that convert scanned and typed text images into machine-readable formats.

In the years following the release of the MNIST dataset, other shared tasks in computer vision appeared to extend the task to increasingly large images and complex categories. The CIFAR-10 (Canadian Institute for Advanced Research) dataset presented a similar task on small color images grouped into ten different things, such as airplanes and dogs.[9] Stanford released the STL-10 dataset based on images in the same categories as CIFAR but at a significantly larger resolution. Caltech-101 and Caltech-256 continued this trend by releasing higher-resolution images in even more categories. While these and other similar datasets include different categories and image resolutions, they all have images that are tightly cropped to concentrate on a single object. Even though human viewers may differ on exactly which linguistic tags to give an object, it would be relatively straightforward to identify what part of the image is intended to be the explicit subject of the images in these collections.

Newer shared tasks in computer vision algorithms have focused on determining the contents of images that are not necessarily focused on a single subject. While small, PASCAL VOC, which consisted of tagged images from Flickr, is an early example of a dataset containing typical examples of digital images found online.[10] The ILSVR Challenge was launched in 2010 with hundreds of thousands of high-resolution images tagged with one thousand different types of objects.[11] More recently, the MS COCO (Microsoft Common Objects in Context) dataset, released in 2014, has become an important benchmark and training source for computer vision algorithms. The emergence of these image collections has shifted the way in which computer vision algorithms categorize the content of an image. No longer is the task to tag each image as belonging to a specific category. Instead, it is now necessary to assign several different tags to each image to represent all known objects present within the frame. Taking the task even further, benchmarks for MS COCO now require algorithms to associate individual pixels in the image with each detected object. In short, the algorithmic goal of answering the question, What is this an image of?, has begun to tackle more of the conceptual difficulties that visual culture scholars have long identified.[12]

The task of assigning pixels in an image to objects has raised an essential question for computer vision research. While the subject of many (though certainly not all) images are people and other objects, objects do not account for the entire frame of a typical image. What about those parts of the image consisting of elements that cannot be individually enumerated, such as the sky, a field of grass, or a body of water? In 2015, a research group added additional tags to a portion of the MS COCO dataset to indicate these other regions.[13] In contrast with the standard categories of *objects*, they presented new categories of *stuff*. The task of simultaneously detecting both objects and stuff quickly became a prevalent task. While the former consists of countable objects, the latter contains unenumerable regions.[14] The expansion to seeing stuff is an addition to computational ways of seeing.

The category of stuff provides another way of viewing and, therefore, a new form of evidence. The focus on object detection only looks at countable features and privileges a specific part of an image: the foreground. Yet, this is just a part of the significant amount of visual information and meaning making in an image. The focus on stuff expands our analysis to another part of the image: the background. Adding the background as a focus expands our ways of seeing. For example, consider an object detection algorithm that has identified a chair in the center of an image. If the remainder of the image contains the sky, sand, and the ocean, we might interpret this as a leisurely scene of a chair positioned at the beach. However, if the image's background contained a wall, windows, and a carpet, we would instead position the chair as being indoors. Further, combining the chair with information about other objects—a table and cups indicating a chair in a dining room, whereas books or a television indicate a living room chair—allows for a richer and more abstract formulation of what is being conveyed within the frame of the image.

In 2016, a fully annotated version of stuff categories was included as the default benchmark within the MS COCO benchmark dataset. The stuff categories were designed in a hierarchical structure to capture a range of innumerable stuff that could appear in a photographic image. The hierarchical structure includes three levels: the first breaks regions into "indoor stuff" and "outdoor stuff";[15] the next level splits these into groups such as "sky," "wall," and "plant"; and the final level makes further distinctions within some groups, such as splitting plants into "flowers," "grass," and "trees." A full list of stuff categories and their hierarchical structure is given in tables 4.3 and 4.4, later in the chapter. Several catch-all groups are designed to capture regions that do not fit elsewhere, such as "solid" and "textile." Also, each final level includes an explicit "other" category to account for anything missed in the specifically assigned tags.

There are several advantages to the stuff and object annotations that make it particularly attractive as an application of distant viewing. The objects included in tasks such as PASCAL VOC and ILSVRC were chosen primarily to make for an interesting modeling challenge. For example, the ILSVRC categories contain nine different dog breeds but not a single class for cows. These categories provide a generative way of seeing how well computer vision algorithms can differentiate between very similar types of dogs but do not result in an algorithm that is particularly well suited to applying as-is to a new collection of images. On the other hand, stuff categories are designed in a hierarchical way that should be able to capture nearly any region that appears in an image. This structure makes it appropriate to apply algorithms trained to detect stuff categories directly to a new task. Even if the most granular categories are only specific for a certain application, the more generic groups can be used instead.

In this chapter, we use an algorithm that performs stuff and object segmentation that has been trained on the MS COCO dataset. Our applications model the different types of analysis possible with varying levels of specificity within the stuff hierarchy. The first application analyzes the detection of people and the first level of the stuff hierarchy (indoor versus outdoor). The second application uses the secondary categories under the outdoor first-level tag. We use the most granular tags available for both objects and stuff in the third application.

Before using the tags automatically generated by an off-the-shelf stuff and object classification algorithm, one must verify that the results can be trusted as a reasonably accurate description of the material. The algorithm we are applying in this chapter learned how to detect objects and stuff using a dataset of modern digital color photographs. This training data is thus significantly different from the black-and-white photographs in The File.[16] To test how well the algorithm works, we randomly selected two hundred images from the collection and looked at all the regions and objects that were assigned by the algorithm. Over 98 percent of the detected stuff tags were present in their respective images and nearly 90 percent of the detected object tags.[17] Every image that was tagged as detecting people did detect people. Only one image containing people was not tagged as such; the people were tiny and hard to identify. This small-scale experiment shows that the automatically generated tags for stuff and people, while not perfect, are sufficiently accurate to use in an aggregative analysis of the collection. The precision of detecting other objects is slightly less accurate; we will address this inaccuracy in the final application at the end of the chapter.

A final detail that needs to be addressed before proceeding to our analysis is the method for summarizing the output of the object and stuff segmentation algorithm. The segmentation model assigns each pixel in an image to a category. From the perspective of the data size, these detected categories are just as complex as the image itself. Some way to summarize all this data is needed to make a distant viewing analysis feasible. In our application, it will suffice to ignore the location of the tags and focus on the overall percentage of the image occupied by each tag. This summary is sufficient for understanding what is captured within the frame of each photograph. If one were interested in understanding the specific composition of the images, a more complex summarization would be needed. This is a topic that we will return to in our analysis of television sitcoms in chapter 5. We will now discuss the history of the FSA-OWI collection to understand the data and metadata that we will be analyzing.

Organizing the FSA-OWI Photographic Collection

The economic crisis ushered in on Black Tuesday in 1929 threatened the very financial stability of the United States. Millions of Americans were unemployed or underemployed as banks failed, capital dried up, and market demand on products plummeted, leading to layoffs and questions about the very foundations of capitalism and the role of government. By 1933, over 15 million Americans were unemployed. With the election of Franklin Roosevelt came a shift in policy from the Hoover years. The government focused first on relief, followed by recovery, and then reform. The set of programs known as the first New Deal created over thirty agencies and an extraordinary expansion of federal-state power.[18] Among the new agencies was the Resettlement Administration (RA), which was established in May 1935 and would be subsumed by the newly formed Farm Security Administration (FSA) in September 1937.

Led by Rexford Tugwell, the agency had the tall task of addressing rural and urban poverty. While October 29, 1929, may have been the tipping point of the global depression, one did not have to tell agricultural workers that there was already a severe problem. After World War I, fluctuating markets—spurred by the rise of mechanization and overproduction that intensified environmental destruction—had only exacerbated the conditions of tenant farming and sharecropping during the early twentieth century. Initially focused on resettling rural families to cooperatives, the RA came under immediate scrutiny from congressmen who labeled the organization socialist. In response, the RA shifted their emphasis toward relief camps. With the passage of the Bankhead-Jones Farm Tenant Act came a focus on loans for purchasing land and investing in mechanization, and the RA became a part of the FSA. To document the work of the FSA, Tugwell created the Historic Section of the RA and hired Roy Stryker to lead it. The result was one of the most iconic documentary photography projects of the twentieth century.[19]

The Historic Section continues to be an object of study because it is considered an important site where we can see how government workers institutionalized and used documentary expression to document and shape US society and politics, as well as negotiated state power. The scholarship and continued circulation of the collection emphasize one of three characterizations of the project: a documentation of rural life during the New

Deal, a portrait of rural poverty in the American South and Dust Bowl, or a technocratic bureaucratic propaganda project that produced progress narratives.[20] These characterizations are methodologically drawn from readings by individuals manually culling through the collection. Yet, as Stryker himself stated, "the work we did can be appreciated only when the collection is considered as a whole. The total volume, and it's a staggering volume, has a richness and distinction that cannot be drawn from the individual pictures themselves."[21] A significant challenge, then, is how to understand the archive at scale.

Distant viewing offers a way to heed his call. We will explore the digitized scans of nearly sixty thousand prints by placing the image-segmentation tags in conversation with the organization of The File. As photos were printed, they were placed in filing cabinets in DC. The initial system organized the photos by state and shooting assignment.[22] A year before Stryker left his position in the US government in 1943, he hired archivist Paul Vanderbilt, who then reorganized the collection. For the next few years, the materials produced by the Historical Unit charted a course through several different government agencies. Eventually, by March 1946, the bulk of the collection was moved to the Prints and Photographs Department at the Library of Congress. There they were further curated, organized, and made available to the public under the direction of Vanderbilt. In early 1950s, the physical photographic prints of the collection were stored in large, publicly accessible filing cabinets housed in the Prints and Photographs reading room. The collection has remained under the supervision of the Prints and Photographs division to this day.

The collection held by the Library of Congress consists of two parts: one set of approximately 80 thousand printed photographs and another of about 175 thousand photographic negatives. Most of the prints in the first collection were originally printed from one of the negatives; many of the negatives, however, were never printed. For our analysis, the composition of both collections is crucial because we will be focusing on the photographs the Historical Section decided to print for circulation in the 1930s and 1940s. The File was arranged to facilitate the use of the collection by government agencies and journalists. The prints are organized first by the location where the photo was taken, grouped into one of several large geographic divisions. Then, the cabinets are arranged according to a hierarchical, three-level subject classification system. The prints were organized into these categories under the direction of Paul Vanderbilt, who was the architect of the organizational strategy. While select photographs and photographers have been studied in depth, the organizational structure of the collection has received less academic study, and we will return to these categories in our following analysis.

Despite containing many exciting records that were not in the prints, the more extensive collection of photographic negatives held at the Library of Congress was not as easily accessible to the public. In the 1990s, the Library decided to undertake one of the earliest mass digitization projects. They chose to digitize the large collection of negatives for this task, making the entire collection available online through the American Memory Project in 1999. Metadata attached to other parts of the collection were meticulously collated and joined to the negatives to form a new digital collection. As digital records have grown in popularity, and as the Library of Congress undertook a second, high-resolution digitization project, the digital archive has increasingly become the most common way to engage with the FSA-OWI collection.

In our analysis, we will use the digitized negatives but limit ourselves to those images that were printed and stored in The File. There is a pragmatic reason for this decision: almost all the metadata from the collection was tied to the photographic prints. Captions, dates, locations, and photographer names were not directly associated with most of the negatives.[23] While it is possible to fill in some of the missing records, much of the information that we would want to explore is missing for most of the unprinted negatives. Our second reason for focusing on the negatives that were later printed as photographs is that they constitute a concrete, deliberate set for which we can draw conclusions. The printed images were manually curated and chosen to create a cohesive whole. On the other hand, the unprinted negatives exist because of the later commitment to save all the work produced by the unit. It is known that many unprinted negatives have been lost. Further, two of our applications investigate the relationship between the images themselves and Vanderbilt's classification system, turning scholarly attention to the relationship between the labels, categories, and photographs. As the classification system was only applied to prints, it is only possible to work with the printed images for those applications.

Finally, we will also limit our dataset of study to include only the fifteen most prolific photographers. This set contains most of the staff photographers hired at some point as full-time photographers by Stryker under the FSA or OWI. It includes all the well-known photographers associated with the collection. By limiting the dataset in this way, we can study questions of artistic control and style as they relate to the content of the images. Also, this limitation has the benefit of removing all the prints from the collection that were not directly taken by the photographic division.[24] After this dataset filtering, we have a collection of 58,642 images and their associated metadata that can be used to understand the composition of the FSA-OWI archive.

Our decision to work with a subset of the collection demonstrates a major consideration of distant viewing and most computational methods. A key question is what we mean by "the whole." Often this does not actually mean analyzing everything. Our approach draws from photography scholar Laura Wexler's advice to "find a set, find a text, read the set against the text."[25] A key component is understanding the parameters and composition of a set and therefore which areas of study it can help explore and which it cannot. Finding a text is an interpretive move that can include reading the set with and against existing scholarship or using a theory such as distant viewing to analyze the set. In our case, we draw on historiography about the collection as well as distant viewing to further understand the selected collection, our set, through interpretation of the visual evidence. Clearly defining the set, and not assuming this means "the whole," is key to selecting the annotations and then interpreting the results.

Building the digitized FSA-OWI collection was facilitated by the Library of Congress's commitment to creating and publishing freely available open data. We used their web-based API to request the metadata associated with all digital images that were part of the FSA-OWI collection.[26] The metadata included URLs linking to the digitized photographs themselves, which we then downloaded and stored. Next, we applied the stuff and object region detection algorithm over the collected images. Our analysis depends only on the overall proportion of objects and stuff detected within the image. We stored the number of pixels associated with each category in every image as structured data. Finally, we cleaned the image metadata and combined the metadata fields with the computer vision annotations. We turn now to our three areas of analysis.

Exploring Themes across The File

Our first analysis studies the digitized negatives corresponding to photographs from The File, starting with the analytical possibilities of producing annotations using the stuff and object region segmentation algorithm. A challenge is mapping a computational way of viewing concepts that facilitate our areas of inquiry. In this section, we focus on how we can select a specific feature—the categories of "indoors," "outdoors," and "people"—and map them onto concepts such as agriculture and cities to analyze the thematic focus of the photography unit. These features help us explore to what degree and how the photographers and archive focused on the built environment, natural environment, and people as visual subjects designed to persuade audiences of the necessity of the New Deal. These concepts map onto the project's stated aims. Questions that our analysis help inform include: Did specific photographers focus on towns and cities? Did certain photographers concentrate on the land, and if so, to what degree were people included? Did photographers' objects of focus change over time? How did the unit's administration shift its focus as the unit moved from the Farm Security Administration, a mainstay of the New Deal, to the Office of War Information amid World War II? These questions guide our broader effort to explore whether the unit's visual story shifted along with the administrative story over time. We then turn to the archival categorization produced by Paul Vanderbilt and his team to further delve into how distant viewing maps onto concepts developed through the manual tagging of physical prints over eighty years ago.

To start, we summarize the region segmentation at a high level. We tag each image to indicate whether at least 10 percent of the image contains outdoor stuff categories. While indoor categories such as buildings and windows can sometimes be photographed outdoors, the outdoor categories are rarely photographed indoors. We also tag each image with the number of people detected within the frame of the photograph. Then, using these tags, we compute the proportion of photographs from each photographer taken outdoors and the ratio of photographs that include people. We will also calculate the average number of people in an image when people are present.

The results of this summarization of the segmentation algorithm are given in table 4.1 and visualized in figure 4.2. Five of the photographers took a substantial number of photographs for both the FSA and OWI. We

Table 4.1

For each photographer in our set, several summary statistics are given: the years active, the number of photographs, percentage of photographs detected as having been taken outdoors, percentage of photographs that were detected to contain people, and the average number of people detected in images that have at least one person. Five photographers who were prominent in both periods and their results are split into two rows. The table is sorted by the percentage of photos taken outside.

Photographer	Years	No.	Outside (%)	People (%)	Avg. people
Dorothea Lange	1935–1939	2246	90.7	62.7	1.8
Marion Post Wolcott	1938–1941	5683	88.4	62.3	2.3
Walker Evans	1935–1938	299	84.8	40.8	1.2
Carl Mydans	1935–1936	783	82.0	53.6	1.7
Arthur Rothstein (FSA)	1935–1942	5510	81.3	65.2	1.8
Edwin Rosskam	1937–1943	448	76.5	82.4	3.1
John Vachon (FSA)	1936–1943	4056	75.3	59.1	1.6
Ben Shahn	1935–1938	1210	75.0	72.6	2.7
Jack Delano (FSA)	1940–1943	5169	70.2	75.9	2.6
Russell Lee (FSA)	1936–1942	15068	68.4	67.6	1.9
John Collier (FSA)	1940–1943	1470	65.6	64.3	2.0
John Vachon (OWI)	1942–1943	2191	64.1	70.8	2.0
Jack Delano (OWI)	1942–1943	3551	64.0	68.3	1.9
John Collier (OWI)	1941–1943	2215	62.0	68.6	1.8
Arthur Rothstein (OWI)	1942–1942	589	55.7	82.9	2.2
Russell Lee (OWI)	1942–1942	905	55.0	70.7	2.0
Arthur S. Siegel	1939–1943	1735	54.1	71.2	2.0
Gordon Parks	1941–1943	1220	45.9	87.7	2.4
Marjory Collins	1942–1943	2321	38.6	88.9	3.0
Esther Bubley	1942–1943	1513	28.2	96.6	3.1

provide the results of these photographers separately for each division using the metadata associated with each negative. This allows us both to see general patterns within each division and to track the trajectory of the work of these five photographers.

When looking at the results, we see significant differences among the photographers along these two dimensions. While over 90 percent of Dorothea Lange's photographs were taken outdoors, Esther Bubley took only 28.2 percent of her photographs outside. Among Bubley's photographs, over 96 percent contain images of people, compared to Walker Evans's 40.8 percent. The patterns we see within these dimensions are not minor

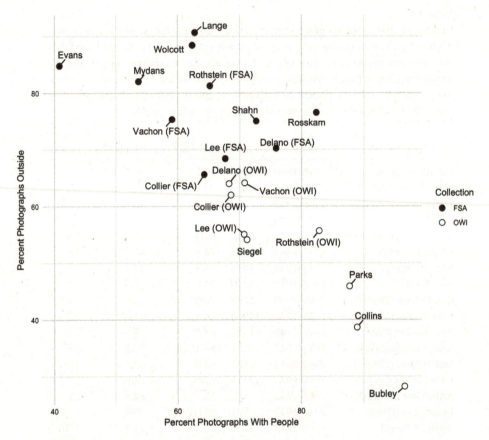

Figure 4.2
A scatterplot showing the proportion of photographs each photographer took where our algorithm detected people (x-axis) and the proportion where our algorithm determined that the photograph was taken outside (y-axis). The color of the dot indicates whether a photographer is associated with the FSA years of the collection or the OWI years. Five photographers who were prominent in both periods have their results split into two groups.

statistical artifacts; they strongly characterize the content and style of the staff photographers. We will look at different clusters of photographers that have similar characteristics along these two dimensions. We pair our analysis with visual culture scholarship and select photos to view closely.

In the upper left-hand corner of the plot, we see a group of four photographers, consisting of Dorothea Lange, Marion Post Wolcott, Walker Evans, and Carl Mydans. All four worked only under the FSA and, except for

Wolcott, were hired in the agency's first year (1935). Their photographs have the highest percentage of being taken outdoors among all the photographers in our dataset; over 80 percent of their photos are tagged as being outside. This group also, along with John Vachon's earlier set of photographs, have the lowest percentage of people in the dataset. Evans is an extreme outlier on this dimension, including people in just over 40 percent of his images, compared with the rest of the group, who are closer to 60 percent. These numbers match the general perception of these four photographers, as they focused on documenting rural poverty in the American South, the Dust Bowl, and California.[27] Iconic images often consist of desolate landscapes and people in front of tiny, worn houses, with careful attention to conveying the dignity of the person while arguing for investment in infrastructure.[28]

Moving down the table, the next group of photographers consists of Ben Shahn, Edwin Rosskam, and the FSA contributions of the five photographers who participated in both projects. This group took slightly fewer outdoor photographs than the first, ranging from Arthur Rothstein's 81.3 percent (very close to Carl Mydans) to John Collier's 65.6 percent. The proportion of images with people is generally larger in than the first group, ranging from 59 percent (Vachon) to 76 percent (Delano). Except for Ben Shahn, all the photographers in this group continued taking photographs for the FSA through 1942 or 1943. At that time, the changing focus can be attributed to Stryker's shift toward showing a more positive and urban image of the nation.[29]

The focus on urban settings challenges broad overgeneralizations in existing scholarship on the unit, which stresses Stryker's nostalgia for Americans residing in small towns who were threatened by modernization.[30] Many of the most well-known images from this set include city scenes such as John Collier's photographs of New Orleans and John Vachon's images from downtown Chicago. Delano and Rosskam had assignments in the Caribbean, Rosskam in Puerto Rico, and Delano in Puerto Rico and the US Virgin Islands. Over 80 percent of the images from these assignments included people. When they included people in their photographs, these two photographers also had a higher average number of people (2.7 and 3.1) than any other FSA photographer.

The next cluster includes the OWI years of the five photographers who participated in both projects, along with Arthur Siegel. This group takes slightly fewer outdoor photographs, ranging from Siegel's 54.1 percent to

64.1 percent (Vachon). The rate of photographs including people is only slightly higher than the previous group, ranging from 68 to 83 percent. Looking at the trajectory of the photographers involved in both projects, we see that all five took fewer outdoor photographs under the OWI than with the FSA. Excluding Delano, the other four also took more photographs of people in the OWI collection. The differences between Rothstein and Vachon across the collections are particularly pronounced. This trend illustrates the changing scope of the project as the United States entered the fray of World War II and the need for images of industrial might sent photographers to the factory floor. The clustering of the strictly OWI photographer Arthur Siegel with this group becomes apparent when looking at a selection of his photographs, about half of which focus on daily life in Michigan. Also, while hired into the OWI, his tenure began in 1939, significantly earlier than the photographers in our final cluster.

The final group in our table consists of Gordon Parks, Marjory Collins, and Esther Bubley. All three were hired directly into the OWI and worked primarily between 1942 and 1943. While they did go on assignments throughout the eastern United States, their work closely centered on the Washington, DC, metropolitan area. These photographers are distinctly separated from the others, with fewer outdoor photographs (less than 46%) and more photographs with people in them (greater than 87%). By the time these photographers took most of these images, the United States had fully entered World War II. The focus on the indoors becomes about manufacturing, military training, education, and government infrastructure—depicting a ready nation defined by strong, able-bodied citizens mobilized for war. This characterization aligns with existing scholarship.[31] Iconic images from these photographers include Alfred Palmer's image of women riveters and Marjory Collin's images of women on the home front working in heavy manufacturing. These all follow the pattern of photographs taken of people indoors. Interestingly, the four female photographers in the first group took both the most extreme proportion of outdoor photographs (Lange and Wolcott) and the largest proportion of indoor photographs (Collins and Bubley).

From looking at these results together, we see that these two relatively simple stuff tags are good proxies for differentiating the types of photographs taken by the FSA and OWI staff photographers. Both indicators exhibit a robust temporal shift throughout the years of the collection as its focus transitioned from support for New Deal policies to a vision of the home front during World War II. The decreasing proportion of out- door photographs is particularly acute, moving from a high point with the earliest photographers, transitioning to those staff photographers present through both the FSA and OWI years, and finally reaching their lowest levels among the photographers hired in 1941 and 1942. Looking at these indicators, we have been able to provide a quantitative measurement that directly aligns with the stated and changing goals of the photographic unit, as described by Stryker. Our two features, which use the highest level of the stuff segmentation categories, also read mostly in line with the general scholarship and understanding of the collection.

To further bolster the conclusions from our analysis, we have an oppor- tunity afforded by the robust metadata provided with the images by the Library of Congress. We now see that the two binary tags applied to images in the FSA-OWI archive strongly differentiate between different photog- raphers and illustrate a temporal change in the photographic unit's goals. We can strengthen our understanding of this relationship by relating the same tags to the specific content shown within each of the images. We can apply the same analysis to the historic Vanderbilt subject categories. These categories, as outlined previously, group all the photographic prints into a three-layer classification based on the subject of each image. By looking at how concentrated these categories are in terms of being tagged as out- .doors or tagged as containing people, we can explore whether the temporal and authorial patterns seen in the previous section might be attributed to changing subject matter.

The results of this analysis are provided in table 4.2 and visualized in figure 4.3. We have used the second level of the Vanderbilt categories, which contains fifty-five unique categories.[32] To simplify the output, we removed from the results the twelve categories that had the fewest number of pho- tographs. As with the photographer results, several clear patterns arise in the data.

Several categories are characterized by a very high proportion of photo- graphs taken outside. All five of the categories under the level-one category *The Land* have 98.7 percent or more of their associated images tagged as occurring outside. These five categories also have a low number of photo- graphs containing people, between 6.3 and 13.4 percent. Other categories

Table 4.2

Several summary statistics shown for second-level Vanderbilt subject classification codes. Several smaller categories are not included in order to fit the table on the page.

V1	V2	N	Outdoor (%)	People (%)	Avg. people
The Land	Mnt, Deserts, Plains	766	99.9	6.3	0.1
The Land	General	327	99.7	4.0	0.1
The Land	Farms, Lands, Conditions	1778	99.1	11.5	0.2
Transportation	Non-mechanized	399	99.0	73.4	1.6
Cities and Towns	Towns & Sm Cities	2883	98.9	35.7	1.0
The Land	Weather & Floods	536	98.7	13.4	0.3
Cities and Towns	City Streets & Buildings	1013	98.5	47.3	1.5
Work	Forest Products	778	95.9	69.5	1.4
Work	Agriculture	6464	94.8	65.8	1.4
Work	Mining, Oil Wells	1048	91.2	49.7	1.0
Work	Engineering & Buildings	1444	90.6	67.8	1.7
Transportation	Water Transport	475	88.7	52.6	1.8
Homes and Living	Temporary Abodes	1272	86.3	55.2	1.3
War	Special Training	506	83.8	84.0	2.4
Transportation	Railroads	1589	78.4	54.0	1.5
Transportation	Road Transport	1582	78.1	73.9	2.1
Social and Personal	Rec. and Relaxation	753	76.3	90.8	4.3
Organized Society	Giving & Other Aid	860	70.4	68.8	2.8
Social and Personal	Entertainments	1032	66.2	92.1	4.9
Organized Society	Labor Orgs	540	62.6	95.6	5.8
Homes and Living	Permanent Homes	2626	60.6	44.1	0.8
Social and Personal	Hotels, etc.	1357	59.3	87.3	3.7
Work	Selling and Distribution	2296	57.8	65.1	2.0
Alphabetical Section	General	416	54.0	56.5	1.6
People As Such	Grps and Ind.	6714	53.6	98.3	3.0
Work	Services	930	52.2	76.3	1.7
War	Civilian Defense	508	51.7	80.5	2.5
Religion	General	839	50.8	72.9	3.8
Work	Processing and Manufacturing	4157	48.5	68.3	1.4
Homes and Living	Household Activities	1389	46.9	79.6	1.3
Social and Personal	Ceremonies	730	45.6	94.4	5.5
People As Such	Children	4791	44.4	95.5	3.4
Organized Society	Government	458	44.1	80.8	3.1
Medicine and Health	General	801	24.5	86.0	2.6
War	Servicemen on Leave	286	24.4	98.6	3.4
Intellectual and Creative	General	662	19.3	80.4	2.0
Work	Research	308	3.0	86.7	1.7

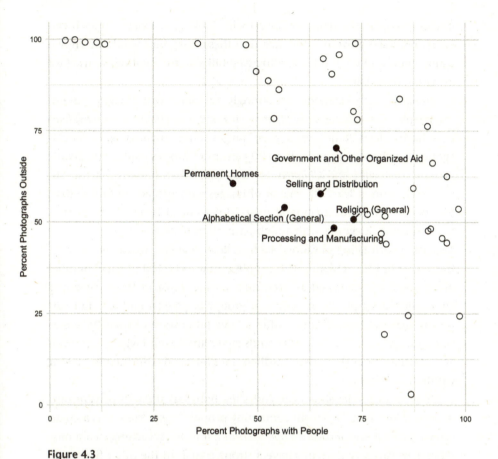

Figure 4.3
A scatterplot showing the proportion of photographs where the algorithm detected people (x-axis) and the proportion where our algorithm determined that the photograph was taken outside (y-axis) for the second-level Vanderbilt subject classification codes. Twelve categories are not included due to a low volume of photographs. Categories for which less than 75% of images are outdoors and less than 75% of images are indoors have been labeled.

with very high numbers of outdoor photos include *Non-Mechanized Transportation* (99%), *Towns and Small Cities* (98.9%), and *Forest Products* (95.9%). In contrast to the photographs under the *Land* level-one category, these other examples include an increased number of people; nonmechanized transportation has over 73 percent of its corresponding photos containing people. Altogether, about half of all the categories consist of at least 75 percent outdoor images, and nearly a quarter consists of at least 95 percent outdoor images. The data, combined with looking at images in each category, provided powerful evidence that these categories would be shown using outdoor photographs, lending credibility to the method we used for assigning these tags.[33]

Similarly, many categories are strongly associated with images containing people. The categories *Servicemen on Leave* and *Groups and Individuals* both have at least 98 percent of their images containing people. Other categories associated with more than 90 percent of images containing people include *Ceremonies* and *Children*. In total, more than one-fifth of the categories contain at least 90 percent of images with people, and more than half of the categories include at least 70 percent of images with people. Some of these categories with a high proportion of people are also strongly associated with being outdoors, such as *Recreation and Relaxation*. In contrast, most of the categories with people contain a typical or small number of photographs identified as occurring outside. Most of these categories are explicit descriptions of people or groups of people, and it is not surprising that the algorithm identifies a large proportion of their images as containing people.[34] This further lends credibility to our tagging algorithm and illustrates that these two classifiers are associated with themes present within the collection.

Only six of the level-two categories are both less than 75 percent outdoors and less than 75 percent containing people. One of these is a catch-all category called *Alphabetical Section (General)*; it is not surprising that a miscellaneous category does not have a strong signal. In the other five cases, which include *Processing and Manufacturing* and *Permanent Homes*, the object of focus is either some form of manufacturing or a building. It is possible to think of typical photos from any of these categories that are taken indoors without any people in them, such as an image of a piece of manufacturing equipment inside of a factory. Looking at the third-level categories again shows a strong correlation to one or both tags. For example, *Farm Houses* contains 288 images of which 99.7 percent are taken outdoors, whereas *Rooms* includes 206 images of which only 0.5 percent were identified as being outdoors. Once again, we see that our generated tags tend to correspond to themes within the collection.

At the beginning of this section, we saw a strong relationship between individual photographers' proportion of outdoor photos and the ratio of their photos containing people. We learned that the distribution of these two binary tags is strongly correlated with the date of the photograph and the credited photographer. Photographers associated with the later stages of the project increasingly took images indoor and with people. Viewing at scale, through nearly sixty thousand photos, indicates a shift in focus—from the land and agriculture to buildings and manufacturing—and therefore, a change in the concerns of the New Deal to those of a nation mobilized for war. Our analysis of these results show that the historical Vanderbilt categories correspond closely to the distribution of the stuff tags. This suggests that our previous results capture thematic elements of what photographers were instructed to focus their work on. In other words, the distribution of these two binary variables allows us to read in alignment with the intended understanding of the collection. It helps us understand a way of organizing both the work of each photographer and the structure of individual photographs along these two dimensions.

The results also show how we work with evidence when distant viewing. We selected a kind of computational vision and mapped the ways of seeing onto concepts and themes that were particular to the exploration of The File. To further bolster the analytical possibilities of our annotations and its application, we used the metadata attached to the photos to check our analysis and to make it more nuanced. By looking at the whole file as Stryker called for, we can see that photographers shifted their gaze as the government goals for the unit changed. At the same time, the data also reveals photographers who did not make this shift, such as Jack Delano and John Vachon, which suggests that there was room for photographers to pursue their own lines of vision. Vachon was among the longest-serving members of the unit, and both photographers made the transition from the FSA to OWI. Still, the fact that working for OWI did not shift their gaze to war mobilization suggests that the photographers were given significant leeway to pursue their interests. Photographers like Vachon may have frustrated OWI officials, but the thousands of photos they sent back to Washington aligned with Stryker and his photographers' expanded vision of the unit. They saw the possibility of creating an archive of everyday life across the United States, which was not defined solely by government expediency. In the next section, we explore further how our stuff and object segmentation algorithms can delve into questions of theme and style among the photographers, a significantly less studied area.

Exploring Photographers' Style

Exactly how to create our annotations and what evidence is produced continues to guide us in our second analysis. As demonstrated in the previous
section, we mapped the stuff categories onto themes in the corpus. We
continue to work with stuff and will now explore how the same feature can
be a strategy for studying style, which is a key aspect of understanding an
image's messages. By identifying and categorizing styles, we can understand
how a person chooses to compose photographs and articulate how framing
and composition shape the image's meaning, areas of inquiry that animate
fields including art history, media studies, and visual culture studies.

The image segmentation algorithms we applied to the FSA-OWI photographic corpus provide far more specific tags than whether a region of stuff is
indoors or outdoors. At the second level of specificity, the outdoor category
is broken down into six groups, and the indoor category is split into eight. We
can use these more specific classifications to capture the content and framing of each photographer's photos more precisely than the two categories we
have already used. Because the secondary categories are influenced by the first
level, using the raw frequencies of these categories risks simply replicating our
previous analysis. To avoid this, we will look at just a subset of the collection.
Here, we will limit ourselves to the subset of outdoor images found within
the Vanderbilt category *Cities and Towns*. With approximately four thousand
photos, this category was chosen because it is one of the categories for which
all the staff photographers in the collection have many photographs.

As before, we will assign a binary variable to each image indicating
whether there is a sufficiently large amount of a particular type of stuff category within the frame. We can then look at the proportion of images from
each photographer categorized as *Cities and Towns* that have each tag. With
some experimentation, we found the most precise results when using a cutoff
of 20 percent; so, an image is tagged with a category if a particular category
takes up at least 20 percent of the frame. Within the outdoor photographs
from our chosen Vanderbilt category, four second-level groups of stuff classification are the most prevalent: plants, sky, ground, and buildings. The first
three are outdoor categories; the final one is described as an indoor group,
but indoor items can exist outside, as mentioned previously.[35] Results showing the proportion of images with each of these four tags by photographer,
using the same photographer categories that were described above, are given
in figure 4.4.

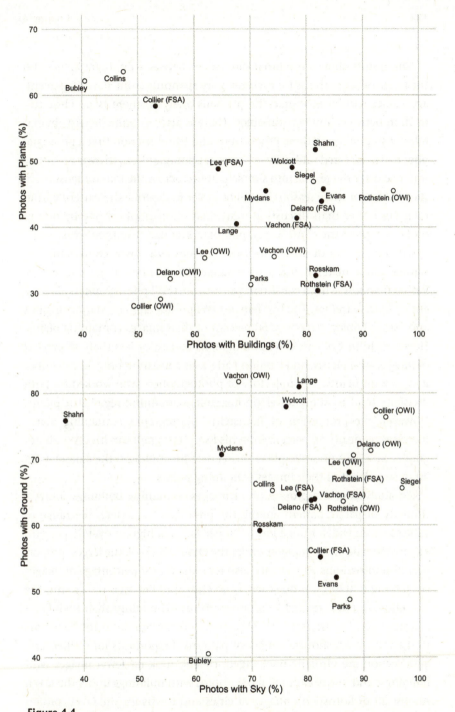

Figure 4.4

Two scatterplots showing the proportion of outside photographs that contain four different stuff categories: plants, buildings, ground, and sky. Five photographers were prominent in both periods. Their results are split into two points, one for each collection, FSA and OWI.

The results show substantial differences between photographers, with the range of proportions for each category spanning from 40 to 60 percentage values. However, unlike the previous analysis, there is no clear correlation between any two variables. There is also no immediately obvious relationship between these proportions and the collection that a photographer had been hired under. Even between photographers, there is no simple way to cluster the results into simple patterns across the four dimensions of the results. For these reasons, it will be easier to describe the pattern within each tag rather than discussing individual photographers one by one in order to explore the control each photographer had over their work.

The proportion of images focused on cities and towns containing substantial plant material has a wide range across different photographers. Rather than following a consistent pattern, the OWI photographers are present on both extremes. The two female OWI photographers, Marjory Collins and Esther Bubley, have over 60 percent of their images containing plants. However, John Collier's OWI photographs consist of less than 30 percent of images with plants, and Gordon Parks's set consists of only 32 percent of images with plants. The trajectory of photographers who worked for both divisions tend to show fewer photographs containing regions of plants. However, the proportion of Rothstein's photographs containing plants increases by nearly 50 percent from his FSA photographs to his OWI photographs. Most FSA photographers cluster near the middle of the dataset, with 40 to 50 percent of their images containing plants.

An analysis of the proportion of images containing buildings shows a similarly disparate pattern among the photographers. Here, the range of values is even wider, from a low of 40 percent to a high of over 95 percent. The two female photographers under the OWI, who took the largest proportion of photographs with plants, also took the fewest percentage of images containing buildings. While there is no clear split between the groups, the FSA photographers tended to photograph more buildings than their OWI counterparts. The trajectory of photographers moving from the FSA years to the OWI years shows a variety of patterns. Proportions for Collier, Lee, and Vachon are virtually unchanged; Delano took far fewer images with buildings; and Rothstein took more photos with buildings under the OWI. Almost all of Rothstein's images of cities and towns for the OWI contain structures. Three photographers known for taking photographs of buildings in street scenes—Delano and Rosskam in the Caribbean, and Vachon in

Chicago and Detroit—all have around 80 percent of their images from this category listed as containing buildings.

Whereas the subject matter could somewhat influence whether each photographer captured the presence of buildings and plants, the distribution of our second two categories should not be as affected by the content of the images. The proportion of photographs that include the sky has a wide range, mainly driven by Ben Shahn, an outlier who framed only 36 percent of his pictures in this category to contain a significant amount of sky. At the other extreme, 97 percent of Arthur Siegel's photographs have a substantial amount of sky. Most of the photographers are closer to the higher end of this range. The trajectory of photographers moving from the FSA to the OWI does not show any consistent pattern, nor does there seem to be any pattern for photographers who worked within only one division.

Our final tag, measuring whether images contain a significant number of regions categorized as ground, also shows a range of values without a clear temporal pattern. Esther Bubley has extreme values for all four measurements and has the lowest proportion (41%) of images classified as containing the ground. Unlike the balance of plants and buildings, though, this extreme value does not follow in work by the other female OWI photographer, Marjory Collins; she has a value that is very close to the average proportion of all photographers. Four of the photographers who crossed between both divisions took a larger proportion of images containing the ground under the OWI; Rothstein continues to go against the pattern of the others with, instead, a small decrease when moving into the OWI years. While plants and ground seem closely related, there is only a minimal correlation between the two proportions by photographer.

Taking together these four elements—the percentage of plants, buildings, ground, and sky—what are we able to learn about the collection and the photographers? Overall, there is a weak correlation between these variables and the divisions under which a photographer worked. However, we also see substantial differences between the photographers, indicating these measurements are not just meaningless noise. Taken together, the proportion of urban photographs framed to contain these four elements seems to be a strong indicator of photographer style, and thus serves as a good starting point for trying to understand the specific style of each photographer. At first glance, for example, we have highlighted three photographers who have strong styles according to these metrics: Esther Bubley, John Collier, and Arthur Rothstein. Let's look closer.

Concepts from visual culture studies and visual semiotics, which theorize how images make meaning, inform our interpretation of the annotations and assessment of style. Compositional elements—such as who and what is in the frame and outside of it, what is in focus, and from which angles—convey messages and values, such as who and what should be documented and how. Formal analysis of such factors as angles, focus, light, and repetition offers concepts that shape the interpretation of how images make meaning. By analyzing style, we are focusing on patterns and outliers in the ways a photographer composes subjects, with attention to how formal elements offer insight into the subject and gaze of certain photographers. When studying The File, looking at style offers a way to analyze how the photographers may or may not have ideologically aligned with the administrative goals of the project as well as a way to compare photographers. And as Stuart Hall theorized, images encode messages that need to be decoded; the way they are decoded is shaped by the way cultural ideologies and power are encoded in formal elements.[36] Distant viewing offers a way to analyze the annotations informed by theories about how images make meaning so that we can compare large amounts of photographs by photographer.

A more in-depth exploration of Bubley's photos in *Cities and Towns* based on our identified features reveals an essential aspect of her style that shapes the message she is conveying. Looking back at her photos with attention to the relationship between ground-sky and plants-buildings shows a prominent characteristic of her images. Five examples are shown in figure 4.5. She tilts her camera toward the sky, seemingly taking the picture from the ground. She is looking up to her subject. Compared to the other photographers, the unusually high proportion of plants indicates the distance that she maintains from her subject. While the primary subject is often a building or statue, she ensures that other features around the building, most often trees, are visible in the frame. Looking up and from a distance, her photos convey the monumentality of her larger subject: the nation's capital. The photos express deference, reverence, and admiration for a nation amid World War II.

For another style, we can look more closely at John Collier's photos for the unit. Collier focused on smaller towns such as Taos, New Mexico, which at first glance could account for his style. Yet, the decision to look up and convey monumentality is a compositional choice that photographers make

Figure 4.5
The top two rows show example photographs taken by Esther Bubley, demonstrating the small amount of ground shown in the background of her images. The bottom two rows are photographs taken by John Collier. In general, Collier includes significant amounts of both ground and sky within the frame of the photograph.

even when photographing small towns.[37] The way that Collier photographs the town is markedly different from Bubley's approach; his photographs' focus has a large percentage of both ground and sky. A closer look at his photos indicates that if one were to draw a horizontal line across the image, most of the photos would be evenly split between the two, as he sought to capture the ground and sky symmetrically and evenly. The buildings take up less visual space in his photographs, while plants are very prominent. The combination of a significant amount of ground, sky, and plants in relationship to buildings reveals the prominence of the natural environment in his depiction of cities and towns. In his photos, buildings fade into the earth. The degree to which they merge with the ground and sky is further captured by the challenges of our algorithm, which did not identify a significant number of buildings that we can see upon closer inspection. Collier's photos thus convey the depicted town's isolation and dissipation as the buildings fade into the natural environment.

At a methodological level, these results highlight the significant impact that small choices in building and aggregating annotations have on understanding the computational analysis results of digital images. Using the broadest level of the stuff region hierarchy shows that the political forces on the FSA and OWI strongly impacted the content matter of the collection. Here, taking the second level of the stuff region hierarchy, we see how the photographers' compositional decisions and practices of looking affect how the United States was depicted. The temporal differences move away, and the strongest influences on the results are due to individual photographers' content and compositional decisions. Distant viewing allows us to toggle between looking at the collection in parts and at individual photographs to look closer at the ways of seeing that shape the work of individual photographers. Their content *and* style influenced how people during their era and today see and understand American life during the Depression and a world war.

To this point, we have been mostly exploring the collection in alignment with its primary organization, rather than across or against the grain for alternative or resistant interpretations. We have been working within Vanderbilt's organization of the collection, and therefore in alignment with a federal government agency which has its own aims and priorities. Yet, what if we used the stuff and object categories to remix and rearrange the corpus? How might we see the collection from a different angle? In the next section, we will continue this methodological path of using other annotations. However, we will investigate the most granular level of the stuff region hierarchy and how the algorithm's ways of seeing can reconfigure the archive to see with, across, and against the state.

Exploring the Breadth of the Collection

Zooming back out to the whole collection of The File, we can remix the archive by distant viewing. The regions detected by the computer vision algorithm we have applied to the FSA-OWI corpus provide a third level of categories beyond those explored in the previous sections. These most granular levels are the labels used to tag the original dataset and to train the algorithm. The two levels that we used in the earlier sections are a way of grouping together and aggregating the more specific tags. We will now use the most specific tags in the algorithm to see if there are themes, subjects, and other connections that may be implicit in or obscured by the current organization of the sixty thousand photographs in corpus.

All of the third-level stuff classes are given in table 4.3 (outdoor classes) and table 4.4 (indoor classes). Along with each class, we indicate the total number of photographs that contain at least some proportion of the associated class. There are a total of twenty classes under the umbrella of outdoor stuff and thirty-three under the umbrella of indoor stuff. Most, but not all, of the second-level groups have a corresponding "other" class that corresponds to anything that does not fit into any other class. These are designated by a class name that is equal to the group name. For the ceiling and sky groups, there is only a single class category. Looking at the class categories shows that some classes appear to be much more specific than others. For example, there are specific classes for mirrors, playing fields, and window blinds. Some of the classes also seem somewhat difficult to distinguish exactly. What, for instance, is the exact cutoff between "gravel" and "dirt"? At what size does a body of water transition from the catch-all class "water" to be called a "sea"?

The challenge of labeling, categorization, and granularity of the third level of the stuff classes brings us back to chapter 1 and the theory of distant viewing. As we try to answer the question, What is this an image of?, we must designate which concept maps onto which pixels. A seemingly straightforward task such as identifying "water" versus "sea" can be

Table 4.3
Summary statistics for photographs containing outdoor third-level stuff category tags. The number of photos that have some amount of the given class is given in the third column. The last two columns give the probability that two randomly chosen photos containing the given category share the same photographer (fourth column) or second-level Vanderbilt subject classification (fifth column).

Group	Class	Count	ProbPhoto	ProbVan2
ground	dirt	17384	15.4	6.6
ground	gravel	1367	14.9	12.0
ground	pavement	10964	9.9	5.2
ground	platform	1002	11.1	12.5
ground	playing field	114	8.6	12.8
ground	railroad	2050	17.6	18.0
ground	road	6942	10.0	6.1
ground	sand	3240	14.6	7.0
ground	snow	2861	11.6	5.8
plant	flower	238	15.4	9.1
plant	grass	20367	13.0	7.4
plant	tree	22995	12.8	6.1
sky	sky	31544	10.9	5.6
solid	mountain	7306	13.3	8.3
solid	rock	2550	17.1	7.0
structural	fence	11397	12.3	5.9
structural	net	25	8.0	4.3
water	river	1337	11.4	6.1
water	sea	2294	9.7	5.9
water	water	1459	11.6	5.1

anything but simple. The building of annotations is packed with decisions that shape our conceptual possibilities, including the decision to view in the first place. The specificity of these tags highlights the degree of human decision-making embedded in computer vision algorithms and how they shape what we can and cannot see.

These challenges do not prevent us from exploring the granular tags. The idea of these more granular classes is to be a bit too specific rather than too general. On the other hand, splitting apart generic classes requires creating an entirely new training dataset and algorithm, a time-consuming and resource-intensive activity. Instead, the granularity can be a benefit. We can aggregate similar categories to pursue analyses as we have done in the previous sections.

Table 4.4
Summary statistics for photographs containing indoor third-level stuff categories. The number of photos that have some amount of the given class is given in the third column. The last two columns give the probability that two randomly chosen photos containing the given category share the same photographer (fourth column) or second-level Vanderbilt subject classification (fifth column).

Group	Class	Count	ProbPhoto	ProbVan2
building	bridge	1663	9.7	7.0
building	building	18284	9.9	5.1
building	house	9954	12.4	7.3
building	roof	3027	15.3	6.3
building	tent	1027	14.1	8.0
ceiling	ceiling	9733	10.4	6.7
floor	floor	10044	12.2	7.9
floor	floor (wood)	3730	20.7	8.4
food	food	802	16.8	15.4
food	fruit	89	16.5	31.9
furniture	cabinet	2418	11.4	7.9
furniture	counter	933	14.3	8.9
furniture	door (stuff)	6880	10.1	7.1
furniture	light	2049	9.8	6.9
furniture	mirror (stuff)	877	10.1	7.3
furniture	shelf	2335	13.1	9.1
furniture	stairs	1889	10.3	6.8
furniture	table	8378	12.3	7.2
raw material	cardboard	1325	18.4	11.0
raw material	paper	5305	12.7	6.6
textile	banner	1739	10.4	6.1
textile	blanket	155	17.7	15.3
textile	curtain	3079	11.7	8.4
textile	pillow	6	26.7	6.7
textile	rug	1658	10.6	10.0
textile	towel	598	17.2	9.9
wall	wall	23997	10.6	7.1
wall	wall (brick)	3565	11.1	6.7
wall	wall (stone)	936	16.4	6.1
wall	wall (tile)	1420	11.7	7.6
wall	wall (wood)	9587	15.6	7.3
window	window	9721	10.8	6.8
window	window-blind	485	10.1	8.0

The results in tables 4.3 and 4.4 also include measurements showing how related each category is to specific photographers or the second-level Vanderbilt subject classifications. Our goal is to learn whether these more granular categories can see beyond these metadata variables; this requires a measurement of the relationship between these categories and the stuff classes. To achieve a measurement for each class, we compute the probability that two randomly chosen images that contain the class will have the same photographer (first column) or the same second-level Vanderbilt subject classification (second column). The higher these numbers are, the more concentrated a particular tag is on a small set of photographers or subject classification codes. Suppose a set is evenly distributed over all the available categories, which results in the lowest possible value for the probability. In that case, there will be a 5 percent probability of selecting two photographs taken by the same photographer and a 2 percent probability of selecting two photographs from the same subject classification. As a better baseline, however, we should consider the fact that neither of these categories is evenly distributed to begin with: two randomly selected photographs from our entire dataset have an 11.2 percent chance of being from the same photographer and a 5.4 percent chance of being within the same Vanderbilt subject classification. We will consider classes close to these baselines to be well spread across photographers or subject classifications; classes with relatively high probabilities are more concentrated within a particular set of metadata levels.

We begin by looking at the distribution of the outdoor classes. The overall frequencies of the classes show a large discrepancy in the number of images tagged with each region type. As mentioned previously, a few classes designate very particular types of stuff, and it seems unsurprising that these have relatively few instances in the collection. There are only 25 images that contain the class "net" and 114 that contain the class "playing field." On the other hand, the most frequent classes correspond to generic classes, such as "sky," and classes that follow the collection's early focus on agriculture, such as "grass," "dirt," and "tree." Perhaps the most interesting frequencies are the categories that fall between these extremes. There are thousands of images in the collection identified as containing "snow," "sea," and "rivers." These tags suggest groups of photographs that are clustered around certain kinds of environments.

The images selected in figure 4.6 illustrate how the stuff category tags can help us find connections across the organizational logic of the FSA-OWI

Figure 4.6
The first two rows show six images that were identified as containing the stuff category "snow," and the second two rows show six images that were identified as containing the stuff category "water."

collection. The first two rows show six examples containing a significant amount of snow. Snow is correlated with winter months and more northern locations; however, the timing of snow is not something that can be precisely planned. The FSA-OWI staff photographers did not seem to be particularly focused on capturing snow itself, and none of the Vanderbilt categories are named for snow. For these reasons, the images containing this category span a variety of years, photographers, themes, and locations. The diversity of topics is apparent in our example images, which include (in order): an aerial photograph of a small town, and photographs of military training, tapping maple trees, sledding, a city scene, and a woman pulling children on a sled.

Collectively, the images capture many of the main themes that guide the collection, such as agriculture, family, city life, and the military. Other than the visual cue of snow, there is no metadata in the collection that would unite these images. Nonetheless, the set of images is united by showing how society endures and even thrives in the presence of inclement weather. It also creates broader temporal and region links—winter and the northern states—that may go unnoticed if we focus only on images that are taken in the exact same place or date. The second two rows in figure 4.6 display a similar set of images, this time united by the presence of water. As with the snow images, we see a variety of different themes and activities here. Themes include images of military vessels, a pond filled with swimming fish, a government worker from the FSA, a burning ship, and a group of young women playing with a beach ball. What do we gain from putting these images together as a set? While not a focus of the FSA-OWI, we can reread these images as an implicit environmental critique. Pairing a tranquil pond of fish and children happily at play with scenes of war and pollution tells a strikingly different narrative from the one of social and industrial strength that is highlighted by captions and Vanderbilt categories. By allowing the computer vision algorithms to help us rethink our exploration of the corpus, new possible connections begin to open between the FSA-OWI and subsequent government photographic projects such as DOCUMERICA, which was run by the United States Environmental Protection Agency throughout the 1970s.[38] The analysis opens up questions about longer histories of environmentalism over the twentieth century in the United States.

Returning to the stuff categories, how concentrated are these tags by photographer and subject classifications? In general, most relationships are weak at best. Keeping in mind that the FSA photographers had a strong bias in general toward more outdoor images, the increased overlap probability of these categories with each photographer is small compared to the baseline. The highest concentration is on the category "railroad," which is driven by the nearly eight hundred photographs that Jack Delano took while crossing the western United States by train. The same story is true for the concentration of Vanderbilt subject classification codes. The highest probability (18.0%) is once again the category of "railroad"; despite there being a dedicated Vanderbilt classification code called *Railroads*, only around one-third of the images containing railroads are found in this category. A few other classes with the highest probabilities also correspond weakly to a specific subject classification, such as "playing field" with *Recreation and Relaxation*. However, as the Vanderbilt categories must put each image in a particular subject—in other words, these were not designed as digital keywords that can be applied freely in many-to-many relations—the stuff categories predominantly find links that are not captured in the historical classification schema.

Whereas some classes are weakly associated with subject classification codes, others offer a view of the collection in ways that are not provided by any of the existing subject categories. This suggests that these most granular stuff categories allow for reading completely against the intended structures and explicit metadata associated with the FSA-OWI collection. A similar pattern arises in the data for indoor classes of stuff. Here, there are a few categories with very few images, such as the six photos with "pillows" and the eighty-nine images with "fruit." Other categories are associated with a large portion of the corpus, such as "floor" and "building." We see that the most common classes are the generic classes that mirror the containing group name. This is the desired behavior; when the algorithm is not certain of a particular subcategory, it seems predisposed to pick the most generic option.

A few classes are slightly more concentrated on specific photographers or the subject classifications, when compared to the baseline probabilities given. Russell Lee took nearly 40 percent of the images with wood floors. Several items that border on object types—blankets, rugs, fruit, and food—are associated with a small group of subject classification categories. The subject categories are not, however, directly associated with the object types. Instead, the relationship is more direct; blankets, for example, are strongly associated with images of children, and fruit with the category *Selling and Distribution*. Even in all these situations, except for the very small number of pillows, no photographer or subject category accounts for more than 40 percent of a single tag. In most cases, the maximum concentration is much smaller.

As with the outdoor classes, one of the most interesting observations is the lack of subject category concentration for some classes that seem to correspond to themes we would expect within this corpus. For example, despite a third-level category for bridges, only 2.5 percent of images tagged by the algorithm to contain a bridge are placed in this category. Similarly, one of the first-level categories is called *Homes and Living Conditions*. Less than half of these are associated with the class "house"; likewise, only 20 percent of images tagged as containing a house are contained under this first-level category. Some of these differences are likely the result of ambiguity between the third-level classes. What exactly is the difference between a "house" and a "building"? How much elevation is needed for a "road" to become a "bridge"? At the same time, some of these differences hint at precisely the question that undergirds the stuff-classification algorithm. The relatively small foreground often drives our understanding of what an image is about, and we forget to take note of the background of the image. The detection of stuff in addition to objects, therefore, allows the annotations to engage with more of the image and further address the task of determining the messages of the image.

Looking at images within the third tier of the object categories can expand our understanding of connections across the collection and what an image is about. Several examples from two categories are given in figure 4.7. The first two rows show images of cakes, though notice that the cake is never the only, or even primary, object in any of the images. These range from a child's birthday party, a child eating a relatively simple meal, community gatherings, holiday celebrations, and commercial kitchens. By seeing how all are connected through a particular food item, we gain an expanded understanding of all the images, spurred by the specificity of the tag "cake." United through foodways, elements of daily family life, community life, special occasions, and work are all connected through a single item.

The second set of images in figure 4.7 of bicycles tells a similar story. This one item is so pervasive in American culture by the 1930s that we find examples such as athletic competitions, medical rehab equipment, and military transportation. Even the way the bikes are used within the rhetoric of each image is different: it is the primary object of focus in the medical office but only a small part of the children's parade in the final image. In

Figure 4.7
The first two rows show six images that were identified as containing the object
"cake," and the second two rows show six images that were identified as containing
the object "bicycle."

the lower-left corner, the bicycles are piled up in a corner outside a building, stressing the absence of their owners rather than the novelty of their
mechanical existence. Yet, despite the differences between the images in
these two sets, the shared status of cakes and bicycles as cultural objects
highlight the interconnectedness of the various elements of American
society in the 1930s and 1940s and the different roles that each played in
American life. These items become a way to see social events and social life,

moments of joy and celebration, which disrupt the typical categorization of the FSA-OWI as a record of loss, isolation, and economic depression.

The most granular level of the stuff region categories provides a way of looking across the typical subject classification codes and image captions. Often these allow us to see background and secondary elements of the images, showing a different but no less insightful way of navigating a collection of images. One way to use these tags is to let them guide us to look more closely at the photo. They can help us notice details in the image that facilitate close looking and add to our understanding of the image's message. These tags can also be used to expose the generated metadata to users through a digital public interface. This provides another form of remixing and serendipity to explore a collection in new ways, a topic that we will briefly address in the following section and take up more fully in our analysis of recommender systems and visual similarity in chapter 6.

Our analysis to this point has focused on the use of stuff categories to understand the FSA-OWI collection. In addition to providing the stuff region categories, most algorithms used for image region segmentation also simultaneously identify objects within the frame. Unlike stuff, it is possible to count the elements in object categories. Consider, for example, objects such as "chair," "TV," and "car" compared to stuff categories such as "furniture," "wall," and "road." Significant work in object detection over the past decade has led to increasingly specific algorithms and cemented these ways of seeing as prominent in computer vision.[39] We have already used one of these objects, the location of people, in our analyses. Given that the objects are already provided as part of the output, we finish our study of the FSA-OWI photographic collection by looking at the objects detected to explore and remix the prints.

Each object instance detected by our algorithm is associated with a confidence score indicating the probability that the detected object is correctly located and identified. Our experimentation with this confidence score shows that it is a good idea to analyze only those objects that are detected with a reasonably high confidence score; in our analysis here, we use a cutoff of 95 percent. In total, there are 79 different object types detected within the corpus. Some have no results above our cutoff score; objects never seen with high confidence include "sandwich," "giraffe," and "carrot." Table 4.5 shows all the objects that do appear in the corpus after filtering by a confidence score. Each object category is given two probability scores similar to

Table 4.5
Summary statistics of objects detected in the FSA-OWI collection. The number of photos that have some amount of the given object is given in each row. The last two columns give the probability that two randomly chosen photos containing the given category share the same photographer or second-level Vanderbilt subject classification.

Object	Count	ProbPhoto	ProbVan2	Object	Count	ProbPhoto	ProbVan2
person	38607	11	7	traffic light	30	8	20
horse	1910	15	28	elephant	25	8.7	20
car	1490	10	11	wine glass	24	19	6.9
chair	1305	11	8.5	toilet	23	44	34
truck	709	17	10	sports ball	22	15	14
cow	631	19	47	motorcycle	21	13	4.8
bottle	580	15	11	baseball bat	18	20	11
train	531	25	45	Frisbee	17	6.6	6.6
bowl	520	24	13	oven	13	15	15
cup	509	15	12	refrigerator	13	13	6.4
tie	285	10	9.3	skateboard	12	14	12
clock	274	13	6.4	cake	11	18	7.3
sheep	246	19	56	baseball glove	10	8.9	2.2
bed	243	19	18	cat	9	25	8.3
dog	242	13	9.5	kite	8	21	3.6
boat	206	7.5	13	cell phone	7	0	0
bench	205	11	5.6	laptop	7	4.8	19
bicycle	197	11	8.3	spoon	7	48	19
bird	197	14	23	tennis racket	7	14	19
airplane	163	18	24	donut	5	60	30
book	142	16	14	knife	5	60	10
bus	135	12	24	stop sign	5	0	10
suitcase	126	12	6.7	teddy bear	5	20	10
umbrella	123	11	6.3	banana	4	0	100
dining table	122	15	11	keyboard	4	17	17
potted plant	107	16	10	surfboard	4	0	17
vase	93	14	16	TV	4	17	100
fire hydrant	59	14	14	fork	3	0	0
handbag	54	9.9	10	parking meter	3	0	0
couch	41	23	39	zebra	3	33	0
sink	40	18	17				

those provided in the previous section, showing how well distributed each object is across the photographer and subject category. As there is no hierarchy of the objects to organize them, we sort the objects by the number of images containing each object type.

The most striking element of the output is how the "people" category dominates the other objects. People occur in over twenty times more photographs than the next most common category (horses), and in general occur in around two-thirds of all photographs in our collection. As discussed above, photographing people amid their homes and places of work was an essential theme of the FSA and OWI photographic units. It is not particularly surprising that people are common in the images; the relative dominance over the other object types is more unexpected. The probabilities show that people are relatively well spread across photographers and subject classifications, with a bit of concentration on certain categories.[40]

On the other end of frequency, we see several objects that appear in only a small number of photographs. Some of these rare categories are interesting as a way of finding surprising links across the collection. For example, the four photographs that feature bananas show this fruit at their source in Puerto Rico, in the truck of a vendor in Texas, at a cooperative store in California, and behind a soda jerker in an ice cream parlor in Corpus Christi. The remixing of the collection reveals an interesting view of the American agricultural supply chain in the 1930s. Other rare categories offer some difficulties in interpretation. While there are some zebras in The File, the three detected zebras shown in table 4.5 are not zebras but instead untitled images of incarcerated people working in black-and-white striped jumpsuits.[41] This is an example of an incorrect result revealing another truth: the existence of the US carceral state. This (mis)categorization in the Vanderbilt system offers evidence of the history of incarceration, which was not an intended theme of the collection.[42]

At the same time, the possibility of remixing the archive comes with cautions. Other found objects are anachronistic, such as the seven cell phones, four (computer) keyboards, and seven laptops. In most cases, one can understand what is being mistaken for the wrong object. The "cell phones" all seem to be detecting rotary telephones, for example. In this case the inaccuracy could be easily fixed by relabeling the category "cell phones" with the less-specific category "phone." In other cases, though, miscategorization can be unhelpful and possibly even offensive.[43] These challenges harken back to chapter 1 where we discussed how computer vision algorithms are encoded with particular ways of seeing that influence their use in distant viewing. Close attention to which parts of an image are categorized with which labels is essential before relying on the results for a domain-specific area of inquiry or a public interface, which we will address in chapter 6.

Our caution extends to the stuff and object segmentation algorithm itself. There are several objects that we would expect to be present in the FSA-OWI collection more frequently than other object types. Looking at the first few object types, we see "horses," "chairs," "cars," "trucks," and "cows." It seems reasonable that these are some of the most frequent objects in the collection; however, the overall frequency of the objects seems low. There are thousands of photographs in the Vanderbilt subject classification for "trains," but only about five hundred photographs that have a detected train in them. Similar arguments can be made for the small number of boats (206), ties (285), and airplanes (163). We would have expected more objects of these types just by looking at keywords in photo captions. The numbers increase if we modify our confidence cutoff, but this causes a corresponding rise in false positives. Perhaps an even more striking example of what is missing in the detected objects are entire categories that are not included in the schema provided by the algorithm.

The object detection algorithm contains less than 80 categories, but clearly, there are many orders of magnitude more objects in the world than just these categories. The fundamental problem here is that rather than creating a hierarchy of different levels of precision, object detection algorithms attempt to detect particular objects precisely. For example, the algorithm is trained to identify horses, sheep, cows, dogs, and cats. It does not know anything about other animals, such as goats and pigs, that appear in the FSA-OWI corpus. When seeing these animals, the algorithm often confidently believes it has found a different animal (usually cows, in this case). Even when the objects present in the image are in the vocabulary of the algorithm, the lack of a hierarchical classification of objects can be a challenge if the objects are difficult to detect. For example, many FSA photographs have lots of animals grazing in the far background. Our image algorithm cannot determine with any degree of certainty whether these are (say) horses or cows, and therefore cannot identify them with a high degree of certainty.

What, then, are we able to do with object detection within the distant viewing framework? Such conditions mean we must be careful about what kind of evidence we have and, therefore, what we know. As one is working with the data, it can be tempting to make claims about the amount to which a particular subject or concept dominates the corpus, for example. Yet, the degree to which these algorithms do not see, or else see "incorrectly," should temper such an approach. We know that a specific category exists. In our case, we checked by looking at photos, and we can map the algorithmic classes onto concepts and features that shape our object of study. The data can show us a theme or element such as compositional features that exist. Still, we need to be incredibly cautious about arguments built upon the prevalence of a feature, particularly when the large size of the corpus exceeds our ability to view the corpus easily. Applying existing algorithms out of the box can find interesting objects—our example of the different images with bananas comes to mind—but their bias toward a small set of specific object types and high error rates make them difficult to use more generally. Algorithms need a lot of framing work to map concepts and ideas that animate the vast areas of inquiry that people want to pursue.

Given the challenges, image segmentation offers a generative way to annotate and view a collection of photographs by providing a way to expand our ways of viewing computationally to include the background of an image. The focus away from "things" also provides a way to see a more abstract idea in images, moving us from counting concrete objects such as clouds to more general concepts such as the sky. Exploring the results requires engagement with theories and areas of analysis that often require mapping an annotation onto another concept or using them in ways that the designer of the algorithm either did not intend or could not imagine. More complex extensions may require retraining existing algorithms on new datasets, or the construction of new techniques may be necessary; this is one reason we need researchers asking questions guided by the humanities and social sciences at the center of developing machine learning. As we pursue distant viewing, tweaking and rebuilding the algorithm for a particular type of image and particular set of objects will often be necessary. We will explore these questions, and possible solutions, further in chapter 6.

Conclusions

In chapter 2, when discussing the challenge of developing annotations, we drew on American studies scholar Alan Trachtenberg's toiling over the question, What is this an image of? Looking at a single photograph in The File, he highlights the challenges of describing a seemingly straightforward photo featuring a horse. At first glance, the content of the print seems clear. The tight framing on the animal's ears, eyes, and nostrils suggests the image is meant to focus on the powerful animal. Yet, Trachtenberg quickly complicates the story.[44] What if we focus on the plume of white next to the nostrils, which suggests moisture due to the difference in temperature between the horse and the air? Another possible framing, he offers, is that the photo is about the weather. Even the most straightforward photo can be read multiple ways, Trachtenberg argues. This challenge scales as we seek to view, classify, and interpret tens of thousands of photos.

Communications scholar Cara Finnegan extends the analysis of interpreting images in The File to the archive itself and the system developed by archivist Paul Vanderbilt. In "What Is This a Picture Of? Some Thoughts on Images and Archives," she discusses the challenges of navigating the sixty thousand prints.[45] Her interests do not directly align with the organization of the archive. She walks the reader through the process of realizing that she must first read with the archive in order to then to read across and against it. The challenge is exacerbated by interpreting a single image, much less tens of thousands of images. Distant viewing offers a way to read with, across, and against the collection. Zooming in and out offers insight into the visual culture of the Depression and World War II as well as the methodological possibilities of distant viewing.

Following Stryker's call to analyze the whole, our application of image region segmentation algorithms in this chapter has produced several insights. Specific patterns have been identified within the FSA-OWI corpus, and we have found ways that image region segmentation can be used in the distant viewing methodology, as well as general techniques that work well for understanding complex image corpora. Within the FSA-OWI photographic collection, we have found patterns that either follow or cut against the governmental logic that funded and directed the project. Patterns of the presence or absence of people within the frame of a photo and whether a photograph was taken indoors or outdoors correlate strongly to the change in the project's focus, ranging from FSA's goal of supporting the New Deal state in its early years through documenting the home front during World War II under the OWI. These patterns also correlate strongly with the organizational logic developed by Paul Vanderbilt throughout the

1940s. In contrast, the framing of photographs—defined by the proportion of buildings, plants, sky, and ground in the image—is most strongly associated with the style of individual photographers, allowing us to identify a particular photographer's ways of seeing and to unpack the cultural and political work of their images. Finally, the presence of more granular regions within images, such as water and snow, can be used to read against the collection's metadata and find new and unexpected relationships that are otherwise hidden by the collection's existing organizational logic. In aggregate, the three areas of exploration offer a path for complicating the cultural work of the file as understood in existing scholarship.

Analyzing the ideologies of the physical archive, Trachtenberg argues that the prints produce a grand narrative that society is generated from the land and grows in complexity. The File reflects and produces the "era's ideology of human history as 'universal' and 'progressive,'" he writes.[46] It is also known that Stryker and the photographers had hoped to build a collection that was a document of everyday life; and many of the photographers, including Dorothea Lange and Gordon Parks, were not interested in a narrative of progress.[47] While Trachtenberg's argument is one reading of the archive and its organization, distant viewing offers a path for complicating and disrupting this cultural work. Our method can be a way to remix the archive to reveal the photographers' themes and ways of seeing that complicate the cultural and historical work that The File can do today. This is a topic that we will delve further into in chapter 6 by using distant viewing and digital public humanities to remix and see differently.

The analysis of The File also offers a methodological intervention. Image region segmentation produces powerful general-purpose features that can be used to understand extensive photographic collections. We were somewhat surprised by the accuracy of these algorithms on black-and-white photography; it seems likely they work well on most twentieth- and twenty-first-century photographic collections. The hierarchical nature of the stuff categories makes them relatively easy to use even if some of the levels are not entirely relevant or accurate for a specific application. In our example, some of the third-level categories were too specific, but this did not get in the way of our analysis. The stuff categories opened ways of seeing at scale, particularly the ability to look at the background of an image, an important part of interpreting visual messages. The out-of-the-box object categories, in contrast, were difficult to make general use of. The results were not particularly accurate, and many exciting object types were not present in the existing schema. The one striking contrast was the detection of people, which seemed to be both very useful and accurate in our collection. The challenge with objects offers productive cautions. We must be careful about not only what an algorithm is trained to see, but also how it is built. Then, we must pay close attention to which concepts we map the computational results onto—the relationship between output and ways of seeing and looking shapes our evidence and therefore what we know.

Finally, our application in this chapter re-enforces the general principles of the distant viewing methodology. The features dictate the direction, possibilities, and limitations of the analysis that we chose to algorithmically extract from the collection. The most exciting conclusions we can make come from intersecting these automatically generated features with existing metadata (here, photographer names and subject classification codes), guided by our knowledge of existing scholarship. At the same time, the distant viewing method is not a prescriptive checklist that should be applied uncritically to a collection of images. Instead, it is a specific way of doing exploratory data analysis, which itself requires iteratively looking at the data from different angles and with other metrics, guided by careful attention to the annotation process. We saw this by looking at several ways to summarize the stuff region tags, the photographer names, and the Vanderbilt subject classification codes. Each of these provided different and mutually beneficial ways of understanding the themes and styles within one of the best-known and widely circulated collections of documentary photography. In the following chapter, we will use a variety of additional annotations to further explore relationships between formal visual elements and the themes and messages within a corpus of US television series.

5 Feast for the Eyes: Locating Visual Style in Network-Era American Situation Comedies

A core research approach in film and media studies is to take a critical lens to the study of formal elements in various forms of media. Consider Ian Cameron and Richard Jeffery's study of the increasingly anxious fade-in and slanted shot angles that Alfred Hitchcock "often used subliminally to undermine our own stability" in films such as *The Birds* (1963) and *Marnie* (1964).[1] Or, how the use of short shot breaks of jarringly different depths of field in the opening scenes of Sofia Coppola's film *Lost in Translation* (2003) "primes the audience for a series of upcoming narrative vignettes in which Bob feels alienated and disconnected," as Brian Ott and Diane Keeling argue.[2] As we explored in chapter 3, even the use of color can have deep symbolic implications. In Goddard's *Une femme est une femme* (1961), for example, the use of a striking blue against an otherwise unsaturated background serves as a leitmotif tying together various narrative threads.[3]

Formal elements of media can be used to study larger implications beyond the space of their narrative frame. There are numerous ways that formal elements of moving images—such as camera angles, sound, and framing—reflect, establish, and challenge cultural norms. The choice of lighting of non-white actors, for instance, can both represent and challenge racial politics.[4] How male and female characters are blocked relative to one another may help demonstrate how gendered power dynamics play out within society. Differences in soundtracks used to establish shots of neighborhoods across parts of a city with different racial and socioeconomic backgrounds can reinforce stereotypes.[5]

Media and television scholars have long argued for the importance of studying a wide variety of visual forms. They have encouraged increased attention to the academic study of so-called low-brow and middle-brow forms of popular film and television. However, these studies often focus on secondary literature and public reception. Close analyses of specific formal elements have, with a few notable exceptions, remained the purview of scholars studying "serious" media, such as award-winning, feature-length films. There are some reasonable justifications for this focus: Hollywood films have significantly larger budgets, time, casts, and crew than most television shows.[6] It stands to reason that these productions can devote more time and energy to a careful consideration of how each shot is taken and carefully edited. However, for the same reasons, there are also significantly more hours of television produced each year than hours of Hollywood films, providing a rich object of study for distant viewing.[7]

TV reaches tens of millions of people, with certain shows enjoying renewal year after year due to their popularity. While films often enjoy caché, TV is one of the most viewed forms of popular culture, sending messages 24/7 about our world. It is a powerful site to study the stories being told about communities, for TV is a mechanism for broadcasting social and cultural values. The quantity of TV shows, however, can make it a challenging medium to study. The amount of TV series produced for a single week often far exceeds the content shown in a movie theater in a single year. The large scale of TV is particularly amenable to distant viewing.

In this chapter, we use distant viewing to study the visual style of two US network-era situation comedies: *Bewitched* (1964–1972) and *I Dream of Jeannie* (1965–1970). We chose the two shows for several reasons. One is that they were two of the most watched series in late 1960s, indicating that the shows' messages resonated and reflected the values of their contemporary US audiences. Second, the two shows were considered innovative for their female lead characters amid the rise of second-wave feminism. The third reason is the fact that *I Dream of Jeannie* was designed to compete directly with *Bewitched* in the networks' battle for dominance over the airwaves. Their development, direct competition, and broad appeal allow us to compare their messages and to see how a generative line of inquiry is animated by fields such as film, media, and TV studies.[8]

We compare the two series to explore how a character's presence on-screen and each show's pacing convey the importance of certain characters. We ask three central questions: Who are the dominant character(s) in each series? What are the characters' relationships? How does shot duration shape the narrative arc? By addressing these questions, we unpack the similarities and differences between the shows and demonstrate how character presence, blocking, and narrative timing convey character centrality, the power dynamics between characters, and cultural messages about the role of women and feminism in 1960s America.

We will work with a corpus containing every broadcast of each series, consisting of 393 episodes and over 150 hours of material. This material contains over 13 million individual frames, significantly larger than the collections considered in chapters 3 and 4.[9] Our analysis will look at how visual forms follow function and how these forms differ between the seemingly very similar series. We start by showing how blocking and screen time are used to establish the most dominant character(s). We then show how shot lengths function throughout each episode to establish different narrative arcs within the series. Finally, we look at how visual forms create different relationships and intimacies between characters and how these contribute to the unique formation of a magical and feminine gaze within the series. The analysis, in aggregate, sheds light on how visual styles shape the social and cultural messages sent by two of the era's most popular and iconic TV shows.

To investigate these questions, we use a distant viewing approach applied to the digitized corpus of materials. In chapters 3 and 4, we harnessed algorithms out of the box. Given the complexity of our research questions in this chapter, we will weave together results of multiple computer vision algorithms. We will use a combination of existing algorithms and one that we built for shot detection. The required features to study visual style are constructed by applying different forms of summarization to the annotations produced by popular computer vision algorithms. We start by breaking the large set of individual frames in each episode into individual shots by comparing the differences between successive frames with our custom-built algorithm. Then, we use out-of-the-box algorithms to detect and identify the people and faces found within each shot. Finally, we define different shot types based on the size and number of people detected. The set of identified characters, shot durations, and shot types can be summarized in various ways to analyze visual style and their social and cultural messages.

Our work builds on previous efforts to computationally study narrative film and television. Beginning with the early work of Barry Salt, a significant focus of this research has focused on the distribution of median shot lengths.[10] Analyses for shot length include Yuri Tsivian's Cinemetrics project, Arclight, and Jeremy Butler's ShotLogger project.[11] Other computational analyses have included the aggregation of language and average shot color, image compositions, and analysis of film scripts.[12] In this chapter, we illustrate the added power of constructing annotations from modern computer vision algorithms.

The chapter begins with a discussion of our annotation decisions, which include shot boundaries and face identification, and how these become the building blocks for our analysis of TV shows. We then turn to ways of aggregating annotations over the individual frames of moving image data. The following sections delve into these methods and detail how to work with time-based media, including potential challenges. Then, we move to an overview of existing scholarship on these two sitcoms, followed by a computational analysis where we explore the data to address our three central questions.

Annotating Shot Boundaries

Working with time-based media is a challenge. We need to account for the form in our analysis by expanding our repertoire of annotations through a consideration of the relationships between individual images. The frames before and after each frame are in direct conversation. To account for this, we begin by looking at shots, a semantic building block of film and TV. To accomplish this task, we built a custom shot detector, which we will now detail. It is the unit by which we will apply face detection and recognition to track when characters are on and off screen.

Working with digitized moving image data presents many of the same computational challenges that we have discussed regarding still images. Due to its large raw file sizes, moving image data are typically saved in highly compressed files designed to store the visual information in as small a format as possible. When we apply computational algorithms to these files, moving images are converted into a sequence of individual frames. Each frame is stored as a rectangular array of pixel intensities; in other words, a frame has the same structure as other digital images. The number of frames corresponding to a particular period of playback time varies, with a typical rate of twenty-four frames per second for standard cinema films and thirty frames per second for broadcast television.[13] Each frame in a particular file has the same dimensions in pixels, which makes frames easy to compare to one another. Moving images also often have soundtracks and subtitles that are synced with the frames. These can also be extracted from the digital file for use in computational analyses. However, we will not use sound or subtitle information in the analyses described in this chapter.[14]

The collection of individual frames from one or more digitized moving image files can be analyzed using computer vision algorithms designed for still images by applying an algorithm to each frame. Industry applications involving video processing, such as analyzing faces in a video chat or detecting pedestrians from the camera of a self-driving car, generally follow this approach. However, successive frames from a film or television series tend to be very similar. Unless there is a period of swift motion, it can be virtually impossible to distinguish two successive frames visually. Also, individual frames are not a meaningful unit of analysis for how moving images are imagined or processed. The frame rate is designed to be sufficiently high enough so that viewers *do not* notice the frames. A more meaningful computational approach involves grouping frames into larger meaningful units.

In film theory, the smallest unit used to describe a portion of a film is a shot. A shot consists of a continuous, uninterrupted sequence of frames that run in continuous time.[15] In the context of physical film, shots are produced by a physical cut in which two different reels of film are spliced together in the editing room. Moving images produced using digital technology simulate the same approach and borrow the same terminology. Most shots are only a few seconds long, though filmmakers have occasionally experimented with *long takes* consisting of significantly longer shots. Classic examples include Alfred Hitchcock's *Rope* (1948),[16] which consists of only ten shots, and the experimental film *Russian Ark* (2002) which consists of one single long shot. Outside of these outliers, longer semantic elements of the film, such as scenes, can be identified by grouping together individual shots.

Several different editing techniques are used to create a transition from one shot to the next. A *hard cut*, by far the most common option, consists of an abrupt change between takes. One frame is the last frame used from one take, and the subsequent frame is the first frame being used from another take. Hard cuts are often employed when multiple cameras are used to shoot the same scene simultaneously; cuts between different angles can jump between participants in a dialogue and highlight a close shot of the actors' reactions. *Gradual transitions* use a more subtle method to transition between shots. These are usually used to signal a more dramatic break, often with a change in location or time, or both. A *fade-in* starts with a blank image and slowly dissolves into the full image of the next shot. A *fade-out*, also known as a *fade-to-black*, ends a shot by slowly dissolving to a fixed image. *Cross-fades* use a similar technique but dissolve from one take to the next instead of from or to a static image. *Wipes*, in which one shot replaces the next by moving across the frame, are less common in feature films but are heavily used as a special effect in sports and news broadcasts. Understanding different editing methods is essential for understanding how we can algorithmically detect and describe shot breaks. Figure 5.1 shows a selection of frames from the first several minutes of an episode of *Bewitched* to illustrate a sequence of hard cuts as well as a fade-out that leads into the opening credits.

The process of algorithmically breaking up a sequence of frames into shots is known as *shot boundary detection*.[17] Several different approaches, ranging from relatively simple thresholds to complex machine-learning algorithms, have been proposed for this task. Shot boundary detection, however, has fewer commercial applications relative to many other computer vision tasks. Also, most approaches seem to work only within a specific domain of moving images. Some work well with complex cut types but break down with noisy or lower resolution inputs. Others handle noise well but struggle to detect gradual transitions, particularly in the challenging case of cross-fades. For these reasons, we found no single standard software implementation that could be reliably applied out of the box to the task of shot boundary detection.[18] Therefore, we trained a shot-boundary detection algorithm specifically designed for the corpus studied in this chapter.

Most shot-boundary detection algorithms function by measuring the differences between two successive frames within a collection of moving images. For most pairs of frames, these differences will be small. However, at the location of a hard shot boundary, we expect to see a relatively significant change between subsequent frames. The trick to this approach involves determining a metric that allows for finding hard breaks between two similar shots while at the same time not accidentally detecting differences between frames within the same shot when the camera or actors are moving quickly. After much experimentation, we found that the best approach for our collection was to compute two different metrics that capture different types of changes between frames. The first metric takes each frame and creates a granular, down-sampled version of the image that is

Figure 5.1
Every tenth frame from a forty-second clip at the start of the *Bewitched* episode "The Magic Cabin" (season 2, episode 16).

only 32 pixels wide and 32 pixels high. The resulting image resembles the upper-right pane in figure 1.4. The difference between pixels in subsequent frames is taken, and the 40th percentile of the differences is used as a metric. The second metric first computes a histogram of the pixel intensities for each image—exactly the same approach used in figure 3.2 for the color analysis of movie posters—and then calculates the total difference between the histograms of subsequent frames. The first metric considers the location of objects in the frame, and the second metric is concerned primarily with color and brightness. We label a shot boundary whenever both metrics fall above a predetermined threshold or whenever either metric individually falls above an even larger threshold. This approach performs well for detecting hard shot boundaries without making many false detections.

Finding gradual transitions requires some additional consideration. Both *Bewitched* and *I Dream of Jeannie* use a single black screen for all fade-in and fade-out effects. Finding these computationally, therefore, does not present any difficulties. A shot boundary is added to those found in the above threshold-based technique whenever a frame consists of entirely black pixels. Cross-fades are more complicated but are relatively rare in these series. The difficulty comes from the fact that no two subsequent frames are notably different, and we cannot easily fall back on detecting a static black frame. To detect these cross-fade events, an additional metric was used that measures the change in image histograms across six different frames. This metric becomes large when two different scenes are superimposed on one another—adding a shot boundary when this value fell above a threshold allowed for detecting this final shot-boundary type from our corpus.

Since we created a custom shot-boundary detection algorithm for our analysis, it is important to verify that it works well to build confidence in our analyses based on this algorithm. To do this, we manually tagged shot breaks for ten episodes of each of the two series in our corpus and then used our algorithm to manually detect shot breaks using the logic described above.[19] Comparing the manual and automatically detected shot boundaries showed a high degree of agreement. Of the automatically detected boundaries, 98.7 percent corresponded to manually detected boundaries. The few errors mainly resulted from falsely detected boundaries when bright strobe lights were used during special effects. In the other direction, 97.2 percent of the manually labeled shot boundaries were found by the algorithm. The remaining errors here resulted from two difficult cross-fades between similar scenes and several hard cuts between characters in dialogue who were framed similarly and wearing similarly colored clothing. Overall, however, the high degree of agreement between manual and automated annotations was more than accurate enough to trust aggregative analyses based on algorithmically produced shot boundaries.

After applying a shot-boundary detection algorithm to digitized moving image data, we can apply other algorithms to the individual frames and then aggregate the information across all of the frames within a single shot. Computer vision algorithms are then applied to the static images to develop a set of annotations describing the type of shot and which characters are present. We turn to these tasks in the following section.

Annotating Faces

Because sitcom narratives consistently advance through character dialogue and action, we can gain a substantial understanding of the visual style implicit in television production, directing, and editing by knowing where specific characters are in each shot. The algorithmic task of identifying the location of characters in an image can be split into two subsequent steps. The first, *face detection*, attempts to find the location of all faces present in each image. Once faces are located, the process of *face recognition* predicts which person is associated with a given face.

Relatively fast and accurate face detection algorithms have existed to detect well-framed faces since the late 1990s. These include the original Haar-wavelet method for general-purpose object detection, the Viola–Jones object detection framework, and the histogram of oriented gradients (HOG) detector.[20] All of these methods identify faces by finding portions of an image that have the shape of a face. This makes the algorithms robust to lighting, skin tone, and shot widths. These methods, particularly the HOG detector, continue to be popular and are often provided in modern image-processing libraries.[21] The downside of shape-based estimators is that they are not able to extend easily to faces in profile. On television shows, wide shots frequently display multiple characters turned inward as they engage in conversation. This is particularly true of sitcoms, which are primarily driven by dialogue rather than action sequences or special effects.

As with many other areas of computer vision, the use of neural networks has enabled a significant improvement in the performance of face detection models. Two prominent examples are the Faster R-CNN and FAREC-CNN.[22] From a series of tests on frames extracted from network-era television series, we determined that the Faster R-CNN is sufficiently accurate to detect many faces without making too many false detections.[23] The neural network algorithm returns a confidence score with each detected face. We decided only to include faces with a relatively high score. This results in an algorithm that occasionally misses a face—about once every twenty frames—but makes very few false detections. We determined this result to be a better balance for subsequent analyses because we will track who is and is not on the screen, so we need to ensure that the face is a face. At the same time, since we have multiple frames per shot, it is okay if it occasionally misses a face. If the face is detected in a few frames in the shot, we can confidently say the person was in the shot.

After detecting where faces exist in individual frames, the next step is to identify which characters are associated with each face. The widespread use of neural networks in face recognition preceded the use of neural networks in face detection by several years, primarily due to the presence of large training datasets and the relatively small size of the images involved. Open-source libraries with neural network-based recognition algorithms include OpenFace and OpenBR.[24] Both libraries are reasonably well known and their respective methods are widely cited. These algorithms, as well as most other face recognition methods, require a preprocessing step whereby a detected face is modified to align key reference points (such as both eyes, the nose, and the mouth) with standardized locations. This approach works well for the high-quality faces detected by algorithms optimized for finding front-oriented faces. Trying to align the faces in profile is impossible, given that only part of the face is visible.

To detect faces that are only partially visible, we have used the VGG-Face2 face recognition model.[25] Unlike other recognition algorithms, this approach did not require the input images to be aligned and was mainly built to handle faces that can be seen only in profile or a low resolution. We hand-labeled faces from the top four characters in five episodes of each of our two series and compared these results to the VGGFace2 predictions.[26] As with the detection of faces, we selected a minimum confidence score for the face recognition algorithm that only labels faces that have a very high confidence score.[27] While the VGGFace2 model for face detection works very well for the subsequent analysis of *Bewitched* and *I Dream of Jeannie*, there are some potential pitfalls. A critical aspect of the current application is the difficulty of VGGFace2 to identify children successfully. While this is often a positive feature given the ethical concerns about training data that includes children, it limits the possibilities of our analysis. Initially, we intended to include Tabitha, the daughter of Samantha and Darrin from *Bewitched*; however, the precision of this task across all available face recognition algorithms made this unworkable.

Work in film and media studies has established a nomenclature for many specific types of shots commonly seen across many genres. Describing different types of shots is important because they can be used to communicate feelings, moods, and relationships between characters. For example, the close shot is a way to build and communicate intimacy. Measuring shot type becomes one decisive way to understand the visual work of media.

Determining shot type typically depends on the relative size of the characters within a frame, the number of characters, the orientation of the characters, and the camera angle. However, many of these specify something about a particular frame but do not describe it in multiple aggregate elements at the shot level. For example, how should we classify a single shot that pans from a close shot of one character to an establishing shot of a building? Suppose one character is standing over another character at a table. Is this a medium-long shot (most but not all of one character is in the frame) or a medium close shot (as only the seated character's upper half is visible)? To algorithmically classify shot types, we need precise definitions with which to build a testing dataset. After carefully parsing through many extracted scenes in our dataset, we decided to use the following four shot types:[28]

- *close shot*: Only one character is present in the foreground of the entire shot and the legs of this character are never shown. Further, if the character is sitting, we can infer that the shot is framed close enough that their face would leave the shot if they were to stand up.
- *two shot*: Exactly the same as a close shot, but there are two characters present in the shot and at some point we see each character's face.
- *group shot*: Any shot that contains at least three characters.
- *over-the-shoulder*: Two characters are shown in the shot but one of the two characters (the one closest to the camera) has their back to the camera and no face showing. This type of shot is likely to arise in the context of a shot/reverse-shot editing sequence in which the camera follows a conversation between two or more characters.

Figure 5.2 shows examples of these four shot types from both an episode of *Bewitched* and an episode of *I Dream of Jeannie*. We refer to any shot that is neither a close shot nor a two shot as a *long shot*. This includes shots that show characters from the waist up—in other studies referred to as a *medium shot*—or the entire body.

All the shot types described above depend on the number of characters present in a shot and their body being shown in the frame. While there is no out-of-the-box algorithm for detecting shot type, we built a hand-constructed algorithm for these four shot types based on the number of detected faces, the placement of the faces, and the size of the faces. To verify that these worked as expected, we hand-labeled the shot types in eight episodes of our series and compared with the results from the algorithm. We found a very high level of agreement between the two methods, with exceptionally high precision for close shots and group shots.[29] Combining the face recognition and detection algorithm with our shot boundary algorithm provides a set of annotations for analyzing visual messages computationally.

Putting two annotation types—shot boundaries and faces—together provides a way to study character dominance, character relationships, the gaze of the camera, and affective space. The annotations can be further explored by combining them with metadata such as time stamps and episode number to understand the TV series at the level of the episode, the season, and the series. We now turn to the history of the shows and the organization of the corpus to analyze the cultural work of these two sitcoms.

Organizing the *Bewitched* and *I Dream of Jeannie* Corpus

The network era of American television (1952–1985) was controlled by just three competing networks: ABC, CBS, and NBC. By the early 1960s, most American households owned a television and had access to the affiliate station from all three major networks.[30] With extensive market penetration and high user engagement, millions of Americans watched television programming on any given evening. The goal for each of the established networks in the oligopoly was to attract the most viewers to their programming over the competition.[31] These market forces caused networks to push out content with a broad appeal to attract viewers and, in turn, to draw the largest percentage of advertising revenue. The result was a relatively uniform stream of programming aimed primarily at white suburban middle-class families.[32]

Figure 5.2
Shot type examples from the *Bewitched* episode "Dangerous Diaper Dan" (season 3, episode 8) and the *I Dream of Jeannie* episode "My Master, the Civilian" (season 2, episode 21).

Situation comedy, or the *sitcom*, has been one of the dominant narrative forms of television shows from the early years of the network era. Unlike sketch comedy and vaudeville, sitcoms focus on a fixed set of characters and usually consist of self-contained episodes. Within each episode, the cast of characters is presented with a new problem that gets resolved by the episode's conclusion. Major plot events, such as extended romances, may be referenced across episodes. However, the sitcom structure makes it easy for a viewer to follow the series even if they miss a particular week's show by producing, as Umberto Eco concisely describes it, "a plot which does not 'consume' itself."[33]

These features made sitcoms an attractive programming choice during the network era. Before the advent of consumer VHS recording technologies in the 1980s, Americans had to watch their favorite programs when they aired or risk missing them entirely. There was no way to fast-forward through commercial breaks, as would later become possible with VCRs, DVRs, and streaming services. These viewing patterns, combined with the desire to integrate commercials, dictated the three-act structure and self-contained narratives that characterize network-era programming.[34] The familiar recurring characters served as a draw for viewers; the fixed cast and sets kept production costs low, and the formulaic narrative assured that consumers would not lose track of the show if they missed an episode.

We now turn to two popular American sitcoms from the 1960s. In line with the genre and time period, both feature a small, all-White cast living in generic suburban neighborhoods. Each week's plot follows a formulaic model: a problem arises that threatens the status quo at home or in the workplace. The first several attempts to address it fail in some comic fashion until ultimately a happy resolution presents itself at the episode's conclusion. However, we will show that the narrative and editing of these series are far from formless. The series have distinct visual elements that serve to challenge and reinforce the narrative structures present in each show.

The sitcom *Bewitched* premiered on ABC in the fall of 1964 and ran for a total of eight seasons. Its central premise focuses on the marriage of the ordinary Darrin Stevens to the supernatural witch Samantha. Samantha does her best to live a "normal" American life, but difficulties from her magical world crop up to make this process challenging. The main cast is completed by Samantha's meddling mother, Endora; Darrin's boss, Larry

Tate; and (from season 3 onward) the Stevenses' magically gifted daughter, Tabitha. *Bewitched* proved remarkably popular. It was the second highest-rated show across all three networks in its first season and enjoyed wide syndication from 1972 to the early 2000s.[35]

To understand the typical structure of an episode of *Bewitched*, we will walk through the plot of a specific example. We can then see how this plot is reflected through the data computationally extracted from its visual contents. Figure 5.3 shows all the detected characters' faces in the episode "Business, Italian Style," the seventh episode in the show's fourth season, which first aired on September 21, 1967. In the opening scene, Darrin and Larry meet with the assistant of a potential new client, an Italian business-man trying to expand into the US market. Through a comic misunder-standing, Larry asserts that Darrin will speak to the assistant's boss in his primary language. Following the credits, Darrin returns home and describes the situation to his wife, Samantha, who confides in her mother, Endora. Endora casts a spell that causes Darrin to speak *only* in Italian, which the Stevenses notice the following day over breakfast around the midway point of the episode. After the commercial break, Larry shows up at Darrin's home and finds that Darrin can no longer communicate in English. After several

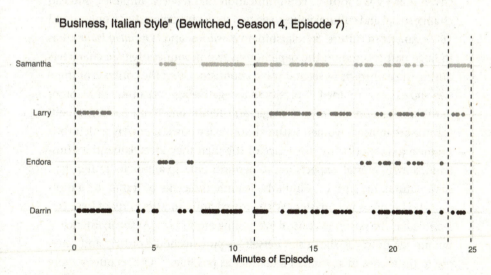

Figure 5.3

Example of the detected characters and narrative breaks from one episode of *Bewitched*.

mishaps, Endora reverses the spell, the business is saved, and all is well with the main characters. The final scene ends with a dinner party that brings together Darrin, Samantha, Larry, and the Italian businessmen, reinforcing the successful conclusion of the episode.

In response to the success of *Bewitched*, in the fall of 1965, NBC debuted *I Dream of Jeannie*.[36] The show features a 2,000-year-old female genie, referred to as Jeannie, discovered by the astronaut Tony Nelson, whom she refers to as her "master." The main cast also includes Tony's friend and fellow astronaut Roger Healey and a NASA psychologist, Dr. Alfred Bellows. A recurring plot device involves Tony and Roger attempting to fulfill their job responsibilities while hiding from and dealing with Jeannie's magical antics. In later seasons, Jeannie and Tony become romantically involved and later marry. *I Dream of Jeannie* ran for only five seasons and did not garner any significant awards.

While *I Dream of Jeannie* did not enjoy the same level of critical success as *Bewitched*, both shows had high ratings and were watched by millions of households. Their design around female characters gave them the potential to be forward-thinking shows amid an era of significant change and anxieties, including the rise of suburbia, liberation movements, and the Cold War. Given that TV is a form of communication that reflects, amplifies, and can change social and cultural values, the two shows become a site to understand 1960s American culture. Scholarship on *Bewitched* and *I Dream of Jeannie* has in large part focused on the depiction of two prominent female characters during the early days of second-wave feminism. Often the contexts of these two shows are combined, typically in a negative light, as in Karen M. Stoddard's analysis on the role of magic and feminism: "Both Samantha and Jeannie are unusual women with extraordinary powers, powers which they promise to curtail at the insistence of the men they love. Samantha's husband, a mere mortal, expects her to perform tasks in a human, rather than supernatural, manner. . . . Similarly, Jeannie the genie is 'found' by a mortal, who becomes her 'master.' With crossed arms and the blink of her eyes, Jeannie has the power to control everything around her. At the insistence of her master, however, she busies herself keeping his house orderly and catering to his wishes in as human a manner as possible."[37] Others offer a more complex reading of the show's gender and sexual politics. Lynn Spiegel noted that in *Bewitched*, "the woman's alien powers serve to invert the gender relations of suburban domesticity, and with this, the consumer lifestyles that characterize the suburbs are also parodied."[38] While the male characters are attempting to subvert the powers of the female characters, at the very core of each show's premise is the idea that women's magic or power cannot be contained and periodically "escapes" domestic or marital constraints. *Bewitched* can also be read as a queer metaphor, in which "mortal" norms take the place of heteronormative thought.[39]

These two shows form an excellent duo for our study of form in television, as network-era sitcoms have small casts and a small repertoire of sets, making both relatively easy to analyze computationally. The prominence of both shows and their repeated presence in television studies research speaks to their cultural importance. Taking into account the historical and industrial context allows our work to engage with broader conversations about the medium and genre. Further, the scholarly disagreements over the relationship between the shows and whether or not their representation of women is feminist make our analysis even more revealing in broader conversations about television, genre, and gender. Distant viewing offers a method for engaging with the scholarly debates from TV and media studies. Our analysis will now turn to how we can use our annotations and combined metadata to explore dominant characters, shot types, and character relationships.

Exploring Dominant Characters

An open question about the two series is understanding which characters are considered the "main" characters of the show. Elizabeth Montgomery (Samantha) and Barbara Eden (Jeannie) are undoubtedly the most well-known actors in our corpus. They feature prominently in the shows' marketing materials. However, it is not immediately apparent to what extent this visibility and name recognition translate into centrality in the narratives of their respective series. For example, a large proportion of plot lines revolve around the careers of their romantic counterparts. The series' titles even hint that this may be the case by establishing agency with the ordinary, career-oriented male characters: Darrin is "bewitched" by Samantha, and Tony is the one "dreaming" of Jeannie.[40] To what extent are these less-recognized male characters central points of the show? How does visual style reflect or potentially undermine narrative centrality across these series?

One straightforward way to assess to what extent visual style correlates to character centrality is to quantify the frequency that each actor appears on-screen, a type of shot semantics. For every shot in our corpus, we created an annotation tagging every character face that appeared in at least one frame. This information was aggregated with shot durations to compute the average minutes per episode that each character was visually present.[41] Table 5.1 shows the computed averages. *Bewitched*'s Samantha and Darrin share the lead with an average of seven minutes of screen time per episode, suggesting not only that their marriage lies at the heart of the show but that theirs is an equitable and egalitarian coupling. At just under eleven minutes per episode, Tony is the most visually present character across both series. On *I Dream of Jeannie*, Jeannie, seen for less than an average of four minutes per episode, is the least visually displayed major character. This inequality is a point in favor of *Jeannie*'s retrograde feminism: while she may act out and rebel in these episodes, the form of the show often transforms her into different objects or screens her (and her controversial costume that some audiences saw as too sexy for TV) from the viewer. By contrast, Tony's coworkers—Roger (5.9 minutes) and Alfred (4.7 minutes)—are seen for longer average durations than Jeannie.

These results highlight a significant difference between the two shows and raise a host of related questions. The character relationships on *Bewitched* are more balanced, indicating the show's twin focus on work and home. Larry is Darrin's boss, but Endora is Samantha's mother. Samantha is absent from the workplace throughout the series, and Darrin is often absent from the magical and family plot elements. Tony's persistent visual presence in *I Dream of Jeannie* underscores how all the lead characters are connected to him, not to one another: Roger is Tony's best friend, Alfred is

Table 5.1
Average minutes per episode for which a character is visible

Series	Character	Mean screen time	Episodes
Bewitched	Samantha	7.0	254
Bewitched	Darrin	6.9	240
Bewitched	Larry	4.1	166
Bewitched	Endora	2.8	148
I Dream of Jeannie	Tony	11.0	131
I Dream of Jeannie	Roger	5.9	124
I Dream of Jeannie	Alfred	4.7	122
I Dream of Jeannie	Jeannie	3.9	131

Tony's boss, and Jeannie is his genie. As a result, usually most of the action, within both the work and domestic spheres, substantially involves Tony.

Understanding when each character is most likely present within an episode indicates how the narrative structure reinforces character central- ity. Each episode can be broken into four parts. The first part, a "cold open," occurs from the start of the episode until the title sequence and lasts approx- imately two to three minutes. The main actions that build and resolve the plot occur in two long blocks lasting around ten minutes each; we refer to these as Act 1 and Act 2. These acts are set off by a mid-episode commercial. Following the final commercial break, a short resolution scene reaffirms the successfully resolved plot and subsequent return to normalcy.[42] We show the proportion of episodes for which each character was detected in each narrative part in table 5.2. By narrative part, Tony's presence dominates the other *I Dream of Jeannie* characters. Most notably, he is almost always pres- ent during Act 2. Samantha is also shown to be present in more acts than Darrin, particularly in the cold open. Though their overall screen time may be similar, we rarely go too long without seeing Samantha.[43]

One way to establish the importance of a particular character is to make a character the first person seen in the opening of an episode. From the opening shot, all the subsequent actions and characters are linked to the perspective of this starting character. This effect is closely related to the cog- nitive bias of *anchoring* in which a set of potential options in a decision- making process are all judged in relationship to the first option presented.[44] Table 5.3 counts the number of times each character was the first detected

Table 5.2

Number of episodes for which a character was seen by narrative act, ordered by total number of occurrences

Series	Character	Introduction	Act 1	Act 2	Resolution
Bewitched	Samantha	189	242	250	125
Bewitched	Darrin	116	217	226	116
Bewitched	Endora	55	100	70	10
Bewitched	Larry	13	132	130	28
I Dream of Jeannie	Tony	47	131	129	32
I Dream of Jeannie	Roger	23	101	98	13
I Dream of Jeannie	Jeannie	23	99	82	11
I Dream of Jeannie	Alfred	10	95	92	21

Table 5.3
Number of episodes where each character is associated with the first face detected in an episode

Series	Character	Number of episodes
Bewitched	Samantha	155
Bewitched	Darrin	76
Bewitched	Endora	21
Bewitched	Larry	1
I Dream of Jeannie	Tony	81
I Dream of Jeannie	Jeannie	18
I Dream of Jeannie	Roger	18
I Dream of Jeannie	Alfred	11

face in an episode.[45] Tony (81 episodes) and Samantha (155 episodes) are overwhelmingly the most likely to be first seen in an episode; Darrin is about half as likely to be featured first compared to Samantha. All of the remaining characters, including Jeannie, are featured at the start of fewer than twenty episodes. For *I Dream of Jeannie*, this further reinforces the centrality of Tony in the show. It also re-establishes the overall narrative: the show chronicles the life of astronaut Tony Nelson, as his world becomes disrupted by the sudden and unwelcome intrusion of Jeannie. This focus is echoed by the show's opening animated credits, in which Tony is introduced first, then Jeannie. In *Bewitched*, while the show in many ways focuses on both characters, Samantha takes center stage more frequently than her mortal husband. To what extent this centrality allies viewers with Samantha, inviting them to root for her subversion of her husband's will, is a question we can begin to address through the presence of close shots.

Close shots are yet another visual tool for establishing characters' centrality and subjectivity. In the mid-1960s, television was distributed in standard definition, signals were sent through noisy analog radio transmission, television screen sizes were substantially smaller, and many households watched television in black and white. Viewers could only get a good view of an actor in tightly framed shots that reveal the character's sometimes private thoughts, feelings, and reactions. Table 5.4 shows the average duration per episode that each character is shown in a close shot. Tony once again dominates the other *I Dream of Jeannie* characters, while Jeannie and Larry receive similar average lengths of close shots, opening up

Table 5.4
Average minutes per episode for which a character is visible in a close shot

Series	Character	Avg. minutes	Number of episodes
Bewitched	Samantha	1.64	254
Bewitched	Darrin	1.19	236
Bewitched	Larry	0.72	152
Bewitched	Endora	0.67	140
I Dream of Jeannie	Tony	1.04	130
I Dream of Jeannie	Jeannie	0.64	129
I Dream of Jeannie	Alfred	0.60	110
I Dream of Jeannie	Roger	0.51	106

questions about Tony's boss and his role in the narrative arc. Overall, the longest average close shot duration (1.36 minutes) across both shows are those of Samantha. Along yet another dimension, Samantha dominates the visual space, while Darrin continues to play a more prominent role than the other *Bewitched* characters.

Taken together, these analyses of shot semantics provide insight into the prominence of the characters in our corpus. Tony appears as the center of the narrative structure in *I Dream of Jeannie*, and this centrality is reinforced through the visual style of the series—time on-screen, close shots, and presence at the start of the episode. Surprisingly, the titular Jeannie is far from the most central character; she is no more visually dominant than Roger or Alfred. On *Bewitched*, by contrast, approximately the same number of scenes feature either Samantha or Darrin. However, visual elements, such as screen time and the number of close shots, establish Samantha as the most central character. While the show focuses on the couple, Samantha is visibly featured as the leading star.[46]

Exploring Shot Distribution and Plot

Extracted annotations can also be used to examine how visual style shapes the narrative arc of television series. Tracking stylistic elements throughout each episode makes it is possible to investigate whether and how producers and editors use visual elements to further the plot as it progresses from the cold open through to the episode's denouement. These patterns, if present, provide further evidence of the visual complexity within the style of network-era sitcoms.

Analyzing the typical duration of shots to study style has been a popular computational approach to the study of film and television series.[47] We initially intended to use shot duration metrics to study the relationship between narrative structure and visual style. However, as shown in table 5.5, our first exploration of shot durations revealed that the duration of a shot is highly correlated with the shot type. Therefore, even small differences in shot distribution can affect the median shot length, and it seems that measuring the duration of a shot lengths is not an ideal metric to use without first accounting for shot type.[48]

An alternative way to explore shot semantics is by exploring the distribution of different shot types. Table 5.6 gives the proportion of close shots and the proportion of group shots for each narrative act. The distribution of shot types changes between narrative acts in both *Bewitched* and *I Dream of Jeannie*; these distributions also differ between the two series. The proportion of close shots is lowest in the introduction and denouement for both series, though the drop-off is noticeably more significant for *I Dream of Jeannie*. This finding likely speaks to how these acts function as either establishing sequences or book-ending the conflicts that characterize the drama of Acts 1 and 2. On *Bewitched*, there is a significant drop in the proportion of close shots between Act 1 and Act 2; there is almost no difference between Act 1 and Act 2 in this metric on *I Dream of Jeannie*. One possibility for these findings is that Act 1 involves the women characters using their magic powers (as an instigating event), and Act 2 centers on the complications that

Table 5.5

Median shot length (MSL) and average shot length (ASL) in seconds for each series, separated into close shots, two shots, and long shots

Series	Shot type	MSL	ASL	Shot count
Bewitched	Close shot	2.64	3.34	26927
Bewitched	Two shot	3.04	4.25	3798
Bewitched	Long shot	4.07	6.74	40548
I Dream of Jeannie	Close shot	2.23	2.84	10857
I Dream of Jeannie	Two shot	2.74	3.83	2577
I Dream of Jeannie	Long shot	4.05	8.71	17626

Table 5.6
Percentage of all shots classified as "close" or "group shots" based on the series and narrative act

Series	Narrative act	Close shots (%)	Two shots (%)	Group shots (%)
Bewitched	1	28.1	1.9	3.2
I Dream of Jeannie	1	16.8	3.3	5.7
Bewitched	2	41.3	5.0	8.8
I Dream of Jeannie	2	37.1	9.0	12.2
Bewitched	3	36.6	6.7	11.6
I Dream of Jeannie	3	36.4	9.2	15.9
Bewitched	4	33.2	7.8	8.9
I Dream of Jeannie	4	21.1	6.3	21.3

arise from their meddling. To do magic, Samantha wiggles her nose, which is typically revealed to the audience through a close shot on Montgomery's face. Jeannie's magic, triggered when she crosses her arms and nods her head, is better framed by a medium or long shot, which is why we might not expect more close shots in the first act.

Across all narrative acts, the proportion of group shots on I Dream of Jeannie is higher compared to in Bewitched. The rate of group shots increases for both shows from the introduction to Act 1 and again from Act 1 to Act 2. Group shots are less common in the denouement on Bewitched but are at the highest observed level in I Dream of Jeannie. Overall, these results indicate that, as the plot builds, a more significant proportion of wide shots are utilized. These wider shots help to convey the complexity of the conflict. For example, in the example episode "Business, Italian Style," wide shots are used throughout Act 2 to capture the interaction of Darrin, Larry, and their two business clients. In workplace scenes, wide shots provide the opportunity to show NASA as grand and impressive in comparison to Samantha's middle-class home or Darren's office in Bewitched. Act 2 in Jeannie has a significantly larger proportion of wide shots in which three or more characters are present. In both shows, however, these shot changes visually reflect the increasingly complicated relationships unfolding in the episode. The initial problem in Bewitched may involve only two characters, such as Darrin and his boss. However, additional characters are drawn in throughout the episode, creating additional strain and opportunity for comedy. These characters either extend the problem to other relationships, as in the episode "Business, Italian Style," or signal failed initial attempts to resolve the plot. The increase in wide shots serves to represent and visually contain these increasingly involved plot lines.

The shot type chosen for the first and last shots of Acts 1 and 2 reveal distinctive stylistic decisions. All four of these shots occur on the boundary of a commercial break; the opening shots attempt to draw the viewer in, and the closing shots try to keep viewers sticking around until the next act. Table 5.7 gives the proportion of close shots and close two shots used in the opening and closing of each Act, as well as the proportion of other Act 1 and Act 2 cuts for comparison. While overall over 40 percent of shots are framed closely across both series, less than 20 percent of the first and last shots are closely framed.

By putting shot type and median shot length together, we can draw a more precise analysis of shot semantics. Table 5.8 shows that first shots tend to have significantly longer durations. Shot type and duration establish and continue the narrative by expanding the gaze of the viewer: at the start of each act, this widening establishes the mise-en-scène, situating the characters in the spaces of work and home, and at the ends of each act, the wider view increases the tension by gesturing to all the characters and scenarios that remain to play out. Now that we have explored how visual elements help structure the narrative arc of these sitcoms through the increased complexity of shots and relationships throughout the episode, we move toward studying the individual relationships among the series' characters.

Table 5.7
Percentage of shots that were classified as close shot or two shot from both Act 1 and Act 2 as a function of whether the shot was the first in the act, last in the act, or somewhere in the middle

Series	Location	Act 1	Act 2
Bewitched	First	13.4	17.3
Bewitched	Middle	47.7	44.4
Bewitched	Last	8.7	6.3
I Dream of Jeannie	First	6.9	9.9
I Dream of Jeannie	Middle	47.2	47.5
I Dream of Jeannie	Last	16.0	8.4

Table 5.8
Median shot length in seconds of long shots for Act 1 and Act 2 as a function of whether the shot was the first in the act, last in the act, or somewhere in the middle

Series	Location	Act 1	Act 2
Bewitched	First	9.4	10.0
Bewitched	Middle	4.5	4.2
Bewitched	Last	6.5	5.5
I Dream of Jeannie	First	6.5	9.7
I Dream of Jeannie	Middle	4.3	4.3
I Dream of Jeannie	Last	4.4	4.9

Exploring Character Pairs

Our analysis of character centrality has focused on the role of a single character within the visual landscape and narrative of a series. Sitcoms, though, primarily advance their plots through series of dialogues. To better deconstruct these components of *Bewitched* and *I Dream of Jeannie*, we must assess the relationships between characters. As is the case with character centrality, there are many ways to quantify visual relationships between characters. Combining insights from several of these approaches yields a more complete picture of how visual style reinforces the connections between characters.

One straightforward method for assessing the relationship between characters is to compute the amount of time that any pair is observed on-screen together. In other words, we need a version of table 5.1 for each pair of characters. Similar analyses of character relationships have been used to produce social networks in the study of novels and plays.[49] For example, one previous study used television scripts to produce a network analysis of the main characters in the TV show *Friends*.[50] Here, with our visual annotations, we can produce more accurate measurements of the amount of time a pair of characters are involved together in the same scene. This measurement approximately counts periods when both characters are presumed to be present on the set, but the camera may temporarily frame only one of them. For instance, a sequence of close shots alternatively cutting between two characters should count as time that they are seen together.

The first metric in table 5.9 shows the average minutes per episode for which a given pair of characters have both been observed within three shots

Table 5.9

Summaries of character pairs: average time (in minutes) per episode that the two characters are separated by at most three shots, average number of two shots the characters are in together each episode, and the average number of close shots that cut between the two characters in each episode. The names of the character pairs are ordered alphabetically.

Series	Character pair	Avg. time	Avg. two shots	Avg. close shots
Bewitched	Darrin-Samantha	10.39	2.85	12.13
Bewitched	Darrin-Larry	6.88	0.72	3.94
Bewitched	Endora-Samantha	5.31	0.46	3.67
Bewitched	Larry-Samantha	4.98	0.08	1.61
Bewitched	Darrin-Endora	3.84	0.07	0.68
Bewitched	Endora-Larry	1.63	0.00	0.09
I Dream of Jeannie	Roger-Tony	9.36	3.57	5.37
I Dream of Jeannie	Alfred-Tony	7.40	0.72	4.76
I Dream of Jeannie	Jeannie-Tony	7.35	1.56	8.47
I Dream of Jeannie	Alfred-Roger	5.05	0.45	1.36
I Dream of Jeannie	Jeannie-Roger	4.36	0.86	2.03
I Dream of Jeannie	Alfred-Jeannie	2.73	0.01	0.37

of one another. Many of the results confirm expected patterns: Darrin and Samantha are the most connected *Bewitched* characters, followed by Darrin and his boss, Larry, and Samantha with her mother, Endora. The lowest relationship is the connection between Endora and Larry, which is unsurprising given that Larry is unaware of Darrin's magical mother-in-law. The relatively high connection between Larry and Samantha, which at first may appear surprising as she spends so little time at her husband's workplace, is explained by their frequent interactions in the Stevenses' home and over the phone, combined with Samantha's general centrality in the series.

The character pair relationships in *I Dream of Jeannie* provide insight into how the relationship structure between the characters differs from those in *Bewitched*. The three most significant relationships are the connections of each character to Tony, which provides further evidence of Tony's centrality in the series. Tony is seen on-screen most frequently with his friend and colleague Roger, followed by Alfred, and then Jeannie. After Tony's relationships, the next pair with the most time on-screen is the remaining workplace-based pairing of Alfred and Roger. This ordering of characters further challenges the similarity between the structures of these two series.

In contrast to the centrality of the domestic space in *Bewitched*, *I Dream of Jeannie* focuses strongly on male comradery and relationships established in the workplace. The weakest correlation occurs between Alfred and Jeannie: just as Endora is being hidden from Larry on *Bewitched*, so do Tony and Roger work to keep Alfred from meeting the irrepressible, supernatural Jeannie.

Measuring the amount of time characters are on-screen together reflects the overall prominence of the characters in each show and provides evidence of the connections between them. A different approach is needed to uncover how the *nature* of relationships is visually reflected. Cuts that move from a close shot of one character to a close shot of another character establish a connection between the pair. Using the estimated shot classifications in our data, we can estimate the rate of cuts between close shots of character pairs. By eliminating the visual space between the characters, the visual cut affirms an intimacy or emotional intensity between the individuals in question, although, as is the case with comedy, it is "all in the timing." To account for the different amounts of time that each character is present in an episode, the rates can be defined as the number of cuts per minute in which both characters are visually present.

The last column of measurements in table 5.9 displays the observed rates of cuts between close shots for all twelve pairs of characters. The pairs with the highest rates are Darrin-Samantha, Roger-Tony, and Jeannie-Tony. The hidden relationships, Endora-Larry and Alfred-Jeannie, have the lowest rate of being on-screen together. These results mostly follow the patterns observed in table 5.9, though the connection between Tony and Jeannie is significantly greater than Tony's relationship with the other three characters. Further, the relationships revealed by these relative rates indicate the presence of strong visual relationships that strengthen the established narrative-driven connections—sometimes a connection so strong that dialogue is unnecessary. Counting how often two characters appear in nearby shots is primarily a function of the script. However, unspoken exchanges, indicated through eye contact or body language, might not translate to the script and instead come out through performance. Thus, even after the narrative elements are controlled, an important and observable relationship is still only detectable through the show's visual style.

Relationships between characters can also be established through their presence together in a two shot. Standing side by side, facing the camera as a pair, the two shot visually establishes a united front by which two characters engage with the remainder of the constructed space. Rates of the number of two shots relative to the time spent on camera together, for each pair of characters, are shown in the next-to-last column of table 5.9. For *Bewitched*, the highest rate of two shots is associated with Darrin and Samantha, followed by Darrin and Larry, and then Samantha and Endora. These are the same three pairs we have seen at the top of all plots, but the relative ordering is essential. How often do the two characters act as one unit? Darrin and Samantha constantly perform this role when speaking with their daughter, Samantha's family, and Darrin's boss and clients, indicating the strength of their union even when they might be at odds. They are also literally a team, in it together. This visual pattern cues us to the critical pattern of sitcoms: relationships will remain stable, any conflicts resolved or reset by the end of the episode.

Darrin and Larry often function similarly when conversing with advertising clients, while Samantha and Endora occasionally unite to perform spells and incantations together. A similar explanation holds for the pairs in *I Dream of Jeannie*. By far, the highest rate of two shots belong to Roger and Tony. These two are often treated as a singular unit at work, taking whatever blame or praise arises as a collective unit. This pattern is strongly represented through the visual style of a shot closely framing the pair. Is Roger and Tony's bromance, then, the primary relationship of the series, or is *Jeannie* a show in which the conflict between male and female is even more fraught and challenging? Furthermore, might this pattern change as the show progresses and Jeannie ultimately settles for a more sedate domestic existence as Mrs. Tony Nelson?

Taken together, the results presented here illustrate that production and editing techniques on *Bewitched* and *I Dream of Jeannie* visually reinforce the character relationships established by each show's narrative structure. There is a close visual intimacy established through successive close shots and common two shots between Darrin and Samantha, whom we have already shown are, together, the two most central characters on *Bewitched*. A similar intimacy is established between Tony and Jeannie, which is particularly interesting given that the sexual tension between them was hidden in the individual and overall counts. Close relationships between employers and employees are also formed through visual cues, but less so with romantic pairings. Finally, the emotional separation of the "odd" pairings is also established through visual dissonance. While Samantha and Larry appear onscreen for a similar length of time as Samantha and Endora (see table 5.9), they are far less likely to appear together in successive close shots or a two shot.

Exploring Magical and Feminine Gazes

Our final analysis leaves more questions than answers by looking at the feminine gazes of the shows, an important area of analysis in film and media studies.[51] As mentioned, the Samantha and Jeannie characters are similar or parallel; both are magically gifted women trying to navigate stereotypical White suburban life in the 1960s. As we have shown, a closer analysis reveals that Samantha and Jeannie function in dramatically different narrative roles within their respective shows. These differences, in turn, affect the way that each is visually portrayed. Despite these divergent roles, are there stylistic similarities between these two characters? To answer these questions, we investigated those metrics that look at relative relationships between visual style tropes, rather than overall tabulations, as we did with the character centrality analysis.

The proportion of time each main character spent in close shots relative to the time seen in all shots is shown in table 5.10. By taking the relative proportion of close shots, a new pattern emerges. The three magical female characters all have a significantly larger proportion of their total screen time in close shots than do the other characters. The overall ratios for *Bewitched* characters are higher than those in *I Dream of Jeannie*, and Alfred is slightly

Table 5.10

Proportion of time for which each character is shown in a close shot as a ratio of the total time they are present in the show

Series	Character	Proportion close shot
Bewitched	Endora	26.9
Bewitched	Samantha	25.0
Bewitched	Larry	17.4
Bewitched	Darrin	17.3
I Dream of Jeannie	Jeannie	21.2
I Dream of Jeannie	Alfred	12.8
I Dream of Jeannie	Tony	9.3
I Dream of Jeannie	Roger	7.5

more likely to be shown in a close shot than Tony and Roger. Given that the pattern here diverges from those seen in the character dominance metrics, it seems likely that the close shot ratios enforce a different visual characteristic and achieve a different narrative objective.

While there is a clear signal in the data identifying a visual aesthetic uniting Samantha, Endora, and Jeannie through the high proportion of close shots, it is not possible within this corpus to offer a confident hypothesis on the specific meaning of this effect. The high proportion of close shots might be due to a common trope for representing female characters or due to a focus on women's appearances. Because the three are the primary magical characters, this style may instead be an attempt to represent their otherness, with the close shots giving the viewer a chance to gawk at the magical incantations and garish costumes. At the same time, the narrative sets them apart as different, even isolated by their powers. Another, more positively empowering reading would be that these magical women co-opt the screen, stealing the show from their male counterparts. Then again, the large proportion of close shots could be a direct function of the popularity of each actor, Montgomery and Eden being the leading ladies and Agnes Moorehead (Endora) being an established star in her own right. Indeed, all these possibilities are plausible. Archival evidence, studio notes, and interviews with creators would be further evidence to help further address these areas of inquiry.

Conclusions

In many ways, the study of American television is indebted to David Bordwell, Janet Staiger, and Kristin Thompson's formulation of "classical Hollywood cinema," in which all aspects of film form are in service of conveying narrative, and "character-centered . . . causality is the armature of the story."[52] Put another way, all elements of film form—from editing to sound—follow character action, which in turn motivates the story. The hidden complexities of Hollywood classicism have been examined in numerous cinema studies accounts, leading us to ask to what extent the "invisible" style of Hollywood film allows for ideological inconsistencies, generating tensions between benign storylines and quietly subversive forms.

Using facial recognition algorithms and shot boundary detection, we bring these questions to the study of the American television sitcom, itself a character-driven dramatic form and one typically dismissed as middle-brow commercialism, lacking in formal or stylistic rigor. As Jeremy Butler writes, "all television programs employ conventions of the medium,"[53] but we ask what tensions, contradictions, and paradoxes are buried in these seemingly facile conventions? The "schema" of the situation comedy—the "bare-bones, routinized devices that solve perennial problems," to borrow Bordwell, Staiger, and Thompson's language[54]—can be the vehicle for messages that belie the content of the story, speaking to the fissures and frictions that characterize the fraught second-wave feminism of *Bewitched* and *Jeannie*. Given that network-era sitcoms are often dismissed as formless middle-brow fluff, it is striking to find that the visual elements show the noticeable difference between these two series and serve to reinforce and question character relationships and gender politics.

Through our use of automatically generated annotations produced by computer vision algorithms, combined with associated metadata, we have been able to explore the visual style and messages of these two network-era sitcoms. By detecting shot breaks and identifying character faces, we have been able to describe the dominance of each of the main characters in the series, examine the relationships between characters, and describe how the narrative flow is influenced by shot type and shot duration. Specifically, we found that Samantha is the most central character on *Bewitched*, and her strongest visual relationships were with her husband Darrin. Conversely, in *I Dream of Jeannie*, Tony is the most central character, and the most frequently seen pairing on the show are Tony and his coworker Roger, followed by his boss, Alfred. Together, these findings challenge the scholarly and popular categorization of *Jeannie* as a close copycat of *Bewitched*. Rather, we see that the former is largely a workplace sitcom with a strong focus on the particularities of working at NASA in the 1960s. In contrast, *Bewitched* is predominantly centered on the domestic space and suburban family life.

The exploration of these sitcoms leads to additional points about distant viewing. The first is that the approach can be a powerful lens into naturalized and subtle, yet no less powerful features. The repetition of a media form such as the sitcom combined with its scale, such as a decade of a single series, can make it challenging to identify and see a particular feature across the duration of a series. However, it does not mean that there are not weighty, if understated, stylistic choices shaping the narrative. Distant viewing offers one way to surface features and ways of seeing and makes them explicit.

Another insight is how layering custom and out-of-the-box algorithms combined with aggregation of the annotations offers a way to reconfigure computer vision to the ways of seeing that we need for our areas of study, in this case time-based media. While some of the annotations in this chapter are built on existing computer vision techniques, we also used custom algorithms for shot boundary detection and shot type identifications. The building and interpretation of the custom and out-of-the-box algorithms are informed by theories from fields such as media studies and semiotics showing how computer vision, and distant viewing more broadly, are in important conversations and debates with the humanities and social sciences. As this chapter demonstrates, the process of figuring out which annotations to look for and how to map them onto the concepts and theories that guide our analysis is central to distant viewing.

A final methodological note concerns the scale of this collection. In terms of the overall amount of data, the collection studied here is many orders of magnitude larger than those studied in the previous two chapters. It is certainly possible to sit and watch all the episodes of these series. However, it is another task entirely to review specific elements of each series repeatedly as we ask new questions and add more annotations. Watching an entire series takes substantial time, but a computer can review all of its episodes with a relatively high speed and precision that allow us to expand the scope and scale of our analysis. We can then explore with new annotations as our questions expand; a reminder that the steps of the method as outlined in chapter 2 are iterative. Distant viewing provides a method for understanding this process. Of course, as in all our examples, this does not mean we do not look closely as well. All our primary conclusions were only possible through the combination of our numeric evidence with our experience watching these two series and our knowledge of the social and industry conditions that they were produced within. Distant viewing, therefore, is about identifying and accounting for the ways of seeing through computer vision in relationship to the cultural, economic, historical, political, and social context of the algorithms and the corpus. These connections will guide the analysis in the next and final chapter, which focuses on how distant viewing can contribute to the access and discovery of the holdings of a large encyclopedic art museum.

6 Opening the Archive: Visual Search and Discovery of the Met's Open Access Program

Over the past few decades, cultural institutions of all sizes have created digital copies of many of their collections. These include digital scans of documents and visual materials, digital recordings of analog tapes and records, and digital photographs of material objects. Having digital copies of collections serves several purposes. When working with fragile materials, such as nitrate film, digitization creates a long-term preservation copy while also reducing the need to circulate physical objects. Digitization makes feasible the distribution of copies beyond the physical institution. Digital surrogates also allow the use of computational approaches to study collections using distant viewing.

Recently there has been a push for large institutions to make their digitized collections freely available to the public, a model and philosophy called *open access*.[1] Copyright issues can make this problematic for relatively newer works, but organizations have been successful in making collections of out-of-copyright works available for bulk access. The US Library of Congress was an early adopter of this model; they made a version of the FSA-OWI collection studied in chapter 4 available online in 1994 through the American Memory project.[2] As of early-2023, they currently allow public access to several million digital images spanning hundreds of different collections. Other large private and national museums have opened collections of a similar scale. The Netherlands' Rijksmuseum API provides access to metadata and images for several hundreds of thousands of images.[3] Since 2017, the J. Paul Getty Museum has made thousands of images available through their metadata server.[4] The Metropolitan Museum of Art's API released hundreds of thousands of images and associated metadata into the public domain.[5] Following this trend, in February 2020 the Smithsonian released 2.8 million digital images into the public domain.[6] And the Musée du Louvre published metadata for nearly half a million records and one hundred thousand digital images.[7]

The commitment to digitization and open access has led to calls within libraries, archives, and museums (often known as LAM for short) to expand possibilities for accessing their collections. Some LAM professionals call for the idea of "collections as data," which encourages the application of computational approaches.[8] As a result, more recent work has been undertaken on the possibilities for data science and machine learning by organizations such as OCLC.[9] Institutions such as the Library of Congress have been at the forefront of new experiments with how machine learning can facilitate access and discovery, in projects such as the Newspaper Navigator.[10] The publication of large image collections by these LAM institutions has been a key part of enabling the kinds of computational analyses we have seen in the previous chapters. In addition to this kind of academic analysis, however, perhaps the biggest motivating factor for institutions such as the Library of Congress, the Met, the Getty, the Louvre, and the Smithsonian in publishing these images is to engage online with a wide public audience. When institutions make collections available online, visitors can engage with the museum in new ways.

Given that large museums typically display only a small percentage of their holdings at any given time, access to digitized collections provides an opportunity for visitors to see parts of the collection that may otherwise be inaccessible. For example, the Library of Congress has outlined a strategy to expand access through digitization to "throw open the treasure chest."[11] The Smithsonian's 2022 Strategic Plan identifies a goal of "reach[ing] 1 billion people a year with a digital-first strategy" to support their purpose: "the increase and diffusion of knowledge."[12] As institutions that support and create knowledge, their commitments to digital access—particularly open access—offer new opportunities for the public to explore, learn, and research. With the increased focus on access to and discovery of collections, we ask how distant viewing can make digitized collections of materials easier to access, search, and explore.

This chapter demonstrates how distant viewing can help us navigate and understand a collection of digital images from an encyclopedic museum. We accomplish this goal through the creation of a digital public interface, a common tool for facilitating the analysis and exploration of digital archives.

Our interface addresses the challenge of searching through a digital collection. Often, archives are searchable through a single search box, perhaps augmented with several facets such as object type or time period. How can we use computational methods to allow the public to explore and identify patterns and characteristics? Similarly, how can we create interfaces for interpreting collections both in alignment with and against existing organizational structures? A visitor might want to read across an institution's organization of their collection to find expected and unexpected connections, but metadata is based on text fields often inputted by an archivist or curator, leaving out significant visual information in the images themselves. How can we enable search and discovery based on visual elements that are not explicitly coded in structured metadata? Distant viewing offers a method for facilitating access to and discovery within collections, thereby supporting important efforts for open access. This work supports fields such as archive studies, information science, and public humanities.

In addition, distant viewing offers a way to see with, across, and against the organizational logic of collections, opening the collection to questions about categorization, collecting processes, and institutional priorities. The cultural power of social institutions such as museums is a significant area of study in fields such as American studies, library and information science, museum studies, and postcolonial studies. Museums and archives hold immense power over defining what counts as knowledge and which parts of the past and present to collect, preserve, and feature. Examining the holdings of institutions is one way to understand their scope as well as to pose questions about their organization and holdings in line with the questions that animate fields such as museum studies.

To demonstrate how distant viewing can address these areas of inquiry, we turn to the publicly available images published by the Metropolitan Museum of Art in New York. In 2017, the Met made available approximately a quarter of a million images of items in their collection. Understanding the scope of the data is a tall task. Looking individually at each photo is not only time-consuming but makes it challenging to see the larger patterns. A further opportunity and challenge are the organization of the collection by department, such as Musical Instruments and Medieval Art. The organization into departments is also complicated by the different approaches to categorization. For example, some departments are based on a type of object while other departments are organized around a region and time frame. This can make seeing connections across the entire collection based on features such as a certain object type or within the same period of time across departments challenging. Reading the metadata is also difficult because decisions were made that are often specific to each department, making it hard to find certain types of connections across the corpus based on the metadata alone. How do we understand the scope and scale of the collection and make it more accessible and navigable for visitors?

To address these questions, we will focus on two specific objectives. First, we will create a recommendation system that creates connections between images that share related features such as composition, objects, and texture. Designed to suggest content in a large corpus, recommendation systems can guide visitors through the collection in expected and unexpected ways. A recommendation system creates an endless, customized, and interactive path through the collection as visitors iteratively click on recommendations and follow them to subsequent pages. When implemented on a public interface, the system offers visitors a way to browse the collection beyond search and textual metadata, and now through visual connections.

Our second task will be to look holistically at the clusters of images in the collection by drawing on the scale of analysis afforded by image embeddings. Each cluster will contain images that are more similar to each other, in some sense, than they are to most other images in the collection. Looking at example images from each cluster and how the clusters relate to one another offers insights into the scope and components of the collection. This approach moves from individual items to a global view of the collection along different features such as materiality and not just department. We can remix the collection in ways that offer a range of themes, categories, and connections. Together, these two tasks allow us to see the shape of the collection both locally, through recommendations from specific starting images, and globally, through the analysis of large-scale clusters. The overall goal is to see how distant viewing opens avenues of exploration to facilitate access to cultural institutions.

Any of the features constructed in the previous chapters could be used to create both the recommendation system and image clusters. For example, as in chapter 3, we could recommend images that use a similar color palette, and cluster images based on their most dominant hues. Alternatively, as already briefly mentioned in chapter 4, we could recommend images that have a similar set of detected regions of objects and stuff. Even the face detection in chapter 5 could be adapted by relating images based on the number, size, and positioning of faces detected in each image within a collection. While each of these options could produce exciting and usable results, there are some cautions. We created the features in the previous chapters to address specific research questions from different fields of visual culture studies. There is a specificity to their annotations that could be less generative to a broad exploration of the Met's collection. Therefore, we turn to another type of algorithm that gives us a more flexible space for our annotations, which will provide multiple avenues of exploration and connections.

While no recommendation system is perfect, we might be best served by finding a more generic set of features to explore a digital collection. To expand our ways of viewing the collection, we will move from supervised to unsupervised methods. *Supervised models* focus on predicting a specific output. Supervised tasks include all the computer vision techniques used in chapters 3 through 5, such as detecting objects, labeling background textures, or identifying faces.[13] *Unsupervised learning* tries to identify general structures within a dataset without a direct predictive task.[14] Common unsupervised learning tasks include determining the similarity between objects in a collection, detecting correlations between annotations, and learning how to group objects into clusters.

Drawing on a more general-purpose approach, this chapter will explore image similarity scores using image embeddings. Our approach offers a different kind of interpretative space to see broad patterns, which the recommender system will help us explore, organize, and communicate. The technique of image embedding allows us to quantify the degree to which two images are similar to one another without relying on a precomputed set of implicit features.[15] Two images may be similar for several different reasons, such as sharing similar textures, using similar compositions, or containing similar types of objects. An embedding can perform all these types of similarity simultaneously, providing a broader set of connections than those that use only color, objects, or faces. We will then show how these similarity scores can be used to identify clusters within the entire collection and then visualize them to find patterns and outliers at scale through a digital public interface built to feature the recommender system.

While powerful, image embeddings should not be seen as a panacea that avoids explicit biases when computing distances between metrics.

The similarity measurements created by unsupervised algorithms remain influenced by the kinds of datasets that were used to develop them. Further, approaches to unsupervised learning are often closely tied to specific supervised learning tasks. For example, the image embeddings created in this chapter are closely related to the supervised task of object detection. Persistent challenges and their possible solutions when using embeddings to generate automatic recommendations to visitors will be explored in the following sections.

The structure of this chapter follows the structure of the previous applications, but the content is slightly different due to differences in the nature of the task. In chapters 3, 4, and 5, we formulated domain-specific research questions and addressed them using a distant viewing approach applied to collections of visual materials. We performed the communication step, described in chapter 2 and featured in figure 2.1 outlining the distant viewing method, by the very act of publishing the text, tables, and figures contained within each chapter. Here, our aim is to create a public digital interface for exploring a collection of images. The communication part takes the form of an interactive digital interface, which can be accessed through the text's supplementary materials, located here: http://distantviewing.org/book. The content of this chapter describes the techniques used to create the public interface and some reflections on patterns found by using it. These are useful for providing a critical eye toward the decisions and underlying assumptions that mediate the work of public interfaces while also serving as a guide for creating a public interface for other visual collections. For the full payoff of distant viewing, visit the digital interface through the link above.

In the following sections, we begin by giving a short description of the underlying techniques used to create image similarity scores and cluster analysis using the technique of image embeddings. We then look at the metadata fields provided as part of the Met's image collection to understand the limitations and possibilities of searching and understanding the collection using the existing textual fields. Following the metadata analysis, we will take up the two main tasks in this chapter by building a recommendation system and image clustering using our image similarity annotations. We will be able to explore the extent to which these annotations, when combined with the existing metadata, can add to our understanding of the collection. Finally, we conclude by connecting our approach to recent scholarship in public humanities as well as library and information sciences.

Annotating Image Embeddings

We have applied several complex and advanced computer vision algorithms throughout the previous chapters. Understanding the environment in which these algorithms developed, and their relative strengths and weaknesses, has been important in considering how they can be used for the computational treatment of collections of digital images. In this chapter, we will be using image embeddings, which are constructed by manipulating the internal structure of another model intended for a different purpose. Describing the nature of these embeddings and gaining an intuition for their application in building recommendation systems and image clustering requires understanding how the original deep learning models are built.[16]

To understand the overarching concepts behind deep learning, we start by thinking about the steps we would go through to build a model that classifies whether a photograph was taken inside or outside based on the average brightness of its pixels. We might begin by manually collecting fifty photographs taken outdoors and fifty photographs taken indoors. Next, we would compute the average brightness of each of these one hundred photographs. If outdoor photographs tend to be brighter, the model we will build consists of finding a cutoff score A, such that any photograph with an average brightness less than A is predicted to have been taken indoors and any photographs with an average brightness greater than A is predicted to have been taken outdoors. The cutoff is selected such that the predictions are as accurate as possible on the one hundred photographs that we have manually labeled. While this model is quite simple and likely to make many mistakes, we can still imagine that a model trained in this way could learn to be significantly better than random guessing in predicting whether an image was taken indoors or outdoors.

The example model has exactly one *parameter* (A) corresponding to one *feature* (average brightness). We could try to make the model more accurate by adding additional features. For example, natural light is bluer than artificial light. We could incorporate a second parameter (B) corresponding to a new feature consisting of the ratio between the average blue intensity of each image divided by the average brightness. We could then build a new model with two cutoff values, A and B, and say that an image was taken outdoors if either the average brightness is greater than A or the ratio of blue light to the rest of the light is greater than B.[17] As before, we would select the cutoff values to maximize the accuracy of the model on our hand-labeled data. By adding features and parameter values in this way, it is possible to develop a fairly accurate predictor of whether a photograph was taken indoors or outdoors.

The algorithm described above is an example of a *shallow model*.[18] It is called this because there is a direct path from each input feature to its impact on the output prediction. The cutoff parameters, in this case, tell us explicitly how each feature (brightness or the ratio of blue light) relates to whether a photograph was taken outside. While the examples here were relatively small, shallow models can be highly complex, with many powerful examples containing hundreds of thousands of features and millions of parameters.

Deep learning takes a different approach to building a predictive model from data. Rather than applying predetermined summaries of the images, deep learning models start with the images themselves. The algorithm adaptively learns to create numeric features from the images while simultaneously choosing the parameters that relate the new features to the output predictions. The features and parameters are chosen together to create a model that accurately predicts the output values on a hand-labeled dataset.

Returning to our indoor/outdoor prediction task, suppose it is true that the ratio of blue light to the rest of the light is a robust predictor of whether an image is taken outdoors. In that case, a deep learning model would adaptively discover that this feature is an excellent way to summarize images. The features are determined using a similar process to determining the cutoff values, as described above. First, we find a way of describing all possible features in terms of a large set of parameter values. Then, we use a series of mathematical techniques to determine values for these parameters that produce models that make accurate predictions on our training data.

Rather than jumping directly from the input images to the final features that we will use to build a set of predictions, deep learning models partition the process of creating features into a sequence of transformations. Starting with input images, a deep learning model may learn several billion meta-features, which are used to construct the final features used in the predictions. Reconsidering our example, we can imagine a model that starts by creating three meta-features: the average intensity of the red, green, and blue pixels in an image. Our two final features take the average value of the meta-features (brightness) and divide the blue intensity by the brightness. The process of creating intermediate steps, or *layers*, within a deep learning model can be iteratively expanded to create as many different steps as desired. The *depth* of a model refers to the number of intermediate layers.[19] The term *deep learning* comes from the fact that these models, unlike shallow learning, undergo several intermediate steps before producing predictions.

Modern deep learning models typically have many intermediate layers. Theoretical and empirical results have shown that deeper models can be more predictive at the expense of being more difficult to build.[20] The art of designing deep learning models often comes down to finding the ideal balance between these two competing properties that are inherent in increasing the depth and complexity of a model.

To describe how deep learning can be used to produce a generalized notion of image similarity, we will first look at the structure of a typical deep learning model used in computer vision. Figure 6.1 shows the structure of a model called VGG19, which was designed to identify the probability that an image contained any one of one thousand different kinds of objects.[21] The number 19 refers to the number of layers in the model. The diagram describes how a single image would be transformed through each of the nineteen layers to produce a set of one thousand different probability scores. First, the image is scaled to be 224 pixels high and 224 pixels wide. Then, a series consisting of two different sets of transformations is applied to the image. These preserve the two-dimensional structure of the image and act locally on parts of the image. The resolution of the features is then reduced by half, and the process of applying two sets of transformations is repeated once more. The successive series of transformations and shrinking of the image is done a total of five times. In the final two layers of the model, the dimensionality of the input image is removed, and we are left with a final set of 4,096 (two to the power of twelve) numeric features. These features can be summarized to produce probabilities that an image contains a specific instance of any of the one thousand objects.

The intermediate features created within the interior of a deep learning model tend to exhibit an important behavior. If the model task is sufficiently broad and the dataset sufficiently diverse, the intermediate features will learn to detect general properties of images that are meaningful outside of the original specific task used to train the model. When researchers have looked at the features generated by models such as VGG19, they have found that the first few layers capture elements such as color, texture, and edges.[22] In contrast, the remainder of the layers put these elements into

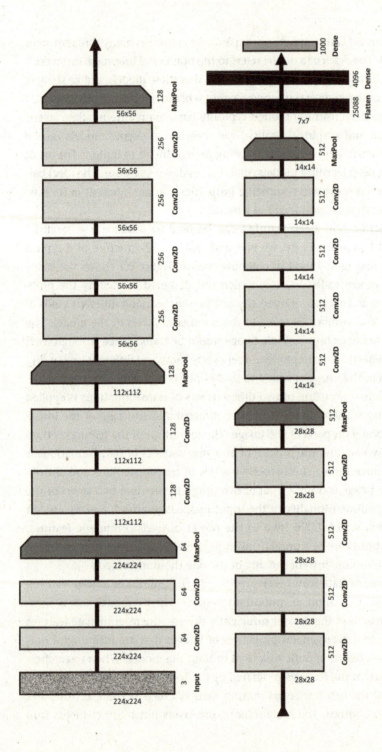

Figure 6.1

Diagram of a deep learning model, VGG19, for image recognition. An input image is placed into the layer on the left-hand side of the diagram, and a set of one thousand probabilities are output on the right-hand side, corresponding to the categories in the ILSVRC. Image created by authors.

increasingly large and complex shapes and objects. The specific categorization into the object types predicted by VGG19 is primarily achieved in the
final layer of the deep learning model. This feature of deep learning models
has important implications for annotating and exploring digital images,
and it is perhaps the most important aspect for their widespread use in
computer vision research.[23]

While a model like VGG19 takes millions of images and a substantial
amount of computing power to train from scratch, the generalizability of
the internal features allows one to build a model that detects or classifies
different kinds of objects with only a few hundred example images using
the method of *transfer learning*.[24] This process is similar to the method we
described above. First, we would take a model, such as VGG19, trained on
a sizeable predictive modeling task. Then, we apply the existing model to
each of our new images. Rather than saving the output probabilities, we look
only at the 4,096 automatically generated features produced by the second-
to-last layer of the model.[25] Finally, we would build a relatively simple,
shallow model that relates these generated features to our manually tagged
data. This approach has been shown to work surprisingly well on various
tasks, such as classifying lung tumors on chest scans, identifying musical
instruments in Italian Renaissance art, and distinguishing the slight differences between hundreds of different types of songbirds.[26] These examples
were done with at most one hundred examples from each category, modest
computing power, and relatively simple models built on top of the features
learned from entirely different predictive modeling tasks. The application
of transfer learning allows researchers to re-train on a new object of study
and customize annotations to explore new research questions.

How does all of this relate to our primary goal of determining whether
two images are similar to one another? The internal features learned by a
large deep learning model can be transferred to another task, often resulting
in a predictive model even though the model was initially trained for a completely different task. This indicates that the internal features capture generic
aspects of the images. Therefore, if two images have similar features, there
may be a salient similarity between the two images. Generalizing this idea,
we can define the similarity between two images by the distance between
their sets of automatically generated features. This technique is called *image
embedding*.

We can use image embeddings to generate a recommendation system based on visual similarity. A visitor to a digital public interface looking at a specific image in the collection, for example, can be recommended the other images in the collection that are closest within the embedding space. This approach creates annotations by noting relationships between objects and images with broad similarities that were not explicitly accounted for or searched for. When combined with metadata, the image embedding annotations allow for an exploration of the relationships between visual similarity and existing archival information. While an image embedding will not make the reasons for the connections explicit, we can infer which features guide the recommendations by exploring the results.

Image embedding provides a way to automatically produce a set of recommendations that show which images in a collection are (in some sense) closest to each other. We can expand on the recommendations to build an understanding of the entire collection of images. To start, we associate each image with a fixed number of its nearest neighbors; our applications in this chapter will use a set of fifteen neighbors for each point. Then, we use an algorithm called uniform manifold approximation and projection (UMAP) to represent these neighborhoods within a two-dimensional space.[27] Specifically, the UMAP algorithm tries to spread out points that represent each image in the collection in a two-dimensional box such that the closest neighbors to each point in the two-dimensional space are the same as the closest neighbors described by the full set of automatically generated features from the neural network.[28]

Once relationships between images are described in two dimensions, we can plot the images as points and see the larger shape of the collection. As the data is now in only two dimensions, any standard clustering method will break the data into similar groups of images. We discuss our choice of clustering algorithms and further explain the implications of the UMAP method in the following sections. The more significant point is that we can use it to explore and communicate the results to describe prominent themes and structures of the embedding space. We will check and augment this analysis by looking at the photos in the clusters, which a recommender system also facilitates, and drawing on the metadata to see and understand any patterns, connections, and outliers.

In the following sections, we will apply the technique of image embedding and the UMAP algorithm to a collection of digital images provided by the Met. We will use the final set of features provided by a deep learning model called InceptionV3.[29] This model was also trained to detect the same one thousand objects that was used with VGG19. Our experience using different deep learning models has shown that this specific choice is a good option for producing image embeddings that work well for building recommendation systems. The structure of InceptionV3 is a bit more complicated than the VGG19 model that we used as an example here, but the general concepts are the same as described above.

Organizing the Met's Open Access Collection

The Metropolitan Museum of Art of New York City, more commonly known as "the Met," is located on the eastern side of Central Park. One of the city's most popular tourist attractions, the museum has a permanent collection of over two million works, making it the largest art museum in the United States. The Met's collections contain a wide variety of works. The museum's stated goal is to present "over 5,000 years of art from around the world for everyone to experience and enjoy."[30] Though certainly not without criticism, its commitments to archeological exploration, preservation, and curation have been essential to introducing the public to histories of human creative expression, as well as providing a source of evidence for academic scholarship across a wide range of fields.[31]

In early 2017, the Met announced that they would be releasing an extensive collection of digital records into the public domain as part of their new Open Access program. Where possible under current copyright and donor agreements, several hundred thousand digital images were released along with a significant portion of the collection's associated metadata. Additional objects and data have been added into this collection since then. The original press release explains the rationale behind the publication of the digital collection:

> As of today [February 7, 2017], all images of public-domain works in The Met collection are available under Creative Commons Zero (CC0). So whether you're an artist or a designer, an educator or a student, a professional or a hobbyist, you now have more than 375,000 images of artworks from our collection to use, share, and remix—without restriction.[32] This policy change to Open Access is an exciting milestone in The Met's digital evolution, and a strong statement about increasing access to the collection and how to best fulfill the Museum's mission in a digital age.

The Met has an incredible encyclopedic collection: 1.5 million objects spanning 5,000 years of culture from around the globe. Since our audience is really the
three billion internet-connected individuals around the world, we need to think
big about how to reach these viewers, and increase our focus on those digital tactics that have the greatest impact. Open Access is one of those tactics.[33]

The press release clarifies that the primary audience for the release of this
digital collection is the broadest possible public, and articulates three main
avenues for how releasing the Open Access program would increase public engagement with their collection. By releasing the collection into the
public domain, other outlets such as artists, educators, and writers can now
integrate digital images from the Met directly in their materials. This helps
reach audiences that may not be actively seeking out art historical content
in the first place. Second, the digitized collection is made searchable and
available on the Met's website. This facilitates access for visitors who are
actively searching for materials, a compelling form of access for those who
cannot visit the physical museum. While it is not the primary motivating
factor, the release of the entire digital records opens the possibility for creating novel digital methods for exploring the collection online. This task is
the one that we will investigate in the following sections.

Our focus is to support using, sharing, and remixing a digital collection
of images through distant viewing to further access. How can we view with,
against, and across the organizing logic of the museum? What patterns,
themes, outliers, and absences can we find? An excellent place to start is to
first look at the existing structured metadata associated with our collection of interest. The Met Open Access program provides a downloadable
spreadsheet with one row for each record in the collection. There are fifty-
nine variables in the dataset providing information about catalog numbers,
access restrictions, author information, a title, and several other structured
fields about the record. The collection is periodically updated; as of this
writing, there were over 475,888 items in the dataset, of which 245,104
are in the public domain. The URL locations for downloading the public-
domain artworks were not contained in the dataset. We accessed these
by calling the Met's API, and include them as an additional variable. This
allowed us to download and store a copy of the nearly quarter-of-a-million
digital images associated with the public-domain records.

Several of the variables in the dataset provide access to the organizational and descriptive information found in the physical museum.[34] The

Met's holdings are split into nineteen different departments, with the permanent galleries primarily organized according to these departments. The department associated with each item is provided as one of the metadata variables. For those materials currently on display, a gallery number is also recorded in the data. In addition, the dataset includes information that would help museum staff or researchers link back to all physical objects, such as the object number and the repository name. Finally, additional variables contain the information typically included in a gallery display: title, artist name, and the acquisition date. Together, all these records open the possibilities of creating a digital version of the physical organization of the museum.

The metadata also contains several variables providing the location and period in which each object was created. These variables provide a rich view of the different scopes of the collection. However, we encountered some data challenges because the format for recording space and time depends on the object type and collection. For example, one variable captures the city where the object was presumed to have been created. This field is filled in for most works in the Islamic Collection and many of the records from the American Wing and the Arts of Africa, Oceania, and the Americas. However, it is missing from all records from the Egyptian Art and Greek and Roman Art departments. Instead, the excavation site number and the description are used to describe the location of these materials. Detailed records about where physical objects were found, such as "Pit 763, burial of Senebtisi," are contained in metadata variables "locus" and "locale." Over two thousand records are given locations based entirely on the names of rivers where objects were excavated or found.

The recording of the date on which an object was created is similarly differentiated by its associated department and culture. One unified field called "object date" is filled in for most of the objects. In most examples, the object date is given at the specificity of a century or range of centuries. Some records, particularly print culture, give specific years or narrow year ranges. Perhaps the most promising time records, however, come from other variables in the data. A field called "period" is used to categorize Chinese Art into classical periods used within the field, such as "Ming dynasty," "Meiji period," and the "Middle Kingdom." Likewise, other fields capture the reign and dynasty associated with objects from the Egyptian Art department. In contrast, records associated with the fifteenth century and onward contain their most complete and precise dates in two fields giving the years that an artist was born and died. While the specific creation date for many artworks may not be known, information about the artists is often easier to find and curate. Domain expertise guides the ways that dates are represented in the metadata across the departments. However, the variation in the way dates are given can make it challenging to use the metadata to explore possible connections across departments.

One field in the data contains a set of pasted-together keyword tags associated with each object. The Met has embraced a Linked Open Data model for the tags; they use a controlled set of tags provided by WikiData and link specific tags within the metadata. While some tags explain the object's materiality, most focus on describing what is represented within the artwork. Some tags capture the people represented in the image, such as "Saint John the Baptist," "Buddha," and "Mary Queen of Scots." Other tags, such as "Dresses" and "Dogs," describe specific object types. Many tags also capture relatively abstract qualities of the artworks. There are hundreds of images labeled as "Street Scene," "Ruins," and "Death." The method used to construct these tags is not documented in the API. However, it appears to be primarily automated using the titles and descriptions of each record.

To summarize, there is a lot of rich and interesting information contained in the metadata provided by the Met's Open Access program. Each of the variables of data mentioned above can enable interactive ways of exploring and remixing the current collection. However, the current metadata largely follows the organizational logic of the physical museum, which is primarily organized by department. This creates a challenge when looking for connections across departments and exploring the collection as a whole, and therefore addressing questions about what counts as part of the histories of fine art. The way that place and time are described in Egyptian Art, for example, is entirely different from how these categories are described in the Islamic Art department. At the other extreme, the categories used to describe the records tend to be relatively coarse. This makes it hard for users to quickly find objects that are similar to one another within a specific collection, such as two pages from different illuminated manuscripts that feature very similar patterns. These two tasks—building a recommendation system and clustering the items in the collection—offer significant potential for us to further explore the corpus using a computational approach applied to the images themselves.

How can we build ways to explore and remix the collection as the Met recommends? We now move on to applying the distant viewing method to the public-domain images available from the Met's Open Access program. We start by looking at how image similarity through image embedding— our type of annotation—allows us to find sets of visually similar objects in the collection, and discuss how this augments the structured metadata that accompanies each record. Then, we use a similar technique to explore how image embeddings can map the entire collection by breaking it into concrete clusters of similar items and showing how they intersect. Neither of these techniques replaces the kinds of search and analysis enabled by the structured metadata nor the important context provided by the data. Instead, combining the annotations with the rich metadata fields that we have briefly outlined offers an exciting way to explore the collection across multiple dimensions.

Exploring Image Recommendation Systems

When visitors enter a gallery, they are provided a set of items that a curator has placed in conversation with one another. The curator develops themes, subjects, and messages to communicate to audiences. Influential exhibitions also prompt new questions and subjects to explore, thus speaking to the power of the museum to produce and spur new knowledge. As custodians of many of the objects critical to understanding the human experience and the natural world, museums are potent cultural and social institutions. It is why collections, exhibitions, and even the existence of a museum are often the site of intense debates.[35] While only a fraction of a museum's holdings are on view, digitized access to collections offers its own challenges, with the scale often becoming unwieldy. How can we find ways to navigate the collections that will reveal existing and novel connections across the collections in a manageable way? Image embeddings paired with recommender systems offer one approach.

Using the methods described in the previous sections, we ran all the digitized, public-domain images made available by the Met through the InceptionV3 neural network. Each image was scaled to a square image that is 299 pixels high and 299 pixels wide. We stored the embedding of the second-to-the-last layer of the neural network, consisting of 2,048 numbers, and associated each image with the other images in the collection that had the most similar set of embeddings. To explore and communicate the results, we created a recommender system. As an information filtering system, recommendation systems are designed to suggest relevant items based on the feature chosen. For example, one could build a recommendation system based on characteristics such as colors, objects, image segmentation, or image similarity. Such systems have been popular in domains such as retail. Think, for example, of all the times that an e-commerce site recommends new items based on your previous search or purchase history; or a social media platform suggests a new entity to engage with. Recommendation systems are also increasingly adopted in libraries, archives, and museums, where they might recommend a similar book, film, or artwork.[36] They are compelling systems for trying to filter through large collections and can engage with the interests of a range of audiences.

This section will explore the opportunities and challenges of the image embeddings approach for the automatic generation of object recommendations. There is no catch-all metric for determining how well a proposed recommendation system performs. Determining their effectiveness requires looking at the results, assessing the connections, and thinking about the audience. As with assessing and interpreting the results, domain knowledge about the data is necessary. A recommendation system designed as an exploratory tool for an individual researcher garners different considerations than one made available to public audiences, such as the millions of visitors to the Met. To investigate the recommendations produced by these image embeddings, we will look at several examples of the generated recommendations and qualitatively describe how they perform.

After running the image embedding algorithm, we pulled a random set of one hundred starting images and looked at the first four nearest neighbors. We manually selected ten images that illustrate the breadth of different patterns found in the recommendation system. The results of these recommendations are found in figures 6.2 and 6.3. The first image in each row shows the starting image; the other four images show the images that are closest to the starting image in the embedding space. The images are displayed with equal height and width in order to illustrate the form used in the embedding algorithm.

The first row of results in figure 6.2 starts with an image of a baseball card. The card depicts a pitcher from the Brooklyn Dodgers and is part of

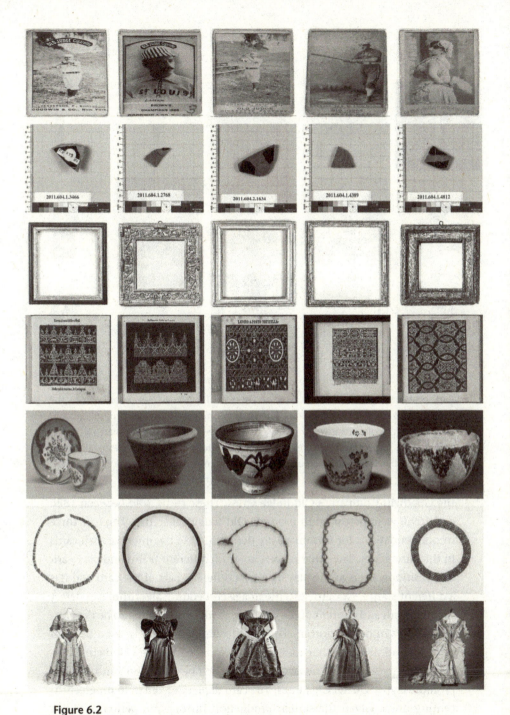

Figure 6.2
Examples of images' nearest neighbors using the penultimate layer of the Inception V3 deep learning model. The first column gives the starting image, and the other four columns give, in order, the four closest images to the starting image. The starting images were selected from a set of one hundred examples to illustrate how the algorithm works across the collection.

Figure 6.3
Further examples of images' nearest neighbors using the penultimate layer of the InceptionV3 deep learning model. The first column gives the starting image, and the other four columns give, in order, the four closest images to the starting image. The starting images were selected from a set of one hundred examples to illustrate challenges that can arise when using automated predictions in a public setting.

the Goodwin Company's Old Judge series. These cards, sold between 1886 and 1890, were produced to promote Old Judge Cigarettes. The first three recommendations for this image are determined to be other baseball cards in the same series. The other players are from different teams and play various positions. Each of the players is in a different part of the card and has a different stance. Nonetheless, the image embedding algorithm can detect that the form and content of the cards are sufficiently similar to be the closest matches in our algorithm. The final recommendation is not a baseball card. Instead, it is another trading card produced by the Goodwin Company: the Actors and Actresses series, produced between 1886 and 1890 to promote Gypsy Queen Cigarettes. The card depicts a woman in nineteenth-century dress. Given the similar production history and period, it is not particularly surprising that the image similarity algorithm finds links between these two collections within the same department. Nevertheless, a closer look at the metadata reveals how it could have been a challenge to move across the two collections, for they share very few metadata terms in common. The image similarity suggests that we should consider looking at both types of trading cards, which could offer insights into topics such as commercialism, popular culture, leisure, and health in the late nineteenth century. An added benefit is that the results offer a good check to ensure the algorithm is making informative connections. Along with helping us check the algorithmic decision-making, our first example highlights how getting outside of the original metadata can produce connections across an extensive, diverse collection of images.

The public-domain collection released by the Met contains many images of Ancient Greek and Egyptian archeological fragments. The second row of results shows an example of the recommendations generated from one of these fragments. The reference image here depicts a fifth-century BCE Attic Greek kylix (small drinking cup) fragment. All the recommendations are also fragments from the exact location and time period. Each image contains the same color and size references on the outer border and a similarly positioned catalog number on a white strip of paper. Because of the uniformity in the composition of the images, even relatively simple types of image similarity algorithms—for example, matching color histograms or even directly comparing pixel intensities of downsampled images—would have been able to relate the archeological fragments to one another. What is impressive about the image embedding technique is that it can connect these pottery fragments even though it is primarily designed to detect high-level semantic elements within images; finding fragments is a way of seeing that is far away from how the model was built. The ability of the embeddings to preserve compositional elements of the input images illustrates how the technique of transfer learning makes it possible to reuse models on tasks that are far outside what the model was initially trained on. Here, it has enabled us to find visual connections across the geographic departments defined by the Met's organizational logic.

The third set of recommendations in figure 6.2 illustrate a similar relationship from a different period. Starting with an image of a wooden, possibly British, picture frame from the eighteenth century, the image similarity algorithm found four other images of frames. These images come from the Robert Lehman Collection and range from the seventeenth to the nineteenth century. The frames are built from various kinds of wood (poplar, pine, and spruce) from different regions (Southern France, Veneto, Lombardy, and Bologna). The recommendation system's links facilitate connections across time and place and opens up questions about the roles of frames and framing as they changed over time, which is an object of study in art history. Visually looking at the recommendations, we see several similarities. The frames are photographed on a white background, feature at least two different components, and are heavily textured. As with the pottery, several different image algorithms would likely relate these images to one another. Interestingly, while image embedding is designed to capture semantic elements in photographic images, it is also able to simultaneously detect lower-level similarities of features such as texture and composition.

The first three examples show that the image similarity algorithm, when applied to an extensive collection of diverse images, can group images based on various semantic and textual elements. They provide a way to access, explore, and remix the collection that can offer expected and unexpected connections. Based on the recommendations, we can explore questions within each set. Are there similarities between these five pottery shards that distinguish them from the seventeen thousand other fragments in the Met's collection? There are nearly four hundred different images of frames. Why are these the four recommendations that were chosen by the image embedding algorithm? Without looking at a more extensive collection of the possible images, these are difficult questions to answer. Our efforts to look within these object types found that the images of trading cards, pottery fragments, and frames were so similar that it was hard, even manually, to find visual elements that distinguish some objects from others. Our close looking, at minimum, offers confidence that the algorithm is connecting similar images. The degree of interest in the specific sets will be driven by the visitors' areas of interest in the collection.

The fourth row in figure 6.2 provides a fascinating example to look at how the image similarity algorithm works within a particular set of objects. The fourth starts with an image from the seventeenth page of a Venetian manuscript of pattern designs. The Met has thousands of images of early modern European manuscripts; as in the first three examples, the image similarity algorithm has found four other images of manuscripts from a similar time and location as the starting image. However, in this case, we can offer a good explanation of the specific pages chosen by the algorithm from the large set of available manuscript pages. The five selected images come from different manuscripts, spanning a variety of national contexts. The manuscripts were all published between 1545 and 1620, and feature design patterns for different mediums. The closest match, for example, comes from the French manuscript *La Pratique de l'Aiguille*, which features seventy-two pages of knitting patterns. The second closest match is a manuscript initially published in Antwerp featuring design examples from Islamic art. Therefore, in this example, we see that the image similarity algorithm has done more than identify a broad category of objects. Instead, it has found a small target set of objects from different manuscripts to produce links between different woodcut pages featuring various design examples. While information about individual manuscript pages is captured in the existing metadata, the image embedding provides a specificity to their similarity that was not captured in the metadata and therefore adds another layer of connections to explore within the manuscripts. The image similarities, therefore, open the possibility for exploring the Met's collection in a way that expands on the existing metadata.

The final three examples in figure 6.2 further demonstrate how image similarity can help surface connections across the collection by cutting across spatial, temporal, and geographical metadata as well as the organizational logic provided by each department. The connections between images are based on the types of objects depicted in each of the images. These are closer to the computer vision task that the InceptionV3 model was trained on. Most of the similarities found in these examples would have been difficult to find using simpler alternatives.

The fifth row starts with an image of a French porcelain cup and saucer dated 1760. The image embedding recommendations show four different cup-shaped objects that come from across the Met's collection. The first is a Coptic bowl from the Medieval Art department, dated between 300 and 700. In the second recommendation, we see a bowl produced in Korea during the fifteenth century. The following recommendation depicts a beaker produced in Japan around 1700; while created in Japan, it was initially intended for the European market, and so the Met houses this object in its European Sculpture and Decorative Arts department. The final object is another bowl held in the Ancient Near Eastern Art department dated between the fifteenth and twelfth centuries BCE. The recommendation system, in this case, has fulfilled the promise of finding meaningful links across the Met's collection. The recommendations span an extremely wide range of time periods and locations, finding cup- or bowl-type objects from four different departments of the museum. While it is important to be culturally specific when naming and describing objects, note that even a textual keyword search would not have associated these five objects with one another, as each department used different terms—saucer, bowl, earthenware, and beaker—to describe them. A person interested in foodways or the domestic sphere would need to search by a plethora of words for the same and similar concepts, while visual similarity provides a way to cluster these connections in a way that can be challenging using the metadata. The recommendations for the French porcelain cup and saucer thus offer a telling example of how image similarity can cut across the organizing logic of a collection.

The sixth example, which starts with an image of an Egyptian string of beads, provides a mixture of the behavior of the connections seen in the previous examples. The second, third, and fourth closest recommendations from the collection are other strings of beads that also come from the Egyptian Art department. These artifacts span from the fifteenth to the twelfth centuries BCE and depict circular objects composed of tiny beads of the mineral carnelian and the tin-glazed earthenware faience. The closest recommendation, however, is a Celtic torc from the fourth or third century BCE. So, while several of the recommendations would have been found based on the metadata, one recommendation creates an interesting link between an ancient Celtic object and one created a thousand years earlier in Ancient Egypt. The heterogeneous mixture of connections, some within and some across the existing metadata fields, is typical of many of the recommendations within this collection. The recommendations build connections across multiple features that we may not have thought to put in conversation. All of which can be explored through the digital public interface.

The final example in figure 6.2 starts with the image of a French evening dress from the early twentieth century. The recommendations produced by the image embedding algorithm find four additional dress images from the Met collection, all of which show silk dresses produced within 150 years of the starting image and held in the department of the Costume Institute. Three of the four dresses are French, and the fourth is American. These recommendations seem quite sensible at first glance and do not appear to cut across the organizing logic of the Met's collection. What makes these images interesting is the metadata attached to the dress in the first recommendation. Both the description of the object and the title of the object mistakenly caption this item as a "suit" rather than a dress. Therefore, creating recommendations based on the metadata would have placed this dress object in with the formal male-oriented costumes in the collection. Here, therefore, we see an example where an image-based algorithm not only opens a new connection that goes across the metadata but a connection that reveals a problem in the structured data associated with the museum's collection.

The examples in figure 6.2 demonstrate a variety of recommendations that offer expected and unexpected connections across time periods, locations, nomenclature, and departments. Rather than assuming which feature to view, we drew on the benefits of an unsupervised model. We let the way the algorithm views, with its more abstract annotations, establish the connections based on kinds of similarities that were not predetermined. We could then map the results onto concepts and features we could establish due to our familiarity with the collection, knowledge of history, and visual culture theory.

We now turn to the second set of recommendations, which highlights some of the potential challenges that arise when allowing an automatically generated recommendation system to create links between objects. In figure 6.3, we have three additional sets of recommendations produced by our image embedding algorithm. As with the first set of images, a glance at the results reveals that the algorithm generally selects images that share some compositional or semantic relationship to the starting image. Yet, this set offers crucial cautions if the system is to be used in a public interface.

The first set of recommendations in figure 6.3 is based on the image of an eighteenth-century Japanese arrowhead. The third recommendation for this image is a bronze Sassanian arrowhead, found in present-day Iran, believed to have been created sometime between the third and seventh centuries. This is a useful recommendation that finds a link between two similar objects from diverse parts of the museum's collection. The other three recommendations come from across the collection; while they have similar shapes to the Japanese arrowhead, these other recommendations depict very different objects. The first is a fifteenth-century German gauntlet, the second is a bone toilet box, and the final recommendation is an eighteenth-century Italian musical instrument. These recommendations would be a tremendous exploratory tool, as they highlight different objects in the collection for the general public, even if most of them are only moderately related to the starting object. For researchers, the benefit of the one connection between the two arrowheads would be worth the time needed to sort through the three additional recommendations that are likely unrelated to the task at hand. However, an interface presenting these results would need to clarify that they are automatically generated and may contain some uninformative and erroneous relationships.

In the second row of figure 6.3, we see a set of recommendations based on an Ancient Egyptian figurine. The object is described as a glass "amulet of baboon in the act of adoration."[37] In some ways, the recommendations generated by the visual embedding in this example provide a great way of exploring other relevant images in the collection. All four of the other images show small figurines from various cultures and time periods. However, the potential difficulty in this example comes from the fact that the visual similarity algorithm associates the figurine of a baboon with figurines of people. The results bring to mind the long history of racialized stereotypes being portrayed through allusions and direct comparisons between groups of people and animals. While the specific example here does not suggest a particular relationship between the images, this example shows the possibility of such a relationship being automatically generated by a computer vision algorithm. Clear labeling of algorithmically generated recommendations, as in the previous example, can help address some concerns along these lines but is by no means a panacea.[38] Upon identifying potentially problematic relationships, we might manually remove such links. We will return to a full discussion of this important question in the final section of the chapter.

Our final example recommendation starts with an albumen silver print photograph of Countess Virginia Oldoini Verasis di Castiglione. The results combine the issues of the first two examples. The first recommendation is a drawing of an English mastiff. The resemblance between the countess and the mastiff is likely due to the similarity in colors and composition between the two images; the original images are also heavily deformed in the process of making them square (the countess is a vertical photograph, and the mastiff is drawn as a landscape). Regardless, this connection again highlights the problems that can arise when automatically generated recommendations intermittently link images of people to images of animals. The second recommendation for the image of the countess is a photograph of a woman in a similar pose but in a very different context, while the third is a photograph of a man posing in a very similar fashion. According to the image embedding algorithm, the fourth closest image in the collection is another photograph of the countess from a different angle. While each of these recommendations could be explained as making sense on their own, there are various aspects of the starting image—composition, objects, and textures—that make the collection of recommendations hard to understand as a set. In addition, we see another example of a human-animal connection that could be upsetting if put into a set of public-facing search results. Attention to how to address and rectify such potentially problematic relationships requires careful consideration when developing a digital public interface. We will return to the solution implemented in our interface in the following sections.

We have seen only a small set of recommendations generated by the image similarity algorithm. The other ninety results we looked at generally produced patterns similar to those in the ten examples shown in figures 6.2 and 6.3. Also, looking at the top twenty-five recommendations for each object produced similar recommendations, but with more room for one or two errant recommendations that were hard to explain based on our understanding of the images. Overall, the results shown here illustrate that image embeddings generate meaningful relationships between different images that can be used to find a variety of different similarities among objects that both reinforce and cut across the structured metadata of a collection.

Exploring the Full Public-Domain Corpus

In addition to providing recommendations of individual items in a collection, image embeddings support the visualization of an entire corpus of images. The scope and scale of the corpus can be visualized to create a more global understanding of the collection. Such a view offers insights into subjects, themes, and connections. Combined with metadata, the approach can reveal explicit and implicit features of the data. In the case of the Met data, we can look with and across the existing organization by department, facilitating exploration by expected and unexpected features.

As described earlier, we can take the closest neighbors of each image in the collection and apply the UMAP algorithm to arrange each image in a two-dimensional space that approximates the closest neighbors of the larger embedding space. In other words, the arrangement puts images that are close together in the 2048-dimensional space close together in a two-dimensional space. Exploring and visualizing the space created by the algorithm provides a way to more holistically view the collection of approximately 228,000 images and the clusters of images that are similar to one another, including seeing how these clusters are related to one another. The approach opens exploration of the scale and scope of the collection, collecting decisions including organization, and the relationships between departments.

The best way to visualize the output of the UMAP algorithm is to view the output using an interactive application. To start, we might have a plot where each image is arranged in a two-dimensional space and represented by a small thumbnail image. Such an application would allow us to zoom in and pan over the space of all the images so we could better understand each part of the embedding. Interactively zooming in and out over different parts of the collection begins to paint a picture of the entire set of images and how they fit together. Tools such as the Yale Digital Humanities Lab's PixPlot offer one solution. At the lowest level of zoom, one can approximately understand the image recommendations themselves. Seeing how these recommendations relate to one another and how we could slowly follow the recommendations from one image in the collection to many others connects the results from the previous section with our larger-scale understanding of the collection.

Since this chapter is constrained to the limitations of static print media, we do our best to understand the structure of the Met's collection using only a few static images. In contrast, the digital version demonstrates how interactive visualizations of the collection at scale using image similarity can be a way to increase access while revealing connections for visitors to explore. This limitation of form does, fortunately, have some positive outcomes. Needing to tell a relatively complex story with limited images has forced us to find new ways to communicate information. Two of the plots, shown in figures 6.5 and 6.6, are relatively original ways of looking at the intersection of metadata and image embeddings. The ideal would be to pair these economical views of the UMAP embedding space with interactive visualization, but we will see that there is still plenty to be learned from

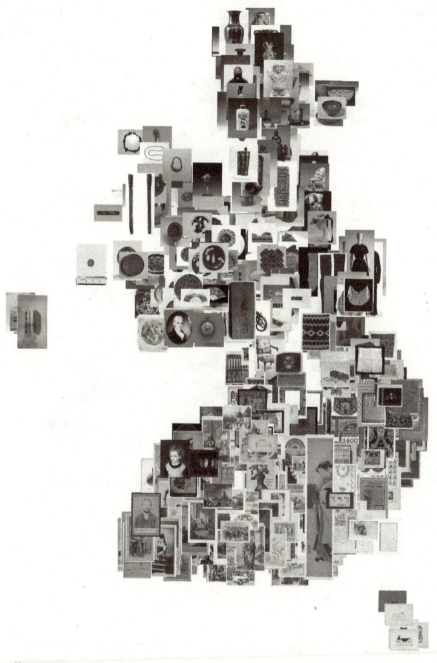

Figure 6.4
A selection of 750 images from the Met's public-domain collection using the UMAP projection of an image embedding induced by the InceptionV3 model. Images are centered on the coordinates of their projection and shown in their original aspect ratio. An additional cluster exists off to the left side of the plot, consisting of archeological fragments, but was removed to allow the rest of the images to be shown at a larger scale.

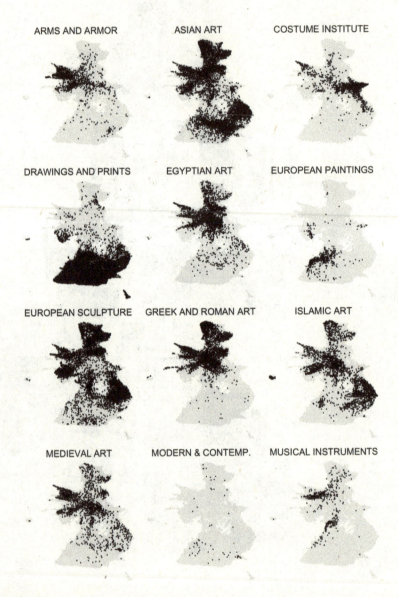

Figure 6.5
Each subplot shows in light gray the location of all the images in the Met's public-domain collection according to the UMAP projection of the image embedding induced by the InceptionV3 model. The black dots highlight where images from each of the twelve selected departments are in the plot. As in the previous figure, an additional cluster off to the left of the plot was removed to increase readability.

them on their own. Before moving on to these visualizations of the collection's metadata, we will look at the image embedding in isolation.

Figure 6.4 gives a visualization of the UMAP embedding using a set of 750 images randomly selected from the Met's public-domain collection. There is no independent meaning to the location where the images are plotted. Instead, the layout has been determined in a way that puts images that have similar embeddings near one another. Looking at the images in the figure, we see that most images are joined together in a large central group. For these objects, it is possible to follow a chain of nearest neighbors to move from any image to another, though the number of required jumps may be significant for images far apart from one another. In addition to the large central group, we see two independent groups: one set of images on the lower right-hand side of the plot and another on the left-most side. There had been an additional third independent group of images off to the far-left side of the plot, but it was not included so that the other images would be more readable. These isolated groups are not an artifact of the 750 images chosen; even if all the collected images were filled in, there would still be a gap between the main group of images and these isolated clusters. Looking closer at the images in these independent clusters will provide an excellent way to understand the global structure of the Met's public-domain collection beyond the institutional organization into departments and existing textual metadata.

The images in the lower right-hand corner in figure 6.4 come primarily from a single collection. These images are nineteenth-century drawings from the American carriage manufacturer Brewster & Co. There are 638 such drawings in the collection as identified by the image embedding model. The drawings include a large amount of white space with a lightly drawn sketch of a carriage, coach, sled, or similar object in the middle. Some images feature more intricate coloring details, but most are done in pencil, black ink, and a small splash of watercolor. Thus, the images in this set have a similar composition and color palette, and feature schematic diagrams of very similar objects. It is not surprising that the image embedding algorithm puts these figures closer to one another, particularly given that the InceptionV3 model we are using was initially trained to detect objects such as cars and bicycles. The new fact that the embedding shows us is that there is no other extensive collection of images in the Met's public-domain collection with a similar set of images. The carriage designs by Brewster & Co. are relatively unique within the museum's public-domain collection, something that would be hard to know based only on the metadata or looking at individual image similarity recommendations. This opens questions such as what features make this collection so unique, why these features are absent from the rest of the collection, and what this might indicate either about art or aesthetics during their period or about collection practices at the Met.

The other two isolated clusters of images feature images of small archeological fragments. These images are similar to the second row of image recommendations in figure 6.2. The large cluster that is not shown in our visualization of the UMAP projection consists of 5,300 objects primarily dated from the sixth and fifth centuries BCE, and nearly all described as terracotta fragments. Most objects within this cluster come from ancient Attica in Greece; there are also several hundred fragments from Etrusca and other cities located in present-day Italy and Greece. The images of these objects are all composed very similarly. They have the same scale in the background, are shot from the same angle, and contain a light-brown grid in their backgrounds. The second cluster of images, the one shown on the left-hand side of figure 6.4, consists of 668 archeological fragments from a different location and time period. These fragments are predominantly from sites in modern-day Iran dated between the twelfth and eighth centuries BCE. Most of the fragments in this group are carved or painted stucco. The first cluster of objects has a consistent composition, with extensive, empty off-white backgrounds and scales at the bottom as size and color references, offering another feature to view the collection through.

By identifying these two clusters of archeological fragments, the image embedding algorithm has helped us understand the Met's collection in two ways. First, we now have a way of identifying and isolating these fragments from the rest of the collection. Secondly, the image embedding has helped show that most of these fragments come from two distinct sets: earlier works of Ancient Iranian stucco and slightly more recent terracotta fragments from Attica. While it may have been possible to identify these sets based on the metadata alone, this is a tricky task because there are many ways these characterizations are made in the data. For example, the stucco fragments are described in over sixty different ways, with no canonical way of finding the term "stucco." Further, even if we could isolate these terms with the metadata alone, we would be left wondering if there were other objects in the collection from different places and time periods that also consist of small archeological fragments. Finally, the image similarity algorithm puts these two clusters on their own, suggesting that they are the only large sets within the Met's public-domain collection. Therefore, the clustering algorithm allows us to create automatically a metadata field with a tag for archeological fragments for all the objects in these two clusters.

Moving on to the large cluster of images in the UMAP plot, several patterns become apparent. The images are broadly divided with the paintings, drawings, and other figurative art at the bottom, and photographs of other pieces of material culture at the top. However, rather than an abrupt break between these two halves, there is an interesting link between them based on a combination of furniture, textiles, and clothing. Though these are photographs of material culture, they have patterns built into them that are connected with the drawings and paintings at the bottom of the plot. Within the art at the bottom of the cluster, we can see the further structure. For example, the left side at the bottom features more realistic artwork (perhaps even some photographs), and the right side consists of more abstract drawings. Above the abstract drawings, forming an additional link to the textiles in the middle, are woodcuts and illuminated manuscripts. There are several distinct clusters of images at the top of the figure as well. We can see groups of vases, cups, jewelry, coins, and pendants. Many of these correspond to the individual recommendations that were shown in the previous section. Over the entire cluster, though, note that there is a tendency toward smooth transitions from one group to another rather than rigid, distinct boundaries.

To get a deeper look at the structure of the images according to the UMAP plot, we need a way of seeing more detail than is possible using figure 6.4 on its own. As mentioned above, a typical next step would be to zoom in to a similar version of the plot with more images, panning in and out to understand how each part connections to one another. As an alternative, we will use the metadata in the Met's collection to understand how the embedding relates different objects to one another. In figure 6.5 we show a set of small figures that highlight where the objects from the twelve largest departments are in the UMAP embedding. Figure 6.6 shows a similar visualization based on twelve of the most used medium types. Looking at these figures together, we will verify and deepen our understanding of the largest component of images in the UMAP embedding.

Many images from the Drawings and Prints department are in the bottom portion of the UMAP embedding. This matches our visual inspection

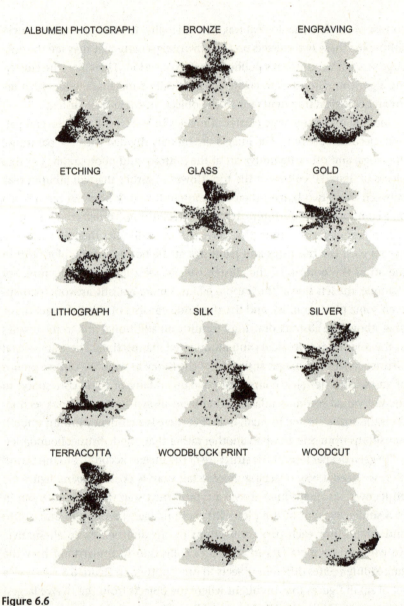

Figure 6.6
Each subplot shows in light gray the location of all the images in the Met's public-domain collection according to the UMAP projection of the image embedding induced by the InceptionV3 model. The black dots highlight where images from each of the twelve selected object types are in the plot. As in the previous figures, an additional cluster off to the left of the plot was removed to increase readability.

of the sample images in the previous figure. Photographs are mostly clustered together in the lower left-hand side of the plot. Next to the photographs are etchings and engravings. These mediums occupy the same space in the plot and appear difficult to distinguish from one another. Further to the right are woodblock prints followed by woodcuts. Slightly above the photographs and slightly overlapping the woodblock prints are lithographs. Finally, paintings are not shown as a specific medium in figure 6.6, but we can infer their location by looking at where the objects in the European Paintings department are placed. These are directly above the photographs, near and partially overlapping the lithographs. Putting all of these pieces together, we have a sense of how the UMAP space is laid out and, in turn, how the images of drawings and paintings visually relate to one another. In a very general sense, the embedding shows increasing realism on the left-hand side of the drawings and increasing abstraction on the right-hand side. Color and brightness are, in contrast, differentiated by the vertical position of the objects.[39] Those objects that are toward the bottom tend to lack color and be relatively unsaturated, whereas those toward the center of the plot are brighter and have more complex patterns. A more global view of the collection, therefore, offers insights into the aesthetic and compositional features that dominate the Met's collection, allowing us to identify patterns that are difficult to discern from a focused analysis of a smaller set of images.

Three departments at the Met focus on objects at the intersection of specific time periods and cultures. These are Arms and Armor, Egyptian Art, and Greek and Roman Art. We can see that these three departments have objects that occupy the upper portion of the UMAP embedding. Arms and Armor is particularly clustered on a specific arm in the upper left-hand side of the plot. The Egyptian department and Greek and Roman Art department have broader swaths of objects. Some overlap the Arms and Armor cluster, while others occupy a slightly lower arm of the embedding or the extreme top. To distinguish the upper section, we need to look at the materiality of the objects. Notice that the gold, silver, bronze, and glass materials roughly overlap different parts of the Egyptian and Greek and Roman Art departments. There is a relatively large intersection between gold and bronze, with silver and glass diverging more toward the top of the plot. Terracotta, likewise, has a similar pattern to glass objects. Taking all these together with the specific images we saw in the previous plot, we see that the material cultural objects have a different pattern than the drawings at the bottom of the embedding. The objects are clustered based on the specific types and shapes of objects: cups are next to cups, which are close to bowls, which are close to plates, which are close to coins. We cannot easily plot this relationship because these object types do not have a consistent description in the metadata, highlighting the value of incorporating visual similarity into the collection. However, we can untangle these connections by putting together various ways of visualizing the UMAP embedding. Along with indicating to the viewer that these forms of material culture are prominent in the collection, this approach opens areas of inquiry about the use of these items over time and enables the comparison of styles and practices that may be unique or shared across cultures and societies.

Two specialized departments provide further insight into how specific object types are clustered at the top of the UMAP embedding. The Musical Instruments department has only 1,668 objects listed in our dataset. In the embedding, these cluster around two different areas on the middle right-hand side. If we were to zoom into these two clusters, we would see that the bottom group consists of pianos and music boxes, and the upper group contains the various string, percussion, and wind instruments. The pianos and music boxes are close to other furniture images, whereas the other instruments are closer to tools and weapons. The Costume Institute has over seven thousand images in the public-domain dataset. Most of these images are placed near one another in a specific arm on the right-hand side of the embedding. We saw these in the previous plot consisting of dresses, hats, and other formal wear. There are also several hundred objects that overlap with the Arms and Armor section. Pulling a few examples shows shirts and hats that closely resemble chain mail shirts and helmets. Along with communicating to the visitor the scope of the collection, the cluster can open questions about clothing aesthetics and practices across communities, moving us from a local to a more global view.

There are also three departments at the Met that are defined primarily based on geography, covering extensive time periods: Asian Art, Islamic Art, and European Sculpture.[40] Except for the areas of the UMAP embedding covered by the Photographs and the Costume Institute, all three collections are spread across most of the large component on the embedding. This matches our understanding of both the top and bottom of the embedding space. All three collections have abstract and figurative art as well as material culture spanning many different types of objects. Recalling the most exciting connections made by the visual recommendations in the previous section, we can see at a large scale how the embedding can lay each of these geographically distinguished collections on top of one another and thus find otherwise obscured connections. There are, of course, some differences between the density of points in the three collections that mirror the different material focuses of each department. For example, the Islamic Art department has very few woodcuts and woodblocks, and the Asian Art department has many objects close to the section corresponding to colored lithographs.

Our extended tour of the UMAP embedding shows that the image similarity measurement has created a high-level structure for understanding the Met's collection. We can see along with and beyond the department structure and observe patterns that are not easily discernable through the metadata. The results complement our understanding of the algorithm and how it builds connections within the collection, which we developed by looking at individual image recommendations in the previous section. Notice that, in both cases, the visual similarity adds an exciting dimension on top of the existing metadata. As with all the applications in this book, the most exciting uses of computer vision usually combine metadata with features extracted from the images themselves rather than being based entirely on automatically constructed features. Our primary motivating factor in applying image similarity algorithms to the Met's collection was to show how image similarity annotations offer another way to explore the collection. We now turn to how this approach can be used in a public humanities interface that makes the collection easier for various audiences to explore and understand.

Communicating through a Digital Public Interface

Now that we have developed a system for creating recommendations based on visual similarity and studied the clustering of images based on an image embedding, we return to the task we outlined at the beginning of the chapter: how to make a digital public interface for search and discovery using this information. Given the scale and breadth of the Met's collection, a single search box or set of faceted searches can be overwhelming. A visitor to the site might struggle without an understanding of the collection's organizational logic and its ontologies. To address the challenge of using the search function, Mitchell Whitelaw proposes the idea of "generous interfaces" for digital cultural collections.[41] These interfaces help represent the scale and depth of collections using a variety of approaches. For our purposes, we created an interactive visualization based on image similarity to show recommendations and ways to move through the collection. In this section, we focus on the overarching design decisions behind the construction of our own generous interface.[42]

There is a large amount of research that has focused on the design of digital public interfaces, including within the fields of user experience research, human-computer interaction, communication studies, and the public humanities.[43] These communities have considered questions ranging from detailed decisions on the choice of font colors through complex considerations about what is meant by the term "public" and how that effects our work.[44] The research in these areas is important to consider whenever developing a digital public interface. Here, we focus on a specific set of considerations we found particularly interesting for this collection and that were integrated into the exploratory tool we built of the Met's collection.

Our public interface consists of three main types of pages.[45] The first page is a landing page that greets anyone first arriving at the site. Our goal with the landing page is to provide context for the data and instructions on how to navigate the public interface. We included a summary of the Met's collection, the goals of our work, suggestions for some initial queries, and a link back to this book. A particularly important goal of the landing page is to clarify that we are not officially working with the Met, but rather are working with the collection they generously allowed to be published under a public-domain license. Placing all the contextual information on a single page allows us to provide a lot of detail while not taking up valuable screen space on the subsequent pages, which are focused on the exploration and visualization of the collection. While most of the content on the landing page is textual, we include a background with images from the Met's collection to invite visitors to click through to the next page.

After clicking on the Enter button on the landing page, visitors are taken to the second type of page in the digital interface. This page has a grid of randomly selected thumbnails from the Met's collection on the left-hand side and a UMAP embedding of thumbnails on the right. Unlike the static images provided in this text, the embedding space enables visitors to scroll through and pan over the images. The sets of images in the embedding space are broken into specific clusters which can be clicked on. When a cluster is selected, images on the left panel are updated with images from the selected cluster. In the upper-right corner of the page are pull-down menus that allow visitors to change the embedding visualization by either recreating figures 6.5 and 6.6 or creating an alternative UMAP embedding with different tuning parameters. To take a closer look at an individual image, visitors can click on any of the thumbnails found in the left-hand panel of the page.

Clicking on an image thumbnail opens the third and final type of page in our digital interface, which focuses on a single image in the collection. A large version of the image is displayed on the left side of the page, with additional metadata shown to the right. A screenshot of the page is shown in figure 6.7. The image metadata includes both archival information taken directly from the Met and algorithmically produced information created by computer vision algorithms. A link back to the Met's page is also listed. To clarify which fields are algorithmically created and which were produced by archivists, we separate the two types by a thick horizontal line and label them clearly as "Archival Data" and "Algorithmic Annotations." To provide additional context, each field is followed by a question mark icon. When one hovers over the icon with one's mouse, a text appears describing the field and how it was generated.

At the bottom of the final page type are thumbnails of the images recommended by our visual recommendation system. The recommendations show other images in the collection that are most similar to the image whose page we are currently looking at, based on the image embedding algorithm. Clicking on a thumbnail opens the image-specific page for the selected image. These images are titled "Recommendations" rather than "Similar Images" to avoid making too strong a connection between the images. This helps contextualize the occasional difficult cases, but still does not fully solve the problem with cases such as those seen in the previous sections, where links are sometimes made between images of people and images of animals. To further prevent these kinds of issues, we ran the people detection algorithm from chapter 4 over the corpus and removed any links that were formed between images of people and images without people. As a final check, we have a link next to the recommendations to report any additional problems that still arise. Through user testing, we found that visitors often got stuck in a small part of the collection through following a series of recommendations. To help them cut across the entire

Visual Search and Discovery of the Met's Open Access Program

Taylor Arnold and Lauren Tilton

This interactive visualization was created to accompany our the book *Distant Viewing* (2023). More information about each element of the visualization can be displayed by hovering over the question mark icon. For more information, see the project's main page.

X

ARCHIVAL DATA [?]
Title: Frontispiece for Champfleury's "Les Amis de la Nature"
Year: 1922
Collection: Metropolitan Museum of Art, New York, NY
Department: Drawings and Prints
Artist: Félix Bracquemond
Artist Bio: French, Paris 1833–1914 Sèvres
Medium: Etching; fourth state of four
Dimensions: Sheet: 7 3/4 × 5 5/8 in. (19.7 × 14.3 cm)
Tags: Musical Instruments | Men | Portraits | Leaves

ALGORITHMIC ANNOTATIONS [?]
Dominant Colors: #7c5d3f ▪ ; #f0d2a3 ▪ ; #ba9460 ▪ ;
Brightness: 0.3
Detected Objects: face; tree
UMAP Cluster ID: 30

Recommendations [?]

Other Recommendations [?]

Figure 6.7

Screenshot from our digital public interface to the Met's open-source collection. The image shows information about an example image, including recommendations to similar images in the collection. A live, interactive version of the site can be seen at https://distantviewing.org/book.

collection, we decided to also include five randomly selected recommendations in addition to the five recommendations based on visual similarity. Finally, a prominent Exit button in the upper corner of the page returns visitors to the UMAP embedding page.

The existing public digital interface hosted on our website provides a working tool for exploring the Met's digital collection and understanding the potential applications of visual similarity and image embeddings for exploratory analysis of a digital collection of images. Of course, many additional aspects could be integrated into the site, such as more contextualization of the materials and faceted search across the archival metadata fields. As with software development, digital projects are never really finished. Instead, they continuously move through various phases from creation, iteration, and eventual retirement.[46] In this specific case, we are fortunate to have the existing search and archival functionality provided by the Met's digital website. Our goal is certainly not to replace the existing site. Instead, our aim is to offer a "generous interface" by "represent[ing] the scale and richness of its collection . . . [and] enrich[ing] interpretation by revealing relationships and structures within a collection."[47] Using image similarity and image embedding annotations, paired with the existing Met digital site, our digital public interface offers a way to explore and communicate the breadth and complexity of the public-domain collection through distant viewing.

Conclusions

In this chapter we have demonstrated how distant viewing can support access and discovery through the construction of a digital interface based on image similarity. Understanding which images are similar to one another opens connections, patterns, and outliers through features such as composition, material, and texture. The annotations can be combined with existing metadata to offer expected and unexpected pathways through the collection. Looking at how a small set of images are similar as well as how thousands of images are similar offers a way to explore connections at various scales, moving us from a few objects that we may be able to see inside the walls of a museum to the tens of thousands of items being preserved in storage. It is a particularly powerful approach when we scale up to the hundreds of thousands of images that a prominent encyclopedic museum holds. When incorporated into a public interface as recommender systems, image embeddings offer a way to access, explore, and discover an image collection.

The Met's public-domain collection serves as a great test case for the methods presented in this chapter but is more complex when we consider building a digital project based on the results. The Met's collection contains metadata that is significantly richer than most image collections. This was a benefit in explaining what the image embeddings were doing. For collections with less existing metadata, verification of the results would be more difficult, but the overall benefit may be even more significant. Image similarity is a relatively quick way to build connections, particularly compared to manually identifying features in each image. Whether augmenting existing metadata or serving as the primary way to search through a collection, image similarity can be a way to harness the visual information to recommend, cluster, and explore.

Another benefit of using the Met's collection is that it has a very heterogeneous mixture of objects, including drawings, paintings, material culture, and archeological fragments. Only a tiny part of this collection consists of photographs and realistic figurative art, the formats that most large image embeddings are trained on. Our work with this collection is an excellent testament to the embedding technique. Given the ability of image embeddings to produce reasonable results on a collection as heterogeneous as the Met's, applying it to collections entirely of photographs or a specific domain of art is likely to also produce informative results.

Recent advances in unsupervised learning, computer vision, and data visualization techniques provide a rich set of potential extensions from the analysis presented in this chapter. In applying image embeddings, we made many choices that affected the output. More insights and even richer interfaces may be possible if we evaluated and compared each of these choices. For example, we could use a different embedding model, a different layer from the model, and different uniform sizes of scale for each image. We could tweak various parameters that were used to create the UMAP embedding.[48] Though we treated image embeddings and the metadata as separate dimensions, we could have designed a different recommendation system by considering both simultaneously. As museums and cultural institutions look to computational approaches to facilitate access to and navigation of their extensive collections, there is exciting work ahead to determine best practices for applying embeddings models to generate visually based recommendations.

Unsupervised methods such as image embeddings offer exciting possibilities that come with cautions. Rather than determining the exact feature to view, such as a specific object, this approach allows the data to drive the connections. We can then map the annotations onto concepts informed by domain-specific knowledge. The results can also be revealed through information retrieval systems such as a recommendation system or visualization strategies that allow us to see globally, while literally at a distance. The challenge is that the connections made can be difficult to interpret and some can even be profoundly problematic, a significant consideration when we are scaling the results for public audiences. As we look to the future, being thoughtful and intentional about the ways we create and share will be fundamental for distant viewing.

As we develop and use deep learning models, understanding the algorithms' ways of seeing and practices of looking becomes more complicated. The combination of explicit and implicit decisions makes explaining the results more challenging. Deep learning builds its model from the input data itself; understanding the training set is increasingly key to understanding the ways of seeing through deep learning. When we turn to computer vision algorithms to annotate images, we subject ourselves to the limitations and biases of the type of annotations that have been privileged by the field of computer vision, the methods used to evaluate the algorithms, and the types of training data available. These are important considerations that we continue to grapple with in our own work and hope to highlight through the growing body of work applying computer vision through distant viewing to a diverse range of applications.

The last four chapters each focused on the application of a specific algorithm to a particular corpus. We intentionally grew in complexity to demonstrate how each algorithm brings possibilities and cautions. We also decided to look at a different type of data in each chapter to begin to demonstrate the range of analytical avenues made possible through our method. In each case, we could have continued to build the analysis using additional annotations, which exceeds the scope of this book. With that said, when doing distant viewing, we often find ourselves applying multiple algorithms to a corpus as the exploration of annotations combined with metadata garners new interpretations and new questions. It is in the process of iteratively moving back and forth between the steps that new insights and avenues of inquiry emerge. The method offers a way to see and view at scale. As we use this method, central is the theory of distant viewing outlined in chapter 1. Computer vision is a way of seeing that encodes and decodes meaning, and how we choose to view our data is a careful, cautious process accountable to the cultural, historical, political, and social conditions that infuse the algorithms, shape our data, and animate our areas of inquiry. When the humanities, social sciences, and sciences collaborate, we can build a better computational world. Let's go distant viewing together.

Conclusion

In the introduction, we opened with our experience building the digital project *Photogrammar* and explained how this project motivated our book. We released a third iteration of *Photogrammar* in 2021, which can be found at photogrammar.org. In addition to an updated map, timeline, and other ways to explore the archival metadata, the new site now includes a recommendation based on visual search using the methods presented in chapter 6. After more than a decade of work, we can present to visitors a way of visually exploring this important archive of documentary photography. The years spent on *Photogrammar* led to this book guided by two questions: How do computer vision algorithms view images and what information and evidence do they offer?

To answer these questions, we presented a theoretical framework for *distant viewing*, the application of computer vision methods to the computational analysis of digital images. We drew on semiotics, media studies, and visual culture theory to offer a critical understanding and a theoretical framework for how computer vision functions as a way of viewing and mode of communication in chapter 1. We demonstrated how the theory has guided us to a method for computationally working with digital images in chapter 2. Answering the question, What is this an image of?, is complex. Distant viewing asks us to slow down and ask pressing questions about how algorithms are designed with certain ways of seeing and then how they encode and decode messages from images. The theory and method hold us accountable to the ways of seeing and viewing through algorithms while offering a way to explore images in exciting ways.

We have offered four examples of how the method of distant viewing can be applied to different research questions. The applications focused on our own research interests in twentieth-century visual culture in the United

States and, in chapter 6, the public digital humanities. Each chapter discussed the careful decision making behind which ways we decided to view using computer vision algorithms. The applications built in complexity to demonstrate how everything from the seemingly straightforward annotations such as color in chapter 3 to 2048-dimensional neural network embeddings in chapter 6 involves nuanced decisions. We addressed the kinds of evidence algorithms can produce and demonstrated how interrupting the algorithmic results is informed by understanding the context of the data as well. The process of decoding messages from digital images is a series of human decisions supported by algorithms. The method—annotating with computer vision, organizing metadata, exploring the results, and communicating the findings—asks us to pause at key moments to think carefully about exactly what we are encoding and decoding. While we focused on digital images such as photography and TV, the method and theory presented can be applied to the study of any collection of digital images, which we hope others will do in the near future.

The affordances provided by computer vision are likely still in the early stages, and there is far more material available from both print and born-digital collections than have been studied so far. We have only begun to scratch the surface of what is possible in terms of building connections across institutions and domains of expertise. These connections allow us to imagine a world where algorithms and computations are not solely defined by the needs of for-profit technologies and surveillance organizations. We have had, for example, the great privilege of working with organizations like the Library of Congress, who are looking instead to put distant viewing in service of access to cultural heritage. What might be possible when we think about how our computational world might be in the service of a broader public good? As we do this work, toggling between out-of-the-box and custom algorithms will require a reconfiguration of who it as the table in developing computer vision. What ways of seeing do we want to build? What are the stakes? Who is affected? What can we learn? These are questions that distant viewing asks us to pause and address.

We hope that this work serves as a starting point for continued scholarship on the theory and application of distant viewing. As described in the sections at the end of this text, we have made several datasets available for readers to replicate and extend the explorations described in the preceding chapters. Readers interested in applying distant viewing to their own collections of digital images can make use of the distant viewing toolkit, open-source software that we have created and maintain.[1] Links and tutorials are available on the book's website. We now conclude with four provocations for future work that we think will be particularly fruitful.

First, we hope to see more computer vision tools explicitly designed for and guided by humanistic inquiry become available. As we have mentioned throughout, large private corporations currently produce the most popular software. Despite their origin, we have seen many examples of how these tools can be used to explore visual messages. At the same time, there is a lot of lost potential for applications that do not line up with industry needs. For example, we saw how the analysis in chapter 5 required building a custom shot-break detector. We need a broad and diverse range of people breaking, building, and reimagining computer vision.

Second, more work needs to be done exploring the possibilities of working with material that is under copyright. We made efforts in this book to include work on freely available data in the public domain in the United States, where copyright law is often shaped by for-profit corporations. However, this focus significantly reduces the available materials of study, particularly within film and television studies. Therefore, we had to work with material under copyright in chapter 5's study of television. It is possible that computer vision could help solve its own problem in this domain. Many annotations could be considered a form of transformative use under US copyright law.[2] Putting these pieces together requires more work on creating strong annotations, building tools, and working closely with scholars from a variety of domains.

Third, we hope to see more interdisciplinary collaborations such as ours working in this space. The challenges of applying computer vision to the study of digital images transcend traditional boundaries. Core questions require engaging with scholarship from engineering, the sciences, the social sciences, the humanities, law, and the arts. As we have seen, the computational exploration of images is a rewarding but challenging task. To extend existing work and realize the full potential of distant viewing, we need more people willing to work at the intersection(s) of these existing spaces. We have no doubt those collaborations will offer new methods and theories that will guide the future of our computational world.

Finally, distant viewing has the potential to intervene in current discussions about the role of algorithms in society. As computer vision algorithms

are deployed by governments and companies, how and what these algorithms see is becoming a pressing issue with high stakes. Our theory of
distant viewing disrupts the myth of "neutrality" through algorithms. We
are accountable to the ways of seeing that algorithms encode and decode.
We must think more capaciously and carefully about why and when we use
algorithms. Computer vision reflects our priorities and the computational
visual world we seek to build, and we are all accountable to the impact of
distant viewing.

Glossary

We have written this text to reach readers coming from a variety of different fields. Many of the key terms we use have slightly different meanings and traditions of usage across communities. When we first mention a term within the text, we provide our definition. Here we also aggregate definitions of important terms.

Annotation: Annotations are structured data produced by computer vision algorithms. Examples include dominant colors, predicted categories, bounding boxes, and embeddings.

Computation: Computation is the use of a computer to perform structured calculations and algorithms. Computations include the application of predictive models, production of summary statistics, and the creation of data visualizations.

Computer vision: The interdisciplinary field of computer vision focuses on how computers automatically produce ways of understanding digital images. Most tasks in computer vision are oriented around algorithms that mimic the human visual system. Tasks include detecting and identifying objects, categorizing motion, and describing an image's context.

Data science: The interdisciplinary field of data science addresses the challenges of collecting, understanding, and presenting structured and unstructured data from a variety of domains and contexts.

Deep learning: Deep learning algorithms learn a sequence of transformations that progressively transform an input—often an image or textual document—into numeric forms that offer increasingly higher-level representations of the information stored in the input.

Digital humanities: The interdisciplinary field of digital humanities (DH) addresses the use of computational techniques to research questions in the humanities as well as the humanistic inquiry of computational techniques themselves.

Digital image: A digital representation of an image as a rectangular array of numeric pixel intensities. Grayscale images are given as a single array; color images are described as three arrays that capture the red, green, and blue pixel intensities.

Distant viewing: The application of computer vision methods to the computational analysis of digital images. We provide a theory of the method in chapter 1 and a methodological description of distant viewing—described by the four parts of *annotating, organizing, exploring,* and *communicating*—in chapter 2.

Image embedding: An image embedding presents a way to map any image to a fixed sequence of numbers. The meaning of these numbers is given only in relationship to the embeddings of other images; similar images will have similar embeddings.

Machine learning: The field of machine learning studies the use of algorithms that have been adaptively and automatically constructed using data.

Photography: Any attempt to create a reproduction of a recording of light is considered photography. Our definition includes physical still photography, digital photography, digital scans, and moving images.

Pixel: The smallest addressable component of a digital display is called a pixel. The pixels of color displays tend to contain three subpixels, one each for red, blue, and green light. The same term is used to refer to the corresponding numeric elements of a digital image as stored on a computer. These digital pixels can be created by sensors in a digital camera.

Region segmentation: The process of region segmentation is a task in computer vision that attempts to describe the objects or materials that correspond to every pixel in a digital image.

Shot boundary detection: Within the study of moving images, the process of algorithmically breaking up a sequence of frames into shots is known as shot boundary detection.

Visual culture: Visual culture consists of the expression of culture through any form of visual media, including art, still photography, television, and film.

Notes

Introduction

1. Wu et al., "Detectron2"; Abadi et al., "TensorFlow," 265–283; Chollet, *Deep Learning with Python*; Paszke et al., "PyTorch," 8026–8037; Redmon and Farhadi, "YOLO9000," 7263–7271.

2. Berger, *Ways of Seeing*; Bordwell, *Making Meaning*; Cartwright, *Moral Spectatorship*; Hall, "Encoding/Decoding," 128–138; Manovich, *Language of New Media*; Nakamura, *Digitizing Race*; Raiford, *Imprisoned in a Luminous Glare*; Sturken and Cartwright, *Practices of Looking*; Wexler, *Tender Violence*.

3. Underwood, "A Genealogy of Distant Reading."

4. Jockers, *Macroanalysis*.

5. Piper, *Enumerations*.

6. Salt, *Moving into Pictures*; Tsivian and Civjans, *Cinemetrics*; Butler, "Statistical Analysis of Television Style."

7. Burghardt et al., "Film and Video Analysis in the Digital Humanities"; Flueckiger, "Methods and Advanced Tools"; Masson et al., "Exploring Digised Moving Image Collections."

8. Arnold et al., "Introduction."

9. We were unaware of Bender's contemporaneous use of the term when we also started using it in 2015 in relationship to our early work on the Distant Viewing Toolkit. Bender, "Distant Viewing in Art History."

10. Van Noord, Hendriks, and Postma, "Toward Discovery of the Artist's Style"; Thompson and Mimno, "Computational Cut-Ups."

11. Additional technical details and references are included throughout in notes.

Chapter 1

1. For work on documentary and truth claims, see Nichols, *Representing Reality;* Nichols, *Speaking Truths with Film;* Kahana and Musser, *The Documentary Film Reader.*

2. Abel, *Signs of the Times;* Berger, *Ways of Seeing;* Gray, *Watching Race;* Wexler, *Tender Violence.*

3. For a small sample of scholars studying the visual methods of a set of images in relationship to a larger whole, see Campt, *Image Matters;* Hirsch, *Family Frames;* Raiford, *Imprisoned in a Luminous Glare;* Smith, *Photography on the Color Line;* Hartman, *Wayward Lives.*

4. Neuendorf, *The Content Analysis Guidebook.*

5. Wevers and Smits, "The Visual Digital Turn," 207.

6. Manovich, *Cultural Analytics,* 9.

7. For example, see Barthes, *Image—Music—Text;* Metz, *Film Language.*

8. Saussure, *Cours de Linguistique Générale,* 159.

9. The concept and terminology of a *symbol* originates for Charles Sanders Peirce's first trichotomy of signs into *icons, symbols,* and *indices.* See Peirce, "Of Reasoning in General," 11–26. His later work would further divide semiotic signs into ten categories. See Peirce, "Nomenclature and Divisions of Triadic Relations," 289–299.

10. Barthes, *Image—Music—Text.*

11. In Peirce's trichotomy, this kind of sign is called an *icon.* The concept is so closely tied to visuality that Peirce occasionally uses the alternative name *image* in place of *icon.* Peirce, "Of Reasoning in General," 13, 19.

12. Throughout, we use the term *photograph* to broadly include manual and digital still photography, film, video, and any other methods for recording a measurement of light to replicate the human visual system.

13. Scott, *The Spoken Image.*

14. Barthes, *Image—Music—Text,* 17.

15. Other semioticians—including Umberto Eco, Jean Baudrillard, and Group μ—have extended the ideas of Pierce, Saussure, and Barthes presented here. The continued scholarship on visual semiotics offers important new ways that visual materials make meaning; we encourage reading and engaging with this literature. However, these arguments largely consist of nuances and expansions that do not affect our core points here regarding the lack of an explicit linguistic indexical system contained in visual media. For further reading, see Groupe μ, *Rhétorique*

générale; Groupe μ, *Rhétorique de la poésie*; Groupe μ, *Traité du signe visual: pour une rhétorique de l'image*; Eco, "Sémiologie des messages visuels," 11–51; Baudrillard, *Simulacra and Simulation*.

16. It is possible to have an image that itself depicts another set of annotations, such as the scanned image of a textual document. The analyses in this book generally focus on image collections that do not consist of such self-contained annotations.

17. Scott, *Spoken Image*, 20.

18. "Regarder, c'est-à-dire oublier le nom des choses que l'on voit." Translation by the authors. Paul Valéry, *Degas, Danse, Dessin*, 178.

19. Barthes, *Image—Music—Text*, 19; Barthes, *Camera Lucida*.

20. Hall, "Encoding/Decoding," 128–138.

21. Hall, "The Whites of Their Eyes: Racist Ideologies and the Media."

22. Bonilla-Silva, "The Invisible Weight of Whiteness," 173–194; St. Clair, "Social Scripts," 171–183; Taylor, *The Archive and the Repertoire*.

23. *Oxford English Dictionary*, s.v. "pixel."

24. The first known use of the term comes from a 1965 edition of the *Proceedings Society Photo-optical Instrumentation Engineers*. *Oxford English Dictionary*, s.v. "pixel."

25. There is a complex relationship between the color perceived by a digital sensor, the color stored in a digital file, and the color displayed on a digital screen. These differences are not crucial for our analysis; we simplify the discussion by focusing on the way the image is stored. For more information, see Poynton, *Digital Video and HD*.

26. Lyon, "A Brief History of 'Pixel,'" 2–16.

27. For example, in UTF-8 encoding, the sequence (01110100) indicates the lower-case letter "t," and the sequence (11001111 10000000) indicates a lowercase Greek letter "π" (pi).

28. A study by NASA showed that the JPEG algorithm was able to store an image in a file that was ten-times smaller than the original pixel intensities with no detectable difference in the end product. See Haines and Chuang, "The Effects of Video Compression."

29. Saussure, *Cours de Linguistique Générale*, 23. Some preprocessing must first be applied, as the text typically needs to be split apart into words by the process known as *tokenization*. For written text, however, this process can usually be accomplished unambiguously through a simple deterministic algorithm. Languages that make use of a syllabary, such as Japanese and Cherokee, require additional work.

30. The call to create structured annotations to describe the messages conveyed by digital images may seem reminiscent of the theory and practice of structuralism. While we are advocating for the need to approximate visual messages using a structured system, our application is driven by the limitations of existing computational techniques. One of the defining features of our methodology is the post-structural critique that these structured annotations are at best an incomplete and imperfect approximation of the visual messages.

31. While there is no single agreed-upon definition of the term *content analysis*, nearly all frame it in the language of the inferential analyses and the scientific method. See, for example, Neuendorf, *Content Analysis Guidebook*; Mayring, *Qualitative Content Analysis*; Riffe, Lacy, Watson, and Fico, *Analyzing Media Messages*.

32. While the terms *annotations* and *annotation* are also often used for labels created directly by human input, through the remainder of the text we will use these terms to describe the automatically produced annotations created by computer vision algorithms. When referring to labels that are not produced algorithmically, we will explicitly mention *manually* constructed annotations.

33. Mitchell and Gillies, "Model-Based Computer Vision System," 231–243.

34. Jin et al., "Methodology for Potato Defects Detection," 346–351.

35. Zhang, Li, and Zhang, "Boosting Image Orientation Detection," 95–99.

36. Ahmed, *The Cultural Politics of Emotion*.

37. Dhall et al., "Emotion Recognition," 509–516.

38. Berger, *Ways of Seeing*; Sturken and Cartwright, *Practices of Looking*.

39. Hall, "Encoding/Decoding."

40. Barthes, *Image—Music—Text*; Hill and Helmers, *Defining Visual Rhetorics*; Kress and van Leeuwen, *Reading Images*.

41. Shannon, "A Mathematical Theory of Communication," 379–423.

42. As further evidence of the duality between textual and visual messages, the guiding example throughout Shannon's article is the transmittance of a short passage of text.

43. Porter, *Trust in Numbers*; Wernimont, *Numbered Lives*.

44. There is extensive scholarship in visual culture studies on the topic. Works include Berger, *Ways of Seeing*, Mirzoeff, *The Visual Culture Reader*; Sturken and Cartwright, *Practices of Looking*.

45. Hall, "The Whites of Their Eyes," 89–93.

46. Sturken and Cartwright, *Practices of Looking*.

47. Berger, *Ways of Seeing*, 10.

48. Hall, "The Whites of Their Eyes"; Nakamura, *Digitizing Race*. See also Chun, *Updating to Remain the Same;* Joanna Drucker, *Graphesis.*

49. Smith, "Visual Culture Studies," 1–16; Rogoff, "Studying Visual Culture," 24–36.

50. Zylinksa, *Nonhuman Photography.*

51. Marblestone, Wayne, and Kording, "Deep Learning and Neuroscience."

52. Research in this area is quickly expanding. For example, see Rettberg et al., "Mapping Cultural Representations of Machine Vision," 97–101.

53. For examples, see Ruth Kim, "Top 4 Beauty Apps,"; Smith, *Photography on the Color Line;* Mulvey, *Visual and Other Pleasures*, 14–26.

54. Selbst et al., "Fairness and Abstraction," 59–68; Noble, *Algorithms of Oppression;* Eubanks, *Automating Inequality;* O'Neil, *Weapons of Math Destruction;* Broussard, *Artificial Unintelligence.*

55. Noble, *Algorithms of Oppression.*

56. O'Neil, *Weapons of Math Destruction.*

57. Anderson, *Technologies of Vision.*

Chapter 2

1. Donoho, "50 Years of Data Science," 745–766.

2. Wickham and Grolemund, *R for Data Science,* ix.

3. Wickham, "Tidy Data," 1–23.

4. While our conceptual pipeline begins with the digitized visual material, we echo Lisa Gitelman's caution that this starting point is not outside of our analysis; rather, "the collection and management of data may be said to presuppose interpretation." Gitelman, *"Raw Data" Is an Oxymoron*, 3.

5. The inclusion of an explicit step showing how the annotations are created through computer vision systems draws on a "feminist strategy for considering context" by acknowledging the "cooking process that produces 'raw' data." D'Ignazio and Klein, *Data Feminism*, 160.

6. Arnold and Tilton, "Enriching Historic Photograph with Structured Data."

7. Brightness and saturation are given here on a scale from 0 to 1. We provide a detailed description and application of these measurements of color in chapter 3.

8. Trachtenberg, "From Image to Story," 43–73.

9. On medical imaging, see Hecht-Neilsen, "Neural Networks," 449–460; on medical imaging, see Ramos et al., "Detecting Unexpected Obstacles," 1025–1032, and Bar et al., "Chest Pathology," 294–297; on militarism, see Zuboff, "Big Other," 75–89; on surveillance capitalism, see Zuboff, *The Age of Surveillance Capitalism*.

10. Ramos et al., "Detecting Unexpected Obstacles," 1025–1032.

11. Redmon et al., "You Only Look Once," 779–788.

12. King, "dlib-ML: A Machine Learning Toolkit," 1755–1758.

13. "Panoptic" is short for *panopticon*, a surveillance system designed by English philosopher Jeremy Bentham. Bentham, *The Panopticon Papers*. It also references the Greek word *panoptes*, "all seeing," which is derived from the many-eyed Greek giant Argus Panoptes. The names of the algorithms further indicate entanglement with practices of looking through computer vision.

14. *Oxford English Dictionary*, s.v. "metadata."

15. Hirsch, *Family Frames*, 74.

16. McAuley et al., "Image-Based Recommendations," 43–52.

17. For example, see Arnold and Tilton, "Distant Viewing: Analyzing Large Visual Corpora."

18. For example, see Arnold et al., "Uncovering Latent Metadata."

19. Ni, Li, and McAuley, "Justifying Recommendations Using Distantly-Labeled Reviews and Fine-Grained Aspects," 188–197.

20. Mayer, "Linked Open Data," 2–14.

21. Dijkshoorn et al., "The Rijksmuseum Collection as Linked Data," 221–230.

22. Fear, "User Understanding of Metadata" 26–60.

23. Riley and Shepherd, "A Brave New World," 91–112.

24. Dorman, "Technically Speaking," 116–17.

25. Library of Congress Names, accessed April 15, 2020, http://id.loc.gov/authorities /names.html.

26. Wickham, "Tidy Data."

27. Arnold, Leonard, and Tilton, "Knowledge Creation through Recommender Systems."

28. Donoho, "50 Years of Data Science," 755.

29. Tukey, *Exploratory Data Analysis*.

30. Arnold and Tilton, "New Data?," 293–299.

31. Arnold et al., *Photogrammar*.

32. Hanson, *Mass Communication*.

33. See, for example, Beebe et al., *Interpersonal Communication*; Croteau and Hoynes, *Media/Society*; Martin and Nakayama, *Intercultural Communication*.

34. Whitelaw, "Generous Interfaces for Digital Cultural Collections."

35. Gibbs and Owens, "Building Better Digital Humanities Tools."

36. Wickham and Grolemund, *R for Data Science*, 423.

37. boyd and Crawford, "Critical Questions for Big Data," 662–679.

38. D'Ignazio and Klein, *Data Feminism*, 110.

39. Benjamin, *Race after Technology*.

40. D'Ignazio and Klein, *Data Feminism*.

41. There are also plenty of images that would be traumatizing for people to view and are better analyzed using a computational process. Newton, "The Trauma Floor."

Chapter 3

1. Sargent, *Picture Theatre Advertising*, 59.

2. Smith, *Selling the Movie*, 68.

3. Street and Yumibe, *Chromatic Modernity*, 123.

4. "Six Secrets of Movie Posters," BBC Bitesize, accessed November 1, 2021, https://www.bbc.co.uk/bitesize/articles/zr9s6v4/.

5. Verdesoto, "Movie Poster Color Schemes Explained."

6. Qiang, "A Study on the Metaphor of Red in Chinese Culture," 100–105.

7. Flueckiger, "A Digital Humanities Approach to Film Colors," 71–94.

8. Heftberger, *Digital Humanities and Film Studies*.

9. Vane, "Making 'Dive into Color.'"

10. Palmer, *Vision Science*, 29.

11. Palmer, 338.

12. Palmer, 254.

13. Polarity, the direction(s) that the light oscillates, is an additional property of light waves, but it does not have a significant effect on human perception. However, it is a critical aspect of the visual systems of certain insects, cephalopods, and other animals, where it aids in navigation and communication.

14. Palmer, *Vision Science*, 112.

15. Palmer, 102.

16. Palmer, 113.

17. Palmer, 137.

18. Palmer, 115.

19. Newhall, *The History of Photography*.

20. Hirsch, *Seizing the Light*, 180.

21. Hirsch, 28.

22. Palmer, *Vision Science*, 181.

23. The early speculation on this fact is credited to the trichromatic theory of Thomas Young and Hermann von Helmholtz. The core idea of their theory has turned out to be remarkably accurate, as medical research subsequently discovered the physiological processes behind their observations. Palmer, 180.

24. Palmer, 185–187.

25. Palmer, 187.

26. Palmer, 96.

27. Palmer, 99.

28. Palmer, 97.

29. There are many other color models that could also be argued for. Options such as CIELAB give a more accurate spacing of colors relative to the sensitivity of the human visual system. However, they are more challenging to perform the kinds of aggregative analysis that follow. Likewise, more popular options such as using saturation in place of chroma and value in place of intensity are slightly more difficult to describe mathematically and offer no benefit in the context of our analysis. See Levkowitz and Herman, "Generalized Lightness, Hue, and Saturation," 271–285.

30. Palmer, *Vision Science*, 97.

31. Palmer, 98.

32. While *chroma* is not commonly used in colloquial English and may appear to be a more technical term than *saturation*, it is easier to both define and visualize. For this reason, many online and popular press sources show color space diagrams using the chroma value but mistakenly label it with the term *saturation*.

33. Palmer, *Vision Science*, 98.

34. Rhodes, "Origin and Development," 228–246.

35. Fuller-Seeley, "Storefront Theatre Advertising," 398–419.

36. There are several extensive histories of the Motion Picture Association of America and early cinema. See, for example, Doherty, *Pre-Code Hollywood*; Jeff and Simmons, *Dame in the Kimono*; Browser, *Transformation of Cinema*.

37. Fuller-Seeley, "Storefront Theatre Advertising," 406.

38. *Moving Picture World: The Film Exhibitor's Guide* (1916), accessed November 1, 2021, https://archive.org/stream/mowor29chal#page/n421/mode/1up/.

39. Fuller-Seeley, "Storefront Theatre Advertising," 417.

40. Staiger, "Announcing Wares, Winning Patrons, Voicing Ideals," 3–31.

41. Cohen, *A Consumers' Republic*, 281.

42. Fuller-Seeley, "Storefront Theatre Advertising," 400.

43. Sargent, *Picture Theatre Advertising*, 68, 250.

44. Franklin, *Motion Picture Theater Management*, 258.

45. Sargent, *Picture Theatre Advertising*, 64; Fuller-Seeley, "Storefront Theatre Advertising," 412.

46. Fuller-Seeley, "Storefront Theatre Advertising," 264.

47. Smith, *Selling the Movie*, 17.

48. Rhodes, "Origin and Development," 232.

49. Rhodes, "Origin and Development," 242.

50. "21 Poster Exchanges Added to Centralized Accessories System," *Motion Picture Herald*, February 17, 1940, 17, accessed November 1, 2021, http://lantern.mediahist.org/catalog/motionpictureher138unse_0635/.

51. Lawlor v. National Screen Service Corp., 349 US 322 (1955).

52. For more on the studio system, see Schatz, *The Genius of the System*. For information on the impact of television, see Anderson, *Hollywood TV*.

53. Poole and Poole, *Collecting Movie*, 110.

54. Bogart, *Artists, Advertising, and the Borders of Art*, 81–89.

55. Karal Ann Marlin, quoted in the film *The Man Who Drew Bug-Eyed Monsters* (1994), dir. Mel Bucklin.

56. Fuller, "The Arts Desk."

57. Bordwell, "It's the 80s, Stupid."

58. Handel, "Hollywood Market Research," 304–310.

59. Street and Yumibe, *Chromatic Modernity*, 27.

60. Handel, "Hollywood Market Research," 308.

61. Films are associated with the year in which they were first released, but box office sales were computed over all time, as of February 2020.

62. For more details about the role of exploratory data analysis, see the discussion in chapter 2.

63. Fisk, *Television Culture*.

64. As a thought experiment, we can take the percentages of white and black in each half-decade and assume that all posters are three-tone: white, black, and a shade of gray with an intensity of 50. This would yield an average intensity of 60.3 for the half-decade between 1970 and 1974 and an average intensity of 34.2 for the years 1995 to 1999. The actual median intensities are very close to this, with values of 60.9 and 34.0, respectively. This further provides evidence that our chosen cutoff values offer reasonable summary statistics for the data.

65. Rhodes, "Origin and Development of the American Moving Picture Poster," 230.

66. We could also account for this difference by using more complex multivariate regression models. However, these require more explanation and are more prone to detect spurious correlations that arise from the multitude of different ways of specifying a multivariate model. We will attempt to use the most easy-to-understand and straightforward approaches to addressing each task throughout this text.

67. Verdesoto, "Movie Poster Color Schemes Explained."

68. There are other relatively rare tags that exist on IMBd but are not present in our data. For example, "Short" appears as a genre for *Serta Perfect Sleeper* (1972), one of the earlier films in our larger fifty-year dataset.

69. Throughout this chapter, we will use capitalized terms to refer to the genre categories in the dataset. Lowercase forms are used to refer to a genre in a general or abstract sense that is not necessarily tied to this specific corpus.

70. Before looking at the results, our intuition was that pairs such as Biography and History, or Thriller and Horror, might have a very high degree of overlap and thus require removing one or the other from the analysis. However, on closer examination, each of these genre tags has a specific meaning that is not mutually synonymous with the other. This is an illustration of the utility that computational analysis provides to challenge seemingly obvious assumptions about a corpus. Even when the analysis confirms our assumption, it is still a valuable exercise to rule out cases such as the example here.

71. As an alternative, we could study the ways in which the genre tags intersect with one another by investigating the full set of many-to-many mappings between the films and tags. This approach would require the use of more involved multivariate methods.

72. Auster and Mansbach, "The Gender Marketing of Toys," 375–388.

73. Deleyto, *The Secret Life of Romantic Comedy*, 24.

74. Cooper, "Escapist Adventure, Timely Irreverence," 25–26.

75. There are techniques for taking means and distances in meaningful ways for circular values such as hue; these are common when working with data that includes observations at different times of the day. These can be useful for a clustering analysis of hue, but do not solve the general problem of combining hues of very different values across a corpus.

76. Roberson et al., "Color Categories," 378–411.

77. Berlin and Kay's classic study of this phenomenon proposes a hierarchical view of how languages evolve terms for color types. See Berlin and Kay, *Basic Color Terms*. More recent work has challenged this hypothesis through the use of additional field methods and experimental research. See Wierzbicka, "The Semantics of Colour: A New Paradigm," 1–24.

78. Winawer et al., "Russian Blues," 7780–7785.

79. Pemberton et al., "CSS Color Module Level 3."

80. Eden, Grizzard, and Lewis, "Disposition Development in Drama," 33–47.

81. Smuts, "The Desire-Frustration Theory of Suspense," 281–290.

82. While outside the scope of this chapter, we could use another set of more advanced computer vision algorithms to detect people, which would be a potential avenue for a future study.

83. Yoon, "Color Symbolisms of Diseases," 1–4.

84. Byrnes, "Color Associations of Children," 247–250.

85. It may seem that the color percentages of each genre in table 3.3 should match the percentages in table 3.5. They have a similar pattern but are measured in different ways. Table 3.3 uses medians to be consistent with the other metrics on the same table; in contrast, table 3.5 uses averages to be consistent with its other measurements. Also, table 3.5 does not include posters that have less than 3 percent of their area covered with colorful pixels. This is the reason that the total count columns are slightly lower in this table.

Chapter 4

1. For a classic overview of the project, see Fleischhauer and Brannan, eds., *Documenting America*.

2. Howells and Negreiros, *Visual Culture*.

3. Sabatelli et al., "Advances in Digital Music Iconography."

4. Wevers and Smits, "The Visual Digital Turn," 194–207.

5. Bermeitinger et al., "Deep Watching."

6. The photo was taken in Cimarron County, Oklahoma, in April 1936.

7. Neural networks, which are currently the most popular approach to computer vision research, were largely dismissed and ignored for over fifty years based on the initial difficulty in getting them to "beat" other techniques.

8. Elgendy, *Deep Learning for Vision Systems*, 263.

9. Elgendy, 264.

10. Elgendy, 310.

11. Elgendy, 266.

12. Finnegan, "What Is This a Picture of?," 116–123.

13. Caesar, Uijlings, and Ferrari, "COCO-stuff," 1209–1218.

14. The original paper uses the terminology of *stuff* and *things*, but we will continue to refer to the latter category as *objects* to coincide with the terminology of other methods.

15. The indoor stuff categories consist of all human-made materials that are not roads or railroads, including regions such as windows and walls, which can of course be photographed from the outside just as easily as they are from the inside.

16. We were, in fact, very skeptical that the stuff algorithm would work well on black-and-white photography, as the algorithm could easily have learned to identify some categories, such as sky, through the detection of color. The positive results were an exciting surprise.

17. These are what are known as false positive rates and are based on whether the tags were reasonable given the image. Not all categories are easy to distinguish properly; for example, what is the exact cutoff in rock size between a dirt road and a gravel road? For a similar reason, it is tough to accurately get false negative rates, which we did not attempt to do outside of the detection of people.

18. For examples of work on the evolution of state power during the New Deal, see Cebul, Geismer, and Williams, eds., *Shaped by the State*; Fraser and Gerstle, eds., *The Rise and Fall of the New Deal*.

19. Finnegan, *Picturing Poverty*.

20. Finnegan, *Picturing Poverty*; Fleischhauer and Brannan, *Documenting America*; Tagg, *Disciplinary Frame*.

21. Stryker and Wood, *In This Proud Land*, 14.

22. Fleischhauer and Brannan, *Documenting America*, 331.

23. Arnold et al., "Uncovering Latent Metadata."

24. Fleischhauer and Brannan, *Documenting America*, 335.

25. Wexler, private communication (2010).

26. The API can be found here: https://libraryofcongress.github.io/data-exploration/.

27. Alpers, *Walker Evans*.

28. Gordon, *Dorothea*.

29. Fleischhauer and Brannan, *Documenting America*.

30. Allred, *American Modernism*, 5.

31. Strange, *Symbols of Ideal Life*.

32. The first level contains only thirteen categories and the third is far too large, containing 1,153 unique values. Using the middle set of categories allows us to give a wide range of topics while still fitting all the results on a single table.

33. To explore the photos in each Vanderbilt system category, visit https://photogrammar.org.

34. We might even expect larger proportion for some categories, such as the 99 percent and greater percentages of outdoor photographs corresponding with *The Land* categories. Manually looking at a sample of one hundred images from the *Children* category reveals that some of these misclassifications are the result of an algorithmic error—a person was present but not detected—but just as many are the result of images that seem to be given a category either in error or because no other better tag existed.

35. In our experiments with the FSA-OWI data, "building" is most usually used to tag a building framed in an outdoor scene. A building from the inside is generally classified with more specific categories, such as a ceiling or wall.

36. Hall, "Encoding/Decoding," 128–138.

37. For example, Russell Lee and Walker Evans photographed small towns and communities. They often focus on one building or a few buildings, taking the photo as if the viewer were looking straight at the building. Evans's compositional approach would become known as "straight documentary" for its seemingly impartial point of view, due to the lack of angles, shadows, and related compositional features. Curtis and Grannen, "Let Us Now Appraise Famous Photographs," 1–23.

38. Berman and Cronin, "Project DOCUMERICA," 186–197.

39. Caesar et al., "COCO-stuff," 1209–1218.

40. Our previous analysis indicated that there was a difference in the proportion of images with people among the photographers, which may at first seem to contradict the observation here. The apparent contradiction is explained by the difference in what each metric is measuring. Before, we looked at the specific probabilities by photographer; here, we measure how spread out the photographs with people are over the photographers. The distribution is changing (it focuses more on OWI photographers and less on FSA photographers), but the overall spread is still large.

41. The images were in the form of a cartoon painting on the side of a circus wagon in Alger, Montana. This can be found by slightly decreasing the cutoff confidence score.

42. For a powerful example of how a small set of photographs can open histories, see Grace Elizabeth Hale's study using a set of FSA-OWI photographs to argue how the rise of consumer culture challenged existing race relations in the American South. Hale, *Making Whiteness*.

43. Buolamwini and Gebru, "Gender Shades," 77–91.

44. Trachtenberg, "From Image to Story," 50.

45. Finnegan, "What Is This a Picture of?," 116.

46. Trachtenberg, "From Image to Story," 45.

47. Gordon, *Dorothea Lange*, 264.

Chapter 5

1. Cameron and Jeffery, "The Universal Hitchcock," 271.

2. Ott and Keeling, "Cinema and Choric Connection," 370.

3. Sharits, "Red, Blue, Godard," 24–29.

4. Dyer, "Lighting for Whiteness," 282; DuVernay, "Lighting the Black Body."

5. Everett, "The Other Pleasures," 26–38.

6. Some recent television series, such as HBO's *Game of Thrones*, have been produced and funded more in line with feature-length films than a typical television series. However, we focus on the far more "typical" television series that dominate both synchronous and asynchronous television. See Mittell, *Complex TV*.

7. This relationship seems to be described well by Ernie Kovacs's (likely misattributed) joke that "television is a medium. So-called because it is neither rare nor well done."

8. An earlier version of the analysis in this chapter appeared in the *Journal of Cultural Analytics*; see Arnold, Tilton, and Berke, "Visual Style in Two Network Era Sitcoms." It was co-written with our collaborator, film and TV scholar Dr. Annie Berke, who has graciously supported our extension of the analysis here; see Berke, *Their Own Best Creations*.

9. For a sense of scale, consider the collected works of William Shakespeare. The digitized text of all his plays, sonnets, and other materials can be saved in a file taking up under 7 megabytes of storage space. In comparison, the standard size of just a single photo on a modern smartphone is currently between 5 and 12 megabytes. Even heavily compressed, a half-hour video file digitized in standard definition requires over 1000 megabytes of storage.

10. Salt, "Statistical Style Analysis of Motion Pictures," 13.

11. Tsivian and Civjans, *Cinemetrics*; Acland and Hoyt, *The Arclight Guidebook*; Butler, "Statistical Analysis of Television Style," 25–44.

12. Burghardt, Kao, and Wolff, "Beyond Shot Lengths"; Ferguson, "Digital Surrealism." Burges, Dimmock, and Romphf, "Collective Reading."

13. These are standard playback frame rates. Slow-motion or time-lapse effects are created by recording at a different frame rate than the playback frame rate. Julie Turnock provides an excellent summary of the history and theory behind frame rates in her analysis of *The Hobbit*, which was known for being played at the unusually high 48 frames per second. Turnock, "Removing the Pane of Glass," 30–59.

14. While not used in the analysis shown in this chapter, the distant viewing toolkit includes algorithms for the analysis of both sound and subtitle information.

15. Butler, *Television*, 30.

16. Miller, "Anal Rope," 119–172.

17. Due to the centrality of this task in video processing, many competing terms are used in the literature, including *shot transition detection*, *shot detection*, and *cut detection*.

18. We became aware of a very accurate, pretrained algorithm for shot boundary detection that was published well after we completed the work presented in this chapter. We would recommend this algorithm for others looking to perform a similar analysis on another dataset. Souček and Lokoč, "TransNet V2."

19. There are a few other minor technical details in the algorithm, such as how to avoid making shots that are too small. These are described in the implementation included in the supplementary materials. Also, note that the introductory cartoon sequences to both series (shown with the titles) were excluded in this and subsequent analyses.

20. See, respectively, Papageorgiou, Oren, and Poggio, "A General Framework for Object Detection," 555–562; Viola and Jones, "Rapid Object," 1–8; Dalal and Triggs, "Histograms of Oriented Gradients for Human Detection," 886–893.

21. For example, a trainable HOG detector algorithm is provided by the popular OpenCV library, dlib library, and the scikit-image Python package.

22. Sun, Wu, and Hoi, "Face Detection Using Deep Learning," 42–50; Sharma, Shanmugasundaram, and Ramasamy, "CNN Based Efficient Face Recognition Technique Using Dlib,"192–195.

23. We applied the Faster R-CNN to every ten frames in six episodes of each of our two series and labeled where the algorithm had mistakenly identified objects as positive faces or had failed to detect faces when present. For the latter, we only considered a face as being missed if at least one eye of a face was present in the frame, and we excluded any extraneous actors (extras) in the far background and removed from the main action. Compared to the hand-labeled faces, the algorithm performed well, with a *precision* (proportion of detected faces that were faces) of over 98.3 percent and a *recall* (proportion of faces that were correctly identified) of 95.1 percent. For comparison, the HOG detector had an overall recall of only 55.2 percent.

24. Baltrusaitis, Zadeh, Lim, and Morency, "OpenFace 2.0," 59–66; Klontz et al., "Open-Source Biometric Recognition," 42–50.

25. Cao et al., "VGGFace2,"67–74.

26. The algorithm can be applied to faces that are not in the training set by supplying a single *reference* image for every character of interest. The algorithm returns which faces in the dataset appear to be the same as one of the reference images.

27. Defining precision as the proportion of assigned faces that were correctly identified and recalled as the proportion of main characters correctly identified, our choice of cutoff values yields an overall precision of 92.8 percent and recall of 87.0 percent. Similarly, a precision of 99.0 percent can be achieved while maintaining a recall of only 67 percent. Kaiming He et al., "Deep Residual Learning," 770–778.

28. We are aware of only one prior attempt to offer an algorithmic taxonomy of film shots. The presented taxonomy mainly related to camera movement in action films and was not very relevant to the features we are interested in classifying. See Wang and Cheong, "Taxonomy of Directing Semantics," 1529–1542.

29. Close shots were identified with a precision of 99.0 percent and recall of 93.5 percent (F1 Score: 0.962); group shots were classified with a precision of 98.25 percent and recall of 95.73 percent (F1 Score: 0.969); and over-the-shoulder shots had a precision of 88.24 percent and recall of 95.74 percent (F1 Score: 0.918). Much of our analysis focuses on the timing and presence of close shots. The precision is exceptionally high because of the conservatively chosen logic in our algorithm.

30. Edgerton, *The Columbia History of American Television*,178.

31. Edgerton, *255*.

32. Lotz, *The Television Will Be Revolutionized*, 51.

33. Eco, "The Myth of Superman," 17.

34. Lotz, *The Television Will Be Revolutionized*, 101.

35. Metz, *Bewitched*, 14–16.

36. Metz, 17.

37. Stoddard, "Bewitched and Bewildered," 50.

38. Spigel, *Welcome to the Dreamhouse*, 132.

39. Fairfield-Artman, Lippard, and Sansom, 27.

40. As further evidence of the uncertainty about the centrality of characters in these series, translations of the title into other languages often reverse the perspective of the original. For example, in Italian, *Bewitched* is called *Vita da Strega* (The life of a witch). The original working title of the script, in fact, was *The Witch of Westwood*; see IMDb, https://www.imdb.com/title/tt0057733/releaseinfo.

41. The character of Darrin on *Bewitched* was played by two actors: Dick York (seasons 1–5) and Dick Sargent (season 6–8). We created separate face detection algorithms for both actors. However, in this and all other results, we have combined them to their common character.

42. This four-part structure roughly follows the chart provided by Jeremy Butler and very accurately matches the structure of our two series. We were able to automatically extract the narrative parts through the chapter breaks encoding in our DVD materials. Butler, *Television*.

43. A common trope on the show involves fast cuts between Darrin and Samantha as they talk over the telephone between the office and home.

44. Sherif, Taub, and Hovland, "Assimilation and Contrast Effects," 150.

45. Only 1.04 percent of the dataset started with a shot containing multiple faces; in these cases, none of the characters was counted.

46. It is unclear from this analysis whether her centrality is due to the magical abilities of Samantha Stevens or the star power of Elizabeth Montgomery. Likely both contribute in some way.

47. Salt, *Moving into Pictures*.

48. Regression analysis can be used to detect how strongly various factors influence median shot length. Predicting shot length first as a function of the series and then

as a function of shot length reveals that the latter explains two orders of magnitude more variation. Series has an R2-value of only 0.000055, whereas a regression model using shot type provided an R2-value of 0.0534. Following prior work on shot lengths, we assumed that shot length followed a log-normal distribution, and ran each regression of the logarithm of each shot length. Cutting, DeLong, and Nothelfer, "Attention and the Evolution," 432–439.

49. Stiller, Nettle, and Dunbar, "The Small World of Shakespeare's Plays," 397–408; Xanthos et al., "Visualizing the Dynamics of Character Networks," 417–419.

50. Blatt, "Which Friends on *Friends* Were the Closest Friends?"

51. Mulvey, *Visual and Other Pleasures*.

52. Bordwell, Staiger, and Thompson, *Classical Hollywood Cinema*, 13.

53. Butler, *Television*, 369.

54. Bordwell, Staiger, and Thompson, *Classical Hollywood Cinema*, 374.

Chapter 6

1. Brennan, "Public, First," 384–390.

2. Digital Collections, Library of Congress, accessed November 4, 2021, https://www.loc.gov/collections/.

3. Rijks Data, Rijksmuseum, accessed November 4, 2021, https://data.rijksmuseum.nl/object-metadata/api/.

4. Baca, *Introduction to Metadata*.

5. Metropolitan Museum of Art Collection API, updated November 17, 2020, https://metmuseum.github.io/.

6. Smithsonian Open Access, accessed July 17, 2022, https://www.si.edu/openaccess.

7. Louvre Collections database, accessed November 4, 2021, https://collections.louvre.fr/.

8. "The Santa Barbara Statement on Collections as Data, Version 2" (2020), accessed November 4, 2021, https://collectionsasdata.github.io/statement/.

9. Padilla, *Responsible Operations*.

10. Cordell, *Machine Learning + Libraries*.

11. "Digital Strategy for the Library of Congress," accessed November 2, 2021, https://www.loc.gov/digital-strategy/.

12. Smithsonian 2022 Strategic Plan, accessed November 2, 2021, https://www.si .edu/strategicplan.

13. Elgendy, *Deep Learning for Vision Systems,* 6.

14. Elgendy, 406.

15. Elgendy, 402.

16. The terms *deep learning* and *neural networks* are often used interchangeably. Originally, deep learning referred to a general approach to building models through a series of iterative transformations, whereas a neural network was a specific example of a deep learning algorithm. However, neural networks and their variants have remained the only commonly used type of deep learning over time. In this section, we use the term *deep learning* to highlight our focus on the concepts behind the approach rather than the specific details of individual model implementations.

17. There are many other ways of building a classification based on two features; this is just one example. A slightly more complex and general-purpose approach would be to use a logistic regression, which learns to weight the two features together as a model of the probability that the image was taken outdoors.

18. Arnold and Tilton, "Depth in Deep Learning," 309–328.

19. Arnold and Tilton, 311.

20. Montúfar et al., "On the Number of Linear Regions," 1–14.

21. Elgendy, *Deep Learning for Vision Systems*, 213.

22. Elgendy, 253.

23. Bansal et al., "Transfer Learning for Image Classification," 1.

24. Elgendy, *Deep Learning for Vision Systems*, 240.

25. Unlike manually constructed features, it is not possible to assign any meaning to the individual features that are automatically generated. This occurs for two reasons. First, since the final features are themselves generated by many interconnected layers, their relationship to the original image becomes highly obfuscated. Secondly, the model is not incentivized to isolate elements in the image in individual features. For example, rather than a single feature indicating whether a photograph was taken outdoors, this aspect of the image is likely to be captured by a more complex combination of the features.

26. Arnold and Tilton, "Depth in Deep Learning," 317.

27. McInnes, Healy, Saul, and Großberger, "UMAP: Uniform Manifold Approximation and Projection," 861.

28. The formal algorithm is slightly more complicated because it is usually not possible to replicate the neighborhood structure exactly. Instead, an approximation is made that measures how closely the two-dimensional neighbors match the neighbors in the original space. Conceptually, the idea is the same as described in the text.

29. Szegedy et al., "Rethinking the Inception Architecture," 2818–2826.

30. "About the Met," Metropolitan Museum of Art, accessed July 17, 2022, https:// www.metmuseum.org/about-the-met.

31. Charr, "Decolonize This Place Targets New York Museums," *MuseumNext*, October 15, 2019, https://www.museumnext.com/article/decolonize-this-place-targets-new -york-museums; Larkin, "The Met Museum Misses the Mark."

32. The number 375,000 is contradicted elsewhere in the press release as being only 200,000. The latter number more accurately matches the number of digital images in the collection as of 2021. It is unclear whether the first number is a typo, whether the legal policies around some records changed at some point, or whether slightly different things are being counted.

33. Loic Tallon, Chief Digital Officer, "Introducing Open Access at The Met," February 7, 2017, https://www.metmuseum.org/blogs/digital-underground/2017/open-access -at-the-met.

34. As we have seen in our study of the FSA-OWI, access to physical, organizational information can open many possibilities of analysis that would not otherwise be possible.

35. See, for example, "Decolonizing Museum Collections: A Conversation between Colleagues in the Field (CSAAM)," American Alliance of Museums, September 29, 2021, accessed November 4, 2021, https://www.aam-us.org/2021/09/29/decolonizing -museum-collections-a-conversation-between-colleagues-in-the-field-csaam/.

36. Simon Wakeling et al., "Readers Who Borrowed This."; Herlocker et al., "Evaluating Collaborative Filtering Recommender Systems," 5–53.

37. See "Amulet of Baboon in Act of Adoration 525–30 B.C.," The Metropolitan Museum of Art Collections, accessed September 30, 2022, https://www.metmuseum .org/art/collection/search/570613.

38. "Google Apologises for Photos App's Racist Blunder," *BBC News*, July 1, 2015, accessed November 4, 2021.

39. Patterns of color can be difficult to make out in the printed black-and-white image; they can be seen more clearly in the full color version available on the book's website.

40. The name *Islamic Art* might suggest a cultural or religious logic, but according to the metadata in the Met's collection, it is better understood as representing the

geographical regions of Northern Africa and the Near East. For example, the twelfth-century BCE stucco fragments from modern-day Iran are housed in the Islamic Art department, despite being made nearly 1,700 years before the start of Islam.

41. Whitelaw, "Generous Interfaces."

42. For readers looking to reproduce the analysis on a similar dataset, the code to produce our interface is included in the text's supplemental material available at https://distantviewing.org/book.

43. Buley, *The User Experience Team of One*; MacKenzie, *Human-Computer Interaction*; Cox and Tilton, "The Digital Public Humanities," 127–146; Smulyan, *Doing Public Humanities*.

44. Caddick and Cable, *Communicating the User Experience*, 28; Warner, "Publics and Counterpublics"; Black, *Transparent Designs*; Emerson, *Reading Writing Interfaces*; Wardrip-Fruin, *Expressive Processing*.

45. The design and code for the interface was adapted from our project *Access and Discovery of Documentary Images* (ADDI), a project designed to adapt and apply computer vision algorithms to aid in the discovery and use of digital collections, specifically documentary photography collections held by the Library of Congress. Funding and support were provided by the Library of Congress through the *Computing Cultural Heritage in the Cloud* project. See https://github.com/distant-viewing/addi.

46. For more on the lifecycle of a digital project and best practices for sustainability, see Visual Media Workshop at the University of Pittsburgh, *The Socio-Technical Sustainability Roadmap*, accessed April 26, 2022, http://sustainingdh.net.

47. Whitelaw, "Generous Interfaces," 3.

48. One of the most important tuning parameters for UMAP controls whether the algorithm tends to create one giant cluster with all the images or many unconnected clusters that split the images into discrete groups. We chose a value that created just a few independent groups because that seemed to be the most interesting on its own. However, there is a lot to be gained by looking at several different embeddings together.

Conclusion

1. Arnold and Tilton, "Distant Viewing Toolkit."

2. Laws regarding the distribution of annotations under the fair use doctrine are largely untested. For an overview, see Lemley and Casey, "Fair Learning," 743–785.

Bibliography

Abadi, Martín, Paul Barham, Jianmin Chen, Zhifeng Chen, Andy Davis, Jeffrey Dean, Matthieu Devin et al. "TensorFlow: A System for Large-Scale Machine Learning." *Proceedings of the 12th USENIX Symposium on Operating Systems Design* (2016): 265–283.

Abel, Elizabeth. *Signs of the Times: The Visual Politics of Jim Crow*. Berkeley: University of California Press, 2010.

Acland, Charles, and Eric Hoyt. *The Arclight Guidebook to Media History and the Digital Humanities*. Sussex, UK: Reframe Books, 2016.

Ahmed, Sara. *The Cultural Politics of Emotion*. New York: Routledge, 2014.

Allred, Jeff. *American Modernism and Depression Documentary*. Oxford: Oxford University Press, 2010.

Alpers, Svetlana. *Walker Evans: Starting from Scratch*. Princeton: Princeton University Press, 2020.

Anderson, Christopher. *Hollywood TV: The Studio System in the Fifties*. Austin: University of Texas Press, 1994.

Anderson, Steve F. *Technologies of Vision: The War between Data and Images*. Cambridge, MA: MIT Press, 2017.

Arnold, Taylor, Nate Ayers, Justin Madron, Rob Nelson, Lauren Tilton, and Laura Wexler. *Photogrammar* (Version 3.0). 2021.

Arnold, Taylor, Peter Leonard, and Lauren Tilton. "Knowledge Creation through Recommender Systems." *Digital Humanities Quarterly* 32, no. 3 (2017).

Arnold, Taylor, Stacey Maples, Lauren Tilton, and Laura Wexler. "Uncovering Latent Metadata in the FSA-OWI Photographic Archive." *Digital Humanities Quarterly* 11, no. 2 (2017).

Arnold, Taylor, Sefania Scagliola, Lauren Tilton, and Jasmijn Van Gorp. "Introduction: Special Issue on AudioVisual Data in DH." *Digital Humanities Quarterly* 15, no. 1 (2021).

Arnold, Taylor, and Lauren Tilton. "Distant Viewing Toolkit: A Python Package for the Analysis of Visual Culture." *Journal of Open Source Software* 5, no. 45 (2020): 1–2.

Arnold, Taylor, and Lauren Tilton. "Depth in Deep Learning: Knowledgeable, Layered, and Impenetrable." In *Deep Mediations*, edited by Karen Redrobe and Jeff Scheible, 309–328. Minneapolis: University of Minnesota Press, 2021.

Arnold, Taylor, and Lauren Tilton. "Distant Viewing: Analyzing Large Visual Corpora." *Digital Scholarship in the Humanities* 34, suppl. 1 (December 2019): i3–i16.

Arnold, Taylor, and Lauren Tilton. "New Data? The Role of Statistics in DH." In *Debates in the Digital Humanities 2019*, edited by Matt Gold and Lauren Klein, 293–299. Minneapolis: University of Minnesota Press, 2019.

Arnold, Taylor, and Lauren Tilton. "Enriching Historical Photography with Structured Data Using Image Region Segementation." *Proceedings of the 1st International Workshop on Artificial Intelligence for Historic Image Enrichment and Access* (2020): 1–10.

Arnold, Taylor, Lauren Tilton, and Annie Berke. "Visual Style in Two Network Era Sitcoms." *Cultural Analytics* 4, no. 2 (2019).

Auster, Carol J., and Claire S. Mansbach. "The Gender Marketing of Toys: An Analysis of Color and Type of Toy on the Disney Store Website." *Sex Roles* 67 (2012): 375–388.

Bansal, Monika, Munish Kumar, Monika Sachdeva, and Ajay Mittal. "Transfer Learning for Image Classification Using VGG19: Caltech-101 Image Data Set." *Journal of Ambient Intelligence and Humanized Computing* 702 (2021): 1–12.

Bar, Yaniv, Idit Diamant, Lior Wolf, Sivan Lieberman, Eli Konen, and Hayit Greenspan. "Chest Pathology Detection Using Deep Learning with Non-Medical Training." *International Symposium on Biomedical Imaging* (2015): 294–297.

Barthes, Roland. *Camera Lucida: Reflections on Photography*. Translated by Richard Howard. New York: Hill and Wang, 2010.

Barthes, Roland. *Image—Music—Text*. Translated by Stephen Heath. New York: Hill and Wang, 1977.

Baudrillard, Jean. *Simulacra and Simulation*. Paris: Éditions Galilée, 1981.

Beebe, Steven A., Susan J. Beebe, Mark V. Redmond, and Lisa Salem-Wiseman. *Interpersonal Communication: Relating to Others*. Toronto: Pearson, 2017.

Bender, K. "Distant Viewing in Art History: A Case Study of Artistic Productivity." *International Journal of Digital Art History*, no. 1 (2015): 1–14.

Benjamin, Ruha. *Race after Technology: Abolitionist Codes for the New Jim Crow*. London: Wiley, 2019.

Bentham, Jeremy. *The Panopticon Papers*. London: Verso, 1995.

Berger, John. *Ways of Seeing*. London: Penguin Books, 1972.

Berke, Annie. *Their Own Best Creations: Women Writers in Postwar Television*. Berkeley, CA: University of California Press, 2022.

Berlin, Brent, and Paul Kay. *Basic Color Terms: Their Universality and Evolution*. Berkeley: University of California Press, 1969.

Berman, Bruce, and Mary Cronin. "Project DOCUMERICA: A Cautionary Tale." *Journalism History* 43, no. 4 (2019): 186–197.

Bermeitinger, Bernhard, Sebastian Gassner, Siegfried Handschuh, Gernot Howanitz, Erik Radisch, and Malte Rehbein. "Deep Watching: Towards New Methods of Analyzing Visual Media in Cultural Studies." *Digital Humanities Conference Abstracts* (2019). https://doi.org/10.34894/hosp8p.

Black, Michael. *Transparent Designs: Personal Computing and the Politics of User-Friendliness*. Baltimore, MD: Johns Hopkins University Press, 2022.

Blatt, Ben. "Which Friends on *Friends* Were the Closest Friends?" *Slate*, May 4, 2014.

Bogart, Michele H. H. *Artists, Advertising, and the Borders of Art*. Chicago: University of Chicago Press, 1997.

Bonilla-Silva, Eduardo. "The Invisible Weight of Whiteness: The Racial Grammar of Everyday Life in Contemporary America." *Ethnic and Racial Studies* 35, no. 2 (2012): 173–194.

Bordwell, David. "It's the 80s, Stupid." *Observations on Film Art* (blog). November 20, 2008. http://www.davidbordwell.net/blog/2008/11/20/its-the-80s-stupid/.

Bordwell, David. *Making Meaning: Inference and Rhetoric in the Interpretation of Cinema*. Cambridge, MA: Harvard University Press, 2009.

Bordwell, David, Janet Staiger, and Kristin Thompson. *The Classical Hollywood Cinema*. New York: Columbia University Press, 1987.

boyd, danah, and Kate Crawford. "Critical Questions for Big Data: Provocations for a Cultural, Technological, and Scholarly Phenomenon." *Information, Communication & Society* 15, no. 5 (2012): 662–679.

Brennan, Sheila. "Public, First." In *Debates in the Digital Humanities*, edited by Matt Gold and Lauren Klein, 384–390. Minneapolis: University of Minnesota Press, 2016.

Broussard, Meredith. *Artificial Unintelligence: How Computers Misunderstand the World*. Cambridge, MA: MIT Press, 2018.

Browser, Eileen. *The Transformation of Cinema, 1907–1915*. Berkeley: University of California Press, 1994.

Buley, Leah. *The User Experience Team of One: A Research and Design Survival Guide*. London: Rosenfeld Media, 2013.

Buolamwini, Joy, and Timnit Gebru. "Gender Shades: Intersectional Accuracy Disparities in Commercial Gender Classification." *Conference on Fairness, Accountability, and Transparency* (2018): 77–91.

Burghardt, Manuel, Adelheid Heftberger, Johannes Pause, Niels-Oliver Walkowski, and Matthias Zeppelzauer. "Film and Video Analysis in the Digital Humanities—An Interdisciplinary Dialog." *Digital Humanities Quarterly* 14, no. 4 (2020).

Burges, Joel, Nora Dimmock, and Joshua Romphf. "Collective Reading: Shot Analysis and Data Visualization in the Digital Humanities." *DH and Media Studies Crossovers* 3, no. 3 (2016).

Burghardt, Manuel, Michael Kao, and Christian Wolff. "Beyond Shot Lengths Using Language Data and Color Information as Additional Parameters for Quantitative Movie Analysis." *Digital Humanities Conference Abstracts* (2016).

Butler, Jeremy. "Statistical Analysis of Television Style: What Can Numbers Tell Us about TV Editing?" *Cinema Journal* 54, no. 1 (2014): 25–44.

Butler, Jeremy. *Television: Visual Storytelling and Screen Culture*. New York: Routledge, 2018.

Byrnes, Deborah A. "Color Associations of Children." *Journal of Psychology* 113, no. 2 (1983): 247–250.

Caddick, Richard, and Steve Cable. *Communicating the User Experience: A Practical Guide for Creating Useful UX Documentation*. New York: Wiley, 2011.

Caesar, Holger, Jasper Uijlings, and Vittorio Ferrari. "COCO-stuff: Thing and Stuff Classes in Context." *Proceedings of the IEEE Conference on Computer Vision and Pattern Recognition* (2018): 1209–1218.

Cameron, Ian, and Richard Jeffery. "The Universal Hitchcock." In *A Hitchcock Reader*, edited by Marshall Deutelbaum and Leland A. Poague, 265–78. Ames: Iowa State University Press, 1986.

Campt, Tina M. *Image Matters: Archive, Photography, and the African Diaspora in Europe*. Durham, NC: Duke University Press, 2012.

Cao, Qiong, Li Shen, Weidi Xie, Omkar M. Parkhi, and Andrew Zisserman. "VGG-Face2: A Dataset for Recognising Faces across Pose and Age." *Proceedings of the IEEE International Conference on Automatic Face and Gesture Recognition* 13 (2018): 67–74.

Cartwright, Lisa. *Moral Spectatorship: Technologies of Voice and Affect in Postwar Representations of the Child*. Durham, NC: Duke University Press, 2008.

Cebul, Brent, Lily Geismer, and Mason B. Williams, eds. *Shaped by the State: Toward a New Political History of the Twentieth Century*. Chicago: University of Chicago Press, 2019.

Charr, Manuel. "Decolonize This Place Targets New York Museums." *MuseumNext*, October 15, 2019. https://www.museumnext.com/article/decolonize-this-place-targets -new-york-museums.

Chollet, Francois. *Deep Learning with Python*. New York: Manning, 2021.

Chun, Wendy Hui Kyong. *Updating to Remain the Same*. Cambridge, MA: MIT Press, 2017.

Cohen, Lizabeth. *A Consumers' Republic: The Politics of Mass Consumption in Postwar America*. New York: Vintage Books, 2003.

Cooper, Rand Richards. "Escapist Adventure, Timely Irreverence." *Commonweal Magazine*, January 26, 2018, 25–26.

Cordell, Ryan. *Machine Learning + Libraries: A Report on the State of the Field*. Washington, DC: Library of Congress, 2020.

Cox, Jordana, and Lauren Tilton. "The Digital Public Humanities: Giving New Arguments and New Ways to Argue." *Review of Communication* 19, no. 2 (2019): 127–146.

Croteau, David, and William Hoynes. *Media/Society: Technology, Industries, Content, and Users*. New York: Sage Publications, 2018.

Curtis, James C., and Sheila Grannen. "Let Us Now Appraise Famous Photographs: Walker Evans and Documentary Photography." *Winterthur Portfolio* 15, no. 1 (1980): 1–23.

Cutting, James, Jordan DeLong, and Christine Nothelfer. "Attention and the Evolution of Hollywood Film." *Psychological Science* 21, no. 3 (2010): 432–439.

Dalal, Navneet, and Bill Triggs. "Histograms of Oriented Gradients for Human Detection." *Computer Vision and Pattern Recognition* (2005): 886–893.

Deleyto, Celestino. *The Secret Life of Romantic Comedy*. Manchester: Manchester University Press, 2019.

Dhall, Abhinav, Roland Goecke, Jyoti Joshi, Michael Wagner, and Tom Gedeon. "Emotion Recognition in the Wild Challenge 2013." *Proceedings of the 15th ACM on International Conference on Multimodal Interaction* (2013): 509–516.

D'Ignazio, Catherine, and Lauren F. Klein. *Data Feminism*. Cambridge, MA: MIT Press, 2020.

Dijkshoorn, Chris, Lizzy Jongma, Lora Aroyo, Jacco van Ossenbruggen, Guus Schreiber, Wesley ter Weele, and Jan Wielemaker. "The Rijksmuseum Collection as Linked Data." *Semantic Web* 9, no. 2 (2016): 221–230.

Doherty, Thomas. *Pre-Code Hollywood: Sex, Immorality, and Insurrection in American Cinema, 1930–1934*. New York: Columbia University Press, 1999.

Donoho, David. "50 Years of Data Science." *Journal of Computational and Graphical Statistics* 26, no. 4 (2017): 745–766.

Dorman, David. "Technically Speaking: Scheming to Normalize Dublin Core." *American Libraries* 33, no. 6 (2002): 116–17.

Drucker, Joanna. *Graphesis: Visual Forms of Knowledge Production.* Cambridge, MA: Harvard University Press, 2014.

DuVernay, Ava. "Lighting the Black Body and How Black Characters Look in Dark Rooms." YouTube video, 4:46. April 23, 2015. https://youtu.be/W8M3Lyywl8k.

Dyer, Richard. "Lighting for Whiteness." In *Images: A Reader*, edited by Sunil Manghani, Arthur Piper, and Jon Simons, 278–283. London: Sage Publishing, 2006.

Eco, Umberto. "The Myth of Superman." *Diacritics* 2, no. 1 (1972): 17.

Eco, Umberto. "Sémiologie des messages visuels." *Communications* 15 (1970): 11–51.

Eden, Allison, Matthew Grizzard, and Robert J. Lewis. "Disposition Development in Drama: The Role of Moral, Immoral and Ambiguously Moral Characters." *International Journal of Arts and Technology* 4, no. 1 (2011): 33–47.

Edgerton, Gary. *The Columbia History of American Television.* New York: Columbia University Press, 2007.

Elgendy, Mohamed. *Deep Learning for Vision Systems.* New York: Manning, 2020.

Emerson, Lori. *Reading Writing Interfaces: From the Digital to the Bookbound.* Minneapolis, MN: University of Minnesota Press (2014).

Eubanks, Virginia. *Automating Inequality: How High-Tech Tools Profile, Police, and Punish the Poor.* New York: St. Martin's Press, 2018.

Everett, Anna. "The Other Pleasures: The Narrative Function of Race in the Cinema." *Film Criticism* 20, no. 1 (Fall/Winter 1995–96): 26–38.

Fairfield-Artman, Patricia, Rodney E. Lippard, and Adrienne Sansom. "The 1960s Sitcom Revisited: A Queer Read." *Taboo: The Journal of Culture & Education* 9, no. 2 (2005): 27–48.

Fear, Kathleen. "User Understanding of Metadata in Digital Image Collections: Or, What Exactly Do You Mean by 'Coverage'?" *The American Archivist* 73, no. 1 (2010): 26–60.

Ferguson, Kevin L. "Digital Surrealism: Visualizing Walt Disney Animation Studios." *Digital Humanities Quarterly* 11, no. 1 (2017).

Finnegan, Cara. *Picturing Poverty: Print Culture and FSA Photographs.* Washington, DC: Smithsonian Books, 2003.

Finnegan, Cara. "What Is This a Picture of? Some Thoughts on Images and Archives." *Rhetoric and Public Affairs* 9, no. 1 (2006): 116–123.

Fisk, John. *Television Culture*. New York: Routledge, 2010.

Fleischhauer, Carl, and Beverly W. Brannan, eds. *Documenting America, 1935–1943*. Berkeley: University of California Press, 1989.

Flueckiger, Barbara. "A Digital Humanities Approach to Film Colors." *The Moving Image: The Journal of the Association of Moving Image Archivists* 17, no. 2 (Fall 2017): 71–94.

Flueckiger, Barbara. "Methods and Advanced Tools for the Analysis of Film Colors in Digital Humanities." *Digital Humanities Quarterly* 14, no. 4 (2020).

Franklin, Harold B. *Motion Picture Theater Management*. New York: George H. Doran Company, 1927.

Fraser, Steve, and Gary Gerstle, eds. *The Rise and Fall of the New Deal, 1930–1980*. Princeton: Princeton University Press, 1990.

Fuller-Seeley, Kathy. "Storefront Theatre Advertising and the Evolution of the American Film Poster." In *The Blackwell Companion to Early Cinema*, edited by Andre Gaudreault, 398–419. New York: Blackwell, 2012.

Gibbs, Fred, and Trevor Owens. "Building Better Digital Humanities Tools: Toward Broader Audiences and User-Centered Designs." *Digital Humanities Quarterly* 6, no. 2 (2012).

Gitelman, Lisa. *"Raw Data" Is an Oxymoron*. Cambridge, MA: MIT Press, 2013.

Gordon, Linda. *Dorothea Lange: A Life beyond Limits*. New York: W. W. Norton, 2010.

Gray, Herman. *Watching Race: Television and the Struggle for Blackness*. Minneapolis: University of Minnesota, 2004.

Groupe μ. *Rhétorique générale*. Paris: Éditions Larousse, 1970.

Groupe μ. *Rhétorique de la poésie*. Paris: Éditions Le Seuil, 1990.

Groupe μ. *Traité du signe visual: pour une rhétorique de l'image*. Paris: Éditions Le Seuil, 1992.

Haines, Richard F., and Sherry L. Chuang. "The Effects of Video Compression on the Acceptability of Images for Monitoring Life Sciences Experiments." NASA-TP-3239 (July 1992).

Hale, Grace Elizabeth. *Making Whiteness: The Culture of Segregation in the South, 1890–1940*. New York: Pantheon Books, 1998.

Hall, Stuart. "Encoding/Decoding." In *Culture, Media, Language*, edited by Stuart Hall, Dorothy Hobson, Andrew Lowe, and Paul Willis, 128–138. London: Hutchinson, 1980.

Hall, Stuart. "The Whites of Their Eyes: Racist Ideologies and the Media." In *Gender, Race, and Class in Media: A Text Reader*, edited by Gail Dines and Jean M. Humez, 89–93. Minneapolis: Sage Publications, 2003.

Handel, Leo A. "Hollywood Market Research." *The Quarterly of Film Radio and Television* 7, no. 3 (1953): 304–310.

Hanson, Ralph E. *Mass Communication*. New York: Sage Publications, 2016.

Hartman, Saidiya, *Wayward Lives, Beautiful Experiments: Intimate Histories of Riotous Black Girls, Troublesome Women, and Queer Radicals*. New York: W. W. Norton, 2019.

He, Kaiming, Xiangyu Zhang, Shaoqing Ren, and Jian Sun. "Deep Residual Learning for Image Recognition." *Proceedings of the IEEE Conference on Computer Vision and Pattern Recognition* (2016): 770–778.

Hecht-Neilsen, Robert. "Neural Networks for Image Analysis." In *Neural Networks for Vision and Image Processing*, edited by Gail Carpenter and Stephen Grossberg, 449–460. Cambridge, MA: MIT Press, 1992.

Heftberger, Adelheid. *Digital Humanities and Film Studies*. New York: Springer, 2018.

Herlocker, Jonathan L., Joseph A. Konstan, Loren G. Terveen, and John T. Riedl. "Evaluating Collaborative Filtering Recommender Systems." *ACM Transactions on Information Systems* 22, no. 1 (2004): 5–53.

Hill, Charles, and Marguerite Helmers. *Defining Visual Rhetorics*. Mahwah, NJ: Lawrence Erlbaum, 2004.

Hirsch, Marianne. *Family Frames: Photography, Narrative, and Postmemory*. Cambridge, MA: Harvard University Press, 1997.

Hirsch, Robert. *Seizing the Light: A Social and Aesthetic History of Photography*. London: Routledge, 2017.

Howells, Richard, and Joaquim Negreiros. *Visual Culture*. London: Polity, 2019.

Jeff, Leonard, and Jerold Simmons. *The Dame in the Kimono: Hollywood, Censorship, and the Production Code*. Lexington: University Press of Kentucky, 2001.

Jin, Jing, Jinwei Li, Guiping Liao, Xiaojuan Yu, and Leo Christopher C. Viray. "Methodology for Potato Defects Detection with Computer Vision." *Proceedings of the 2009 International Symposium on Information Processing* (ISIP 2009): 346–351.

Jockers, Matthew. *Macroanalysis: Digital Methods and Literary History*. Urbana-Champagne, IL: University of Illinois Press, 2013.

Kahana, Joanna, and Charles Musser. *The Documentary Film Reader: History, Theory, Criticism*. Oxford: Oxford University Press, 2016.

Kee, Kevin, and Timothy Compeau. *Seeing the Past with Computers: Experiments with Augmented Reality and Computer Vision for History*. Ann Arbor: University of Michigan Press, 2019.

Kim, Ruth. "Top 4 Beauty Apps Koreans Can't Live Without." *beautytap*. June 20, 2017. https://beautytap.com/2017/06/top-4-beauty-apps-koreans/.

King, David. "dlib-ML: A Machine Learning Toolkit." *Journal of Machine Learning Research* 10 (July 2009): 1755–1758.

Klontz, Joshua, Brendan F. Klare, Scott Klum, Anil K. Jain, and Mark J. Burge. "Open-Source Biometric Recognition." *Proceedings of the Sixth International Conference on Biometrics: Theory, Applications and Systems* (2013): 42–50.

Kress, Gunther, and Theo van Leeuwen. *Reading Images: The Grammar of Visual Design*. New York: Routledge, 2006.

Larkin, Daniel. "The Met Museum Misses the Mark in Recounting Its Own Complicated History." *Hyperallergic*, November 11, 2020. https://hyperallergic.com/598105/making-the-met-review-metropolitan-museum-of-art/.

Lemley, Mark A., and Bryan Casey. "Fair Learning." *Texas Law Review* 99, no. 4 (2021): 743–785.

Levkowitz, Haim, and Gabor T. Herman. "GLHS: A Generalized Lightness, Hue, and Saturation Color Mode." *CVGIP: Graphical Models and Image Processing* 55, no. 4 (1993): 271–285.

Lotz, Amanda. *The Television Will Be Revolutionized*. New York: New York University Press, 2014.

Lyon, Richard. "A Brief History of 'Pixel.'" *Proceedings of the IS&T/SPIR Symposium on Electronic Imaging* (2006): 2–16.

MacKenzie, I. Scott. *Human-Computer Interaction: An Empirical Research Perspective*. London: Morgan Kaufmann, 2013.

Manovich, Lev. *Cultural Analytics*. Cambridge, MA: MIT Press, 2020.

Manovich, Lev. *The Language of New Media*. Cambridge, MA: MIT Press, 2002.

Marblestone, Adam H., Greg Wayne, and Konrad P. Kording. "Toward an Integration of Deep Learning and Neuroscience." *Frontiers in Computational Neuroscience* 10, no. 94 (2016).

Martin, Judith, and Thomas K. Nakayama. *Intercultural Communication in Contexts*. New York: McGraw-Hill, 2013.

Masson, Eef, Christian Gosvig Olesen, Nanne Van Noord, and Giovanna Fossati. "Exploring Digitised Moving Image Collections: The SEMIA Project, Visual Analysis and the Turn to Abstraction." *Digital Humanities Quarterly* 14, no. 4 (2020).

Mayer, Allana. "Linked Open Data for Artistic and Cultural Resources." *Art Documentation: Journal of the Art Libraries Society of North America* 34, no. 1 (2015): 2–14.

Mayring, Philip. *Qualitative Content Analysis: A Step-by-Step Guide*. New York: SAGE, 2022.

McAuley, Julian, Christopher Targett, Qinfeng Shi, and Anton van den Hengel. "Image-Based Recommendations on Styles and Substitutes." *Proceedings of the 38th International ACM SIGIR Conference on Research and Development in Information Retrieval* (2015): 43–52.

McInnes, Leland, John Healy, Nathaniel Saul, and Lukas Großberger. "UMAP: Uniform Manifold Approximation and Projection." *Journal of Open Source Software* 3, no. 29 (2018): 861.

Metz, Christian. *Film Language: A Semiotics of the Cinema*. Translated by Michael Taylor. Chicago: University of Chicago Press, 1991.

Metz, Walter. *Bewitched*. Detroit, MI: Wayne State University Press, 2007.

Miller, D. A. "Anal Rope." In *Inside/Out: Lesbian Theories, Gay Theories*, edited by Diana Fuss, 119–172. New York: Routledge, 1991.

Mirzoeff, Nicholas. *The Visual Culture Reader*. New York: Routledge, 2012.

Mitchell, Brian T., and Andrew M. Gillies. "A Model-Based Computer Vision System for Recognizing Hand-Written ZIP Codes." *Machine Vision and Applications* 2, no. 4 (1989): 231–243.

Mittell, Jason. *Complex TV: The Poetics of Contemporary Television Storytelling*. New York: New York University Press, 2015.

Montúfar, Guido, Razvan Pascanu, Kyunghyun Cho, and Yoshua Bengio. "On the Number of Linear Regions of Deep Neural Networks." *Advances in Neural Information Processing Systems* 27 (2014): 1–14.

Mulvey, Laura. *Visual and Other Pleasures*. London: Palgrave Macmillan, 1989.

Nakamura, Lisa. *Digitizing Race: Visual Cultures of the Internet*. Minneapolis: University of Minnesota Press, 2008.

Neuendorf, Kimberly. *The Content Analysis Guidebook*. New York: SAGE, 2016.

Newhall, Beaumont. *The History of Photography: From 1839 to the Present*. New York: The Museum of Modern Art, 1982.

Newton, Casey. "The Trauma Floor: The Secret Lives of Facebook Moderators in America." *The Verge*, February 25, 2019.

Ni, Jianmo, Jiacheng Li, and Julian McAuley. "Justifying Recommendations Using Distantly-Labeled Reviews and Fine-Grained Aspects." *Empirical Methods in Natural Language Processing* (2019): 188–197.

Nichols, Bill. *Representing Reality: Issues and Concepts in Documentary*. Bloomington: Indiana University Press, 1992.

Nichols, Bill. *Speaking Truths with Film: Evidence, Ethics, Politics in Documentary*. Berkeley: University of California Press, 2016.

Noble, Safiya Umoja. *Algorithms of Oppression: How Search Engines Reinforce Racism*. New York: New York University Press, 2018.

O'Neil, Cathy. *Weapons of Math Destruction: How Big Data Increases Inequality and Threatens Democracy*. New York: Broadway Books, 2016.

Ott, Brian, and Diane Keeling. "Cinema and Choric Connection: *Lost in Translation* as Sensual Experience." *Quarterly Journal of Speech* 97, no. 4 (November 2011): 363–386.

Padilla, Thomas. *Responsible Operations: Data Science, Machine Learning, and AI in Libraries*. Dublin, OH: OCLC Research, 2018.

Palmer, Stephen. *Vision Science: Photons to Phenomenology*. Cambridge, MA: MIT Press, 1999.

Papageorgiou, Constantine, Michael Oren, and Tomaso Poggio. "A General Framework for Object Detection." *Proceedings of the Sixth International Conference on Computer Vision* (1998): 555–562.

Paszke, Adam, Sam Gross, Francisco Massa, Adam Lerer, James Bradbury, Gregory Chanan, Trevor Killeen et al. "PyTorch: An Imperative Style, High-Performance Deep Learning Library." *Advances in Neural Information Processing Systems* 32 (2019): 8026–8037.

Peirce, Charles Sanders. "Nomenclature and Divisions of Triadic Relations, as Far as They Are Determined." In *Selected Philosophical Writings*, vol. 2 of *The Essential Peirce*, edited by The Pierce Edition Project, 289–299. Bloomington: Indian University Press.

Peirce, Charles Sanders. "Of Reasoning in General." In *Selected Philosophical Writings*, vol. 2 of *The Essential Peirce*, edited by The Pierce Edition Project, 11–26. Bloomington: Indian University Press.

Pemberton, Steven, Brad Pettit, Tantek Çelik, Chris Lilley, and L. David Baron. "CSS Color Module Level 3: RGB Color Values." W3C Standards (2011), Section 4.2.1.

Piper, Andrew. *Enumerations: Data and Literary Study*. Chicago: University of Chicago Press, 2018.

Poole, Edwin, and Susan Poole. *Collecting Movie Posters: An Illustrated Reference Guide*. London: McFarland & Company, 1997.

Porter, Theodore M., *Trust in Numbers: The Pursuit of Objectivity in Science and Public Life*. Princeton: Princeton University Press, 1996.

Poynton, Charles. *Digital Video and HD: Algorithms and Interfaces*. New York: Morgan Kaufmann, 2002.

Qiang, Huang. "A Study on the Metaphor of Red in Chinese Culture." *American International Journal of Contemporary Research* 1, no. 3 (2011): 100–105.

Raiford, Leigh. *Imprisoned in a Luminous Glare: Photography and the African American Struggle*. Chapel Hill, NC: University of North Carolina Press, 2013.

Ramos, Sebastian, Stefan Gehrig, Peter Pinggera, Uwe Franke, and Carsten Rother. "Detecting Unexpected Obstacles for Self-Driving Cars: Fusing Deep Learning and Geometric Modelling." *Intelligent Vehicles Symposium* (2017): 1025–1032.

Redmon, Joseph, Santosh Divvala, Ross Girshick, and Ali Farhadi. "You Only Look Once." *Proceedings of the IEEE Conference on Computer Vision and Pattern Recognition* (2016): 779–788.

Redmon, Joseph, and Ali Farhadi. "YOLO9000: Better, Faster, Stronger." *Proceedings of the IEEE Conference on Computer Vision and Pattern Recognition* (2017): 7263–7271.

Rettberg, Jill Walker, Marianne Gunderson, Linda Kronman, Ragnhild Solberg, and Linn Heidi Stokkedal. "Mapping Cultural Representations of Machine Vision: Developing Methods to Analyse Games, Art and Narratives." *Proceedings of the 30th ACM Conference on Hypertext and Social Media* (2019): 97–101.

Rhodes, Gary. "The Origin and Development of the American Moving Picture Poster." *Film History: International Journal* 19, no. 3 (2007): 228–246.

Riffe, Daniel, Stephen Lacy, Brendan Watson, and Frederick Fico. *Analyzing Media Messages: Using Quantitative Content Analysis in Research*. 4th ed. New York: Routledge, 2019.

Riley, Jenn, and Kelcy Shepherd. "A Brave New World: Archivists and Shareable Descriptive Metadata." *The American Archivist* 72, no. 1 (2009): 91–112.

Roberson, Debi, Jules Davidoff, Ian R. L. Davies, and Laura R. Shapiro. "Color Categories: Confirmation of the Relativity Hypothesis." *Cognitive Psychology* 50, no. 4 (2005): 378–411.

Rogoff, Irit. "Studying Visual Culture." In *The Visual Culture Reader*, edited by Nicholas Mirzeoff, 24–36. London: Routledge, 1998.

Sabatelli, Matthia, Nikolay Banar, Marie Cocriamont, Eva Coudyzer, Karine Lasaracina, Walter Daelemans, Pierre Geurts, and Mike Kestemont. "Advances in Digital Music Iconography: Benchmarking the Detection of Musical Instruments in Unrestricted, Non-photorealistic Images from the Artistic Domain." *Digital Humanities Quarterly* 15, no. 2 (2021).

Salt, Barry. *Moving into Pictures*. New York: Starword, 2006.

Salt, Barry. "Statistical Style Analysis of Motion Pictures." *Film Quarterly* 28, no. 1 (1974): 13–22.

Sargent, Epes Winthrop. *Picture Theatre Advertising*. New York: The Moving Picture World Chalmers Publishing Co., 1915.

Saussure, Ferdinand de. *Cours de Linguistique Générale*. Translated by Roy Harris. Chicago: Open Court, 1998.

Schatz, Thomas. *The Genius of the System: Hollywood Filmmaking in the Studio Era*. New York: Henry Holt and Company, 1988.

Scott, Clive. *The Spoken Image*. London: Reaktion Books, 1999.

Selbst, Andrew D., danah boyd, Sorelle Friedler, Suresh Venkatasubramanian, and Janet Vertesi. "Fairness and Abstraction in Sociotechnical Systems." *Proceedings of the Conference on Fairness, Accountability, and Transparency* (2019): 59–68.

Shannon, Claude E. "A Mathematical Theory of Communication." *Bell System Technical Journal* 27, no. 3 (1948): 379–423.

Sharits, Paul J. "Red, Blue, Godard." *Film Quarterly* 19, no. 4 (1966): 24–29.

Sharma, S., Karthikeyan Shanmugasundaram, and Sathees Kumar Ramasamy. "FAREC: CNN Based Efficient Face Recognition Technique Using Dlib." *Advanced Communication Control and Computing Technologies* (2016): 192–195.

Sherif, Muzafer, Daniel Taub, and Carl I. Hovland. "Assimilation and Contrast Effects of Anchoring Stimuli on Judgments." *Journal of Experimental Psychology* 55, no. 2 (1958): 150–155.

Sherratt, Tim, and Kate Bagnall. "The People Inside." In *Seeing the Past with Computers: Experiments with Augmented Reality and Computer Vision for History*, edited by Kevin Kee and Timothy Compeau, 11–31. Ann Arbor: University of Michigan Press, 2019.

Smith, Ian Hayden. *Selling the Movie: The Art of the Film Poster*. London: White Lion Press, 2018.

Smith, Marquard. "Visual Culture Studies: History, Theory, Practice." Introduction to *Visual Culture Studies*, edited by Marquard Smith, 1–16. London: SAGE Publications Ltd, 2008.

Smith, Shawn Michelle. *Photography on the Color Line: W. E. B. Du Bois, Race, and Visual Culture*. Durham, NC: Duke University Press, 2004.

Smulyan, Susan. *Doing Public Humanities*. New York: Routledge, 2020.

Smuts, Aaron. "The Desire-Frustration Theory of Suspense." *The Journal of Aesthetics and Art Criticism* 66, no. 3 (2008): 281–290.

Souček, Tomáš and Jakub Lokoč. "TransNet V2: An Effective Deep Network Architecture for Fast Shot Transition Detection." *arXiv preprint arXiv:2008.04838* (2020). https://doi.org/10.48550/arXiv.2008.04838.

Spigel, Lynn. *Welcome to the Dreamhouse: Popular Media and Postwar Suburbs*. Durham, NC: Duke University Press, 2001.

Staiger, Janet. "Announcing Wares, Winning Patrons, Voicing Ideals: Thinking about the History and Theory of Film Advertising." *Cinema Journal* 29, no. 3 (1990): 3–31.

St. Clair, Robert N. "Social Scripts and the Three Theoretical Approaches to Culture." *Intercultural Communication Studies* 17, no. 4 (2008): 171–183.

Stiller, James, Daniel Nettle, and Robin Dunbar. "The Small World of Shakespeare's Plays." *Human Nature* 14, no. 4 (2003): 397–408.

Stoddard, Karen M. "Bewitched and Bewildered." *Journal of Popular Film and Television* 8, no. 4 (1981): 50–52.

Strange, Maren. *Symbols of Ideal Life: Social Documentary Photography in America, 1890–1950*. Cambridge: Cambridge University Press, 1989.

Street, Sarah, and Joshua Yumibe. *Chromatic Modernity: Color, Cinema, and Media of the 1920s*. New York: Columbia University Press, 2019.

Sturken, Marita, and Lisa Cartwright. *Practices of Looking*. Oxford: Oxford University Press, 2001.

Stryker, Roy Emerson, and Nancy C. Wood. *In This Proud Land: America, 1935–1943, as Seen in the FSA Photographs*. New York: New York Graphic Society, 1975.

Sun, Xudong, Pengcheng Wu, and Steven C. H. Hoi. "Face Detection Using Deep Learning: An Improved Faster RCNN Approach." *Neurocomputing* 299 (2018): 42–50.

Szegedy, Christian, Vincent Vanhoucke, Sergey Ioffe, Jon Shlens, and Zbigniew Wojna. "Rethinking the Inception Architecture for Computer Vision." *Proceedings of the IEEE Conference on Computer Vision and Pattern Recognition* (2016): 2818–2826.

Tagg, John. *The Disciplinary Frame: Photographic Truths and the Capture of Meaning*. Minneapolis: University of Minnesota Press, 2009.

Taylor, Diana. *The Archive and the Repertoire: Performing Cultural Memory in the Americas*. Durham, NC: Duke University Press, 2003.

Thomson, Laure and David Mimno. "Computational Cut-Ups: The Influence of Data." *The Journal of Modern Periodical Studies* 8, no. 2 (2018): 179–195.

Trachtenberg, Alan. "From Image to Story: Reading the File." In *Documenting America*, edited by Carl Fleischhauer and Beverly W. Brannan, 43–73. Berkeley: University of California Press, 1988.

Tsivian, Yuri, and Gunars Civjans. *Cinemetrics: Movie Measurement and Study Tool Database* (2005). Accessed April 9, 2022. http://www.cinemetrics.lv/database.php.

Tukey, John. *Exploratory Data Analysis*. New York: Pearson, 1977.

Turnock, Julie. "Removing the Pane of Glass: 'The Hobbit,' 3D High Frame Rate Filmmaking, and the Rhetoric of Digital Convergence." *Film Criticism* 37/38, nos. 3/1 (2013): 30–59.

Underwood, Ted. "A Genealogy of Distant Reading." *Digital Humanities Quarterly* 11, no. 2 (2017).

Valéry, Paul. *Degas, Danse, Dessin*. Paris: Gaillmard, 1937.

Van Noord, Nanne, Ella Hendriks, Eric Postma. "Toward Discovery of the Artist's Style: Learning to Recognize Artists by Their Artworks." *IEEE Signal Processing Magazine* 32, no. 4 (2015): 46–54.

Vane, Olivia. "Making 'Dive into Color.'" *Cooper Hewitt Labs* (blog). 2018. Accessed November 6, 2021. https://labs.cooperhewitt.org/2018/making-dive-into-color/.

Verdesoto, James. "Movie Poster Color Schemes Explained." *Vanity Fair*, March 11, 2019. https://www.vanityfair.com/video/watch/movie-poster-color-schemes-explained.

Viola, Paul, and Michael Jones. "Rapid Object Detection Using a Boosted Cascade of Simple Features." *Proceedings of the 2001 IEEE Computer Society Conference on Computer Vision and Pattern Recognition* 1 (2001): 1–8.

Wakeling, Simon, Paul Clough, Barbara Sen, and Lynn Silipigni Connaway. "Readers Who Borrowed This Also Borrowed . . . : Recommender Systems in UK Libraries." *Library Hi Tech* 30, no. 1 (2012).

Wang, Hee Lin, and Loong-Fah Cheong. "Taxonomy of Directing Semantics for Film Shot Classification." *IEEE Transactions on Circuits and Systems for Video Technology* 19, no. 10 (2009): 1529–1542.

Wardrip-Fruin, Noah. *Expressive Processing: Digital Fictions, Computer Games, and Software Studies*. Cambridge, MA: MIT Press, 2009.

Warner, Michael. "Publics and Counterpublics (abbreviated version)." *Quarterly Journal of Speech* 88, no. 4 (2002): 413–425.

Wernimont, Jacqueline. *Numbered Lives: Life and Death in Quantum Media*. Cambridge, MA: MIT Press, 2019.

Wevers, Melvin, and Thomas Smits. "The Visual Digital Turn: Using Neural Networks to Study Historical Images." *Digital Scholarship in the Humanities* 35, no. 1 (2020): 194–207.

Wexler, Laura. *Tender Violence: Domestic Visions in the Age of U.S. Imperialism*. Chapel Hill: University of North Carolina Press, 2000.

Whitelaw, Mitchell. "Generous Interfaces for Digital Cultural Collections." *Digital Humanities Quarterly* 9, no. 1 (2015).

Wickham, Hadley. "Tidy Data." *Journal of Statistical Software* 59, no. 10 (2014): 1–23.

Wickham, Hadley, and Garrett Grolemund. *R for Data Science: Import, Tidy, Transform, Visualize, and Model Data*. New York: O'Reilly Media, 2016.

Wierzbicka, Anna. "The Semantics of Colour: A New Paradigm." In *Language and Culture*, vol. 1 of *Progress in Colour Studies*, edited by Carol Biggam and Christian Kay, 1–24. Philadelphia: John Benjamins Publishing Company, 2006.

Winawer, Jonathan, Nathan Witthoft, Michael C. Frank, Lisa Wu, Alex R. Wade, and Lera Boroditsky. "Russian Blues Reveal Effects of Language on Color Discrimination." *Proceedings of the National Academy of Sciences* 104, no. 19 (2007): 7780–7785.

Wu, Yuxin, Alexander Kirillov, Francisco Massa, Wan-Yen Lo, and Ross Girshick. "Detectron2" (2019). Accessed November 7, 2021. https://github.com/facebookresearch/detectron2.

Xanthos, Aris, Isaac Pante, Yannick Rochat, and Martin Granjean. "Visualizing the Dynamics of Character Networks." *Digital Humanities Conference Abstracts* (2016): 417–419.

Yoon, Sarah. "Color Symbolisms of Diseases: Edgar Allan Poe's 'The Masque of the Red Death.'" *The Explicator* (2021): 1–4.

Zhang, Lei, Mingjing Li, and Hong-Jiang Zhang. "Boosting Image Orientation Detection with Indoor vs. Outdoor Classification." *Proceedings of the Sixth IEEE Workshop on Applications of Computer Vision* (2002): 95–99.

Zuboff, Shoshana. *The Age of Surveillance Capitalism: The Fight for a Human Future at the New Frontier of Power*. New York: Public Affairs, 2019.

Zuboff, Shoshana. "Big Other: Surveillance Capitalism and the Prospects of an Information Civilization." *Journal of Information Technology* 30, no. 1 (2015): 75–89.

Zylinksa, Joanna. *Nonhuman Photography*. Cambridge, MA: MIT Press, 2017.

Datasets

We have made all the data and code needed to recreate all the analyses in this text available under an open-source license as part of the book's supplementary materials. Where possible, we also provide or link to the digital images from which we are working. Our hope is that making this information available will encourage others to continue exploring these collections and to apply distant viewing techniques to new collections of digital images. In many cases we have supplied supplementary annotations in addition to those used directly in the text. The following datasets directly correspond to the analyses presented in the previous chapters:

- *FSA-OWI Color Images*: A set of 1,616 color images that are part of the FSA-OWI holdings at the Library of Congress. Notably, these include the image of a shepherd, horse, and dog featured in the first two chapters. All the images are in the public domain as works of the US federal government. Metadata, image region segmentations, and image embeddings are included in the collection.

- *Movie Posters*: A set of 4,669 color images of movie posters, with approximately 100 posters in each year from 1970 to 2019. Metadata, face bounding boxes, and color information are included. Metadata comes from Wikipedia. Links to images on Wikimedia are provided in the metadata; note that copyright of most posters belongs to their respective creators.

- *FSA-OWI Greyscale Images*: A set of 171,180 grayscale images that are part of the FSA-OWI holdings at the Library of Congress. All the images are in the public domain as works of the US federal government. Metadata, image region segmentations, and image embeddings are included in the collection. Small versions of the images can be directly down-loaded; links to larger versions at the Library of Congress are given in the metadata.

- *Bewitched* and *I Dream of Jeannie*: A summary table with one row for each of the 102,334 shots detected from the runs of the two series is provided, giving information about the length of the shot, the characters in the shot, and the framing of the shot. The original materials are under copy-right, and therefore we are unable to share them.

- *Metropolitan Museum of Art Collection API*: A set of 288,252 images. We provided image embeddings and metadata for each record. Links to download the images are provided in the metadata. Materials have been released into the public domain (Creative Commons Zero license).

To further continue the use of distant viewing, we also include annotations for the additional collections of digitized images listed here:

- *Detroit Publishing Company*: A set of 25,172 documentary photographs held at the Library of Congress. Photographs consist of images taken by staff photographers working for the company. Annotations include object detection, region segmentation, face detection, and image embed-dings. Links to the images are provided in the metadata. All data are images in the public domain.

- *George Grantham Bain Collection*: A set of 41,447 documentary photo-graphs held at the Library of Congress. Created from the archives of one of the earliest news picture agencies in the United States. Annotations include object detection, region segmentation, face detection, and image embeddings. Links to the images are provided in the metadata. There are no known restrictions on distribution of the images and metadata.

- *Harris & Ewing Collection*: A set of 41,542 documentary photographs held at the Library of Congress from the Washington, DC–based news pho-tography firm. Annotations include object detection, region segmen-tation, face detection, and image embeddings. Links to the images are provided in the metadata. There are no known restrictions on distribu-tion of the images and metadata.

- *National Photo Company Collection*: A set of 35,619 documentary pho-tographs held at the Library of Congress. Annotations include object detection, region segmentation, face detection, and image embeddings.

Links to the images are provided in the metadata. All data are images in the public domain. There are no known restrictions on distribution of the images and metadata.

- *Getty Open Content Program*: A set of 75,362 images from the museum's files. Metadata, image embeddings, and links to the images are provided. All images are believed to be free of restrictions for use and distribution.
- *Rijksmuseum API*: A set of 392,725 images from the museum's files. Metadata, image embeddings, and links to the images are provided. All images are believed to be in the public domain.
- *National Gallery of Art*: A set of 136,567 images from the gallery's files. Metadata, image embeddings, and links to the images are provided. All data are in the public domain, though some images may be subject to copyright restrictions.

We plan to release new annotations for additional collections in other venues as we continue to apply computer vision techniques to the study of visual messages.

Index